ROUTLEDGE LIBRARY EDITIONS:
SOCRATES

Volume 4

SOCRATES, THE ORIGINAL AND ITS IMAGES

SOCRATES, THE ORIGINAL AND ITS IMAGES

ALAN F. BLUM

Routledge
Taylor & Francis Group
LONDON AND NEW YORK

First published in 1978 by Routledge & Kegan Paul Ltd

This edition first published in 2019
by Routledge
2 Park Square, Milton Park, Abingdon, Oxon OX14 4RN

and by Routledge
711 Third Avenue, New York, NY 10017

Routledge is an imprint of the Taylor & Francis Group, an informa business

British Library Cataloguing in Publication Data
A catalogue record for this book is available from the British Library

ISBN: 978-1-138-61842-8 (Set)
ISBN: 978-0-429-45011-2 (Set) (ebk)
ISBN: 978-1-138-32296-7 (Volume 4) (hbk)
ISBN: 978-1-138-32307-0 (Volume 4) (pbk)
ISBN: 978-0-429-45163-8 (Volume 4) (ebk)

Publisher's Note
The publisher has gone to great lengths to ensure the quality of this reprint but points out that some imperfections in the original copies may be apparent.

Disclaimer
The publisher has made every effort to trace copyright holders and would welcome correspondence from those they have been unable to trace.

Socrates
the original and its images

Alan F. Blum

Routledge & Kegan Paul
London, Henley and Boston

First published in 1978
by Routledge & Kegan Paul Ltd
39 Store Street,
London WC1E 7DD,
Broadway House,
Newtown Road,
Henley-on-Thames,
Oxon RG9 1EN and
9 Park Street,
Boston, Mass. 02108, USA
Set in 10 on 12 pt Baskerville by
Computacomp (UK) Ltd., Fort William
and printed in Great Britain by
Redwood Burn Ltd
Trowbridge & Esher

British Library Cataloguing in Publication Data

Blum, Alan F.

Socrates, the original and its images.
1. Socrates
I. Title
183'.2 B317 77-30373

ISBN 0 7100 8766 7

Contents

CHAPTER I

Theory and Life

I

One conventional way of understanding Aristotle leads to the conclusion that the first decisive enemy of Socrates was Aristotle. Yet, if we tentatively suspend our inquest into this opinion, we might still begin with a remark of Aristotle with which Socrates is sure to agree. In the *Ethics* Aristotle says, 'Every art and every inquiry, and similarly every action and pursuit, is thought to aim at some good; and for this reason the good has been rightly declared to be that at which all things aim.' Aristotle then proceeds — after this remark which is friendly to the spirit of Socrates — to concretize the very understanding from which the remark issues — to classify and categorize these 'goods', to convert them into predicates, to require their observability, etc. Yet, for the present we can ignore this and try to recollect the friendliness of the remark.

If 'every ... action and pursuit is thought to aim at some good' we might then ask how the action or pursuit that is the life of a man is 'thought to aim at some good'?

If our task is to understand the life of a man, a life is a course of action or a pursuit which we can think of as aiming at some good. In fact Socrates would require us to think of a life in this way or else to be prepared to conceive of a life as an accident or as a collection of incidents the togetherness of which consists only in their collectability.

So Socrates would caution us to understand the life of a man as the good towards which it aims. If the idea of 'life' has any weight he would say — if it is authorized by a distinction that is itself good (instead of the difference between physical existence and non-existence or between things being alive and being dead) — then it must make reference to the aim or good towards which the idea of life aspires.

But this Socratic reminder returns the problem back to us even more forcibly because what the reminder reminds us of is this: that *every* pursuit and action is to be so understood and, consequently, life is no exception to the rule, but an exemplification. The idea of life is no different from any idea: it must be formulated as a pursuit or action that aims at some good. It is only when this understanding is concretized that the notion of the good towards which a pursuit aims is treated as its goal or value and thus, many 'kinds' are predicated.

Furthermore, the reminder implicates us even more seriously in the review of a life for it says that the act of reviewing a life (the art, the inquiry) is like all actions and pursuits in that *it* must aim at some good. When we review the life of Socrates by attempting to formulate its aim or good, we will be doing our review as itself an instance of *its* aim or good. What, then, is the relationship between the end or good of life and the end, aim, or good of re-viewing (of reflecting, discoursing, or theorizing)?

It is at this point that Aristotle would distinguish between the good of life and the good of theorizing, whereas Socrates cautions us to understand that the formulation of the aim of life *is* a display of the aim of theorizing and that the aim towards which theorizing aspires must be understood as itself an exemplification of the good towards which the idea of life is directed.

Socrates brings life and theory together by urging us to remember that our examination and inquiry is our own way of exemplifying a life. The good towards which we re-cognize the idea of life as aiming is the good towards which we ought to understand every art, action, and pursuit as aiming, including the art of inquiring, into this good. This is a formidable responsibility to accept: we elect to review the life of a man whose very life shows its involvement in the question of the relationship between reviewing and living.

If a life means or makes reference to the difference it makes, we might think of the end or good of a life as the end of making a difference. Yet there are many ways of making a difference, i.e., of having effects, consequences, etc. In these cases, in so far as a life makes a difference what it *makes* is a difference between itself and other lives and so, such lives are fertile and demand to be oriented to and honoured. Perhaps the difference which Socrates makes is to make us indifferent to *these* differences except as a way of pointing to the difference between these differences and that which is truly Other or different. Perhaps he tells us that the former differences are inessential (between lives) and that if a life is to make a real difference it will be by pointing to the difference between inessential differences and Real difference.

No one will deny that lives are different, that the differences between lives are many. The multitude is concerned with these kinds of differences and that is how the multitude acquires its name, from its concern with *multis*, manyness, and plurality. But the differences between lives — the issue of manyness — can only make sense if the idea of life is understood. There is only one idea of life and the task of the theorist is to re-achieve and sustain the conversation into that singular idea. The theorist faces the opposition and enmity of *multis*, of the idea that inessential differences are essential. The theorist must respect those differences because he cannot sustain conversation into the idea of life without the occasioning of different lives as precedents and examples. Yet the theorist must re-collect the source of these differences in that which is the same. The theorist then resists the attempt of *multis* to assert the primacy of difference in so far as he is always pointing to the way in which unity underlies plurality. The theorist himself makes a difference only because he shows the difference between what is essential and inessential. What is essential is that all speeches are sheltered by language, even speeches that deny such sheltering; what is inessential are the concrete differences among speeches. And yet, the essentiality of language can only be spoken, i.e., it needs and requires as essential the inessential differences which it originates.

II

Most historians see the Greeks as having made a difference; the principal difference made by the Greeks is viewed as their initiation of an impulse which we have completed. The difference the Greek makes is then between himself and us. Even condemnations of the Greeks acknowledge the need to surpass their legacy; even glorifications of the Greeks stress the need to return to that origin. In the fullest sense then, the Greeks relate to us as predecessors: as predecessors they represent a moment that has preceded us, a moment whose liveliness for us is contingent rather than essential. Whether we revive or annihilate that moment is a matter of choice for us, it is our decision. We stand to the Greeks in the way that followers contingently relate to predecessors and so, our relationship to the Greeks is organized around this difference. We always see the Greeks as a beginning and ourselves as an end.

A good question then concerns what the Greeks began. In the view just mentioned they began a movement towards us. In this way the Greeks would always be formulated in terms of our end: even our praise of the Greeks which sees them as initiating what we could not complete, understands our failure and their success in terms of *our* standard of success and failure.

Yet, what if the Greek beginning was to raise the question of the end? If the Greek beginning was to raise the question of the end, this question itself had to be raised before *we* came to view. Thus, the question of the end is independent of what comes to view and is eternally recollectable from any view.

Do we then stand to the Greeks — to our predecessors — as those who failed or succeeded in raising that question or rather, do we share with the Greeks the opportunity to raise that question? When *we* look (back) to the Greeks we tend to emphasize the difference between us, whereas when the Greeks view others they tend to emphasize a unity which overrides even the difference between Greek and barbarian. In Greek, what we share — the opportunity to raise the question of the end — collects us *vis-à-vis* what is truly different (Other); that is, it collects us in relationship to the end. What we share as men as compared to Other (than man) is our need to raise the question of the end. If the Greek then differentiates himself from others it is only because these others fail to seize the opportunity shared by both them and Greek to raise the question of the end. The Greeks then addressed the essential difference between the communal need shown by the imperativeness of this question and that after which the question quests. The Greek shows the inessentiality of the difference between Greek and barbarian *vis-à-vis* the essential difference between man and that which gives and grants his manliness.

In this way we understand the Greeks as less our predecessors than our fellows: to say that they begin to raise the question of the end is not to say that they are first but rather that they exemplify for us the work of beginning. The Greeks are not first in time, but exemplary in their treatment of what is first. The Greeks exemplify the work required to raise the question of what is first. All who follow the Greeks are not second, third, ..., but equal with respect to the opportunity to raise the question of what is first. All who 'follow' the Greeks then face the choice between conversation and barbarism. Now, 'first' does not refer to the Greeks, but to what is beyond both them and us as that which induces (indeed compels) us to raise the question of what is first. We no longer relate to the Greeks in the way that followers contingently come after predecessors (however flawed or glorious these predecessors) for that is not the real difference; rather, we relate as co-speakers to that which is truly Other than our discourse.

The Greeks show the work involved in raising the question of what is first. This ought to instruct us on how to read the Greeks: let us read them as exemplifying the work involved in raising the question. Let us not read them in terms of a maxim of descriptive and biographic literalness but instead, let us treat them as inviting us to do the work of sustaining *that* question — the work of formulating the requirements for raising the question of what is first. The Greeks then invite us to work instead of doing passive judgment and criticism upon their successes and failures.

Is this not what a friend ought to do — to share the work? To share the communality of the requirement to raise the question of the end by re-collecting and sustaining that question? Is not a friend of the Greeks one who understands the requiredness of raising the question of what is first not as a literal repetition of the Greeks, but out of a full and strong re-cognition of the need of 'what is first' to be continuously re-achieved as a question? And what of the enemies? Are they not those who refuse to face such a question? And shall we not better grasp the imperativeness of the question by analysing this resistance since the overpowering character of what is first is itself the source of the resistance?

If 'life' makes reference to the need to raise this question, Socrates appears to both friend and enemy as a reminder of this need as displayed in work. Socrates reminds us of the meaning of life as our need to work (to discourse) and Socrates' life exemplifies the labour involved in meeting the requirements of such a need. Socrates' life then needs neither biography nor obituary but work

— the work involved in using his life as an illustration of the work required in the raising of the question of what is first. This means that Socrates' life must not be described or reconstructed exegetically but that it ought to be reformulated with violence — as an occasion to raise the question of what is first. The life of Socrates must be fitted to these requirements.

III

If we treat the Greek as exemplary for raising the question of what is first, or what is the end, is Socrates himself not the exemplary Greek? Is it not Socrates who shows us what it means to be Greek?

Aristotle speaks of Socrates as the founder of theorizing as if Socrates was an inventor. In contrast, we shall understand Socrates as an exemplar rather than as an original. The conception of both Greek and Socrates as original rather than as exemplification permits the modern to 'interpret' Socrates — to write his history, biography, obituary — rather than to join with him in conversation. The essence of the original is that he originates, that he succeeds in founding, whereas the exemplar continuously reminds us of the difference between originality and addressing the question of origin. The exemplar takes as his topic the difference between originating and addressing the origin: he exemplifies adequate speech about this difference because what he stands for is the Desire to sustain the question 'what is first?'

IV

If Socrates points to the difference between what is essential and what is inessential, we might say that he points to what is needed or required, i.e., that he points to life. Socrates then keeps the question of life alive. The question of life as the question of what is necessary or essential asks — what is the end of life; what is its good or aim? This question is not asked idly; it is posed within the context of a social encounter, of an eternal conversation. Though no 'answer' awaits the participants as a product for their consumption, they must work together to appreciate the necessity of the question being continually asked. They must theorize to understand the force of the question as that which needs being re-achieved.

And yet, if the question of life presupposes the capacity to theorize, participating in the quest is conditional upon what is essential and necessary in the sense that life — unlike theorizing — is absolute, unconditioned, and has no opposite. Although life needs theorizing to re-achieve its necessity in discourse, life must first be accepted as necessary and absolute before theorizing. This need to re-discover what is first accepted is captured by the Socratic metaphor of *anamnesis*.

Socrates' value was to show that what is essential to life is to keep the question of life — of essentiality — alive. He showed that to make a difference is to keep the question of the difference — between what is essential and inessential — alive, a difference that could only be made through the practice of questioning which needed to presuppose that very difference it was querying.

We shall propose that Socrates stands for the Desire to keep theory and life together and consequently, that friendship to Socrates reproduces this desire. Theorizing needs life in the sense that theory must be guided by a strong version of what is essential and necessary: theory needs life as it needs what is unconditionally absolute rather than what is 'for all practical purposes' essential. Although there are always pressures upon theory to accept what is inessential as essential, the togetherness of theory and life means that the best and liveliest theorizing needs to recognize its dependency upon what is absolute and essential.

In the same way, life needs theory. This is to say that the very understanding of what is absolute and essential only occurs through the practice of discoursing, questing and inquiring. The need of life for theory is not subordinate to the need of theory for life for just as discourse requires a strong sense of its place in relation to what is necessary, the necessity of what is absolute and essential only lives through the reflective discoursing that is theory (what is necessary needs the inessential to display its own necessity). What is inessential is then essential to what is necessary.

V

Friends and enemies are individual persons who can be unlike themselves. Friends can become enemies and enemies can become friends. In this sense, friends and enemies resemble the things of which Socrates speaks to Zeno in the *Parmenides*, for there is nothing essential to their difference, it is a contingent coincidence whether a man is a friend or an enemy.

Friendship or enmity however, as essents, are limited. The idea of a friend cannot be unlike itself (it cannot be like the idea of enemy) and the idea of enemy cannot be unlike itself (it cannot be like the idea of friend). These ideas of friendship and enmity are shown in the ordinary practices of everyday life. Yet, such work never issues in products (the products of friendship or enmity) because that again would be to treat these ideas as if they were things that could become what is their opposite. Friendship and enmity are essents and, as such, are limited by their opposites in a way quite different from a particular person who could be a friend or an enemy. We must then begin to ask how these ideas of friendship or enmity are shown in discourse.

The difference between friendship and enmity towards Socrates is the difference between knowing and not knowing how life and theory belong together. The difference between friendship and enmity is the difference between knowing or not knowing the requiredness of this co-existence. Such knowledge ought to be shown in the work that is conversation and discourse. It should be shown even when the work is directed to the life of Socrates himself. Friendliness to Socrates as the knowledge that life and theory belong together can be shown in the work — the conversation, the discourse — of reformulating the very enmity to Socrates that disregards the co-existence of life and theory. In this sense, such enmity will be re-viewed: its grounds will be re-layed as part of an approach that renounces the impulses towards both unregulated abstraction and description. We reformulate enmity to Socrates — opposition to the idea that life and theory co-exist — by inventing ordinary icons of this enmity in the embodiment of different practices. This reformulation as the work of conversation is intended to display *its* friendliness to Socrates by re-achieving in its own discourse a strong sense of the togetherness of life and theory.

Friendliness to Socrates is then personified in the Desire to keep life and theory together, whereas enmity is reflected in their segregation. Friendliness in this sense is displayed in the work of sustaining inquiry into the issue of beginning regardless of the practice being examined. Enmity then shows itself as a resistance to such work, as a tendency to relate to what precedes mechanically and passively instead of attempting to reformulate and violate it. Enmity to Socrates will always show itself as a resistance to the work of conversing with material.

If Socrates symbolizes the Desire for the co-existence of life and theory it is only because such a desire — such a co-existence — is deemed absolute and necessary for life. We invent the Socrates we need in such a way as to show our own work of inventing as it-self an exemplification of that co-existence. A friendly treatment of Socrates must show its work by combining violence and prudence: by inventing a Socrates that is true to what is needed it keeps both theory (work) and life (what is needed) together. A friendly treatment resists formulating the life of Socrates as either biography or obituary because in its understanding of friendship as entering and sharing in the work which he exemplifies, it understands how it must act with violence rather than react to a Socrates who is secure and unproblematic.

The founder personifies a particular understanding of the meaning of 'one' as firstness rather than as unity. As first, the founder *is* an inventor, a one who gives birth and who is surpassed by that which he produces. The first begins an indefinite plurality which surpasses and completes him, and so his essence is to provide conditions for his being surpassed and rendered obsolete. Because the relation between the founder and what follows is progressive, he is not continuously seen and re-collected in what follows because his being first means that our understanding of him is secure, we reflect 'back' upon him only to appreciate how far we have come. The idea of a founder then includes the notion that the very act of founding prepares the living liquidation of him who so founds by preserving him as only an abstract remembrance. Recall how Socrates claimed that he was not a founder.

In contrast, the idea of 'one' as unity, as personified in the notion of grounding rather than founding, makes reference to the gathering-together of the self-understanding of what we are at its highest point. In this sense, Socrates would re-present the end towards which our work aspires. Whereas the idea of a founder expresses the understanding that time does change language (i.e., that language *as* speech is in the kind of perpetual motion that guarantees the obsolescence of the founder), the idea of Socrates as a re-presentation of unity as grounds says that his moment is the eternal moment because the eternality of language guarantees his omnipresence as a reminder of the continuous re-collectability of our grounds.

If our reason for writing on Socrates was his firstness, his genius, or his 'greatness', he himself would concede that such a reason is not great. Socrates would say that it is our task — expressed in the manner and mode of our relationship to our material which *happens* to be his life — to re-achieve this greatness. He would say: do not study me as if I am a teacher and not simultaneously a pupil[1] — do not treat me as an enigmatic and distant genius — but make of me your pupil as you are mine. Socrates invites us to re-formulate him instead of merely assenting to his greatness or recording and interpreting his opinions. With Nietzsche he might say — instead of 'interpreting' me, *use* me to make something valuable.

We study Socrates then, not because he is first, but for the reason that we are disposed to allow his life to make great demands upon us, the demand that we address through it the question of what is first. We shall use Socrates' life to make something valuable.

If Socrates stands for the co-existence of life and theory this co-existence is shown in discourse which truly converses, in discourse which raises, explores and sustains the quest into what is first. Such a conversation explores the question of beginning and as work, it must display its governance by a commitment to the co-existence of life and theory. While this commitment can be re-collected through any conversation, the effort here will be to re-assert it through talk about enmity to Socrates himself.

We do our best by Socrates and the Greeks — we show our discipleship, our friendship — not by preserving their words through exegesis, nor by agreeing or disagreeing with their conclusions, their speeches. We show our friendship by sharing in the work which they exemplify, the work of exploring the question of what is first. We show our friendship to the Greeks by entering that conversation in the proper spirit of prudence and violence.

The opinions with which we begin re-present our formulation of the enmity to Socrates which is needed to display and sustain the difference between what is essential and inessential. The relationship between Socrates and his enemies should serve as an icon of the difference between knowing and not knowing the difference between exigencies of interaction and communication and the necessity of life. To treat exigencies as necessary is — by confusing concrete interaction or communication with life — to keep theory and life apart by treating what is absolute and essential (life) as that which discourse cannot touch. Knowing this distinction is shown through the practice of the ironic formulation of opinions, a practice whose possibility is only grounded by something other than opinions. Various sorts of resistance to man's necessary ironic sense of his place and to the desire to formulate opinions — various signs of enmity to Socrates — will be addressed.

CHAPTER II

Hedonism

I

To write about Socrates is to interact with him. The possibility of such an interaction means that in some sense Socrates still lives. Our interest in Socrates testifies to that survival. Actually, our interest testifies to the difference between living and surviving, it says that Socrates 'lives' even as he has physically perished. The life of Socrates is then instructive, for just as he — as the Greek — makes the difference between what is essential and inessential the topic, he recreates the question of the difference between life and survival as the foundation and resource for inquiry into that topic. This inquiry can only re-achieve the necessary sense of necessity on the grounds of a conception of the limit to which what is necessary is responsive. If these limits are corporeal — if life is identified with physical survival — the absolute is formulated as those conditions which are essential to survival and the difference between survival and life is buried under a notion of exigencies as the necessities.

To understand the idea of necessity, we might return to the notion of need. Socrates instructs us to begin with what we need and to spend our time in the effort of re-achieving the difference between what is needed because it is valuable and Good and what happens to occur. He reminds us that the difference between the necessary and the inessential is a difference between what is Good and what is coincidental.

The difference which Socrates points to is essential. What is Good, necessary and needed is never what occurs, though we approach it and render it transparent through what occurs. The alterity of the essential and necessary is announced in the coinciding of the familiar.

Thus, to ask the question 'what is necessary?' or 'what is needed?' is similar to asking the question 'what is first?'. That which is needed because of its Goodness is that which *must* be first in the sense that its necessity means that it is essential to What Is (is it Good and needed in so far as it is constitutive of What Is).

If indeed Socrates shows us that what we need is itself to recognize the need — the necessity — for something essential and different from what happens to coincide, he teaches us that what we need is the notion of an absolute and self-sufficient Good. He then tells us that what we need will never coincide with us in the sense of appearing to us and exhausting itself in this appearance. To recognize the need for something absolute and self-sufficient is to recognize something Other than us, for we are men and as such, we are dependent rather than self-sufficient.

Socrates' question 'what is first?' ('what is the origin?') as 'what is necessary, Good and unconditioned?' demands as an answer reference to something Other than exigencies. Exigencies or conditions coincide with man whereas the question 'what is first?' as 'what is needed?' points to something Other than man because it asks what man needs in order to re-achieve and re-assert his place as man (as the dependent being). This means upon what should man depend in order to bring out the best of his manliness? On what notion of the essential, the necessary, and the Good should man require of himself to depend? Socrates says that man must continuously work to show the need for such a commitment and that this work is embodied in the practice of making a difference between what is necessary (what is Other than man) and what is coincidental (what coincides with man).

We say that Socrates keeps theory and life together because these questions accept as their limit a notion of life rather than of survival (that what is Good, necessary and self-sufficient means what is essential for life and not what is technically indispensable for survival or what is instrumental for 'adaptation') and they can only be raised as questions through the work of re-achieving this difference in speech (which is the practice of theorizing). Enmity to Socrates — to theorizing — will be organized in the first instance around a resistance to such questioning.

The question 'what is first?' now understood as 'what is Other than man?' asks for the innate. Enmity to Socrates must deny that anything is Other than man for it must deny the notion of innateness. Furthermore, such a denial can only be prepared by repudiating the difference between survival and life, i.e., because of the identification of What Is with what coincides with man. If this is the case, What Is and What Is-Not are equivalent to being alive and being dead. If there is something Other than man, there must be something Other than corporeal life and death: if anything Other than the facts of life and death are re-collected, there will be something Other than man. Socrates tells us that what we need is something Other than these facts.

Socrates directs our attention to that which limits *these* limits (the limits of life and death) as the limit to which we cannot imagine opposition. Socrates tells us that the Real difference is not between these limits (between life and death) but between these limits and that which limits them. His questions 'what is first?' 'what is needed?' 'what is other than man?' then translate to are there alternative icons of life and death other than surviving and perishing (e.g., like action and passivity, conversation and speechlessness)? The questioning which Socrates directs to the denial of alterity — to the denial of innateness — involves reformulating the positive conception of community which licenses that very denial. In other words, Socrates shows that the denial of alterity is a declaration of that which is being denied, that it — the denial — is only possible because it is grounded in a particular conception of what is necessary, essential and Good. Socrates would then do the work of re-creating conversation about these commitments rather than about the topics that happen to coincide as their products or results.

II

The denial of the innate — the assertion that there is nothing Other than what coincides with man — generates a conception of beginning as essentially variable. This is because all assent to the existence of the innate are opinions and opinions essentially vary. What is first is not that which the assent or dissent intends to ratify or deny, but the act of assenting or dissenting. In the beginning is choosing and so, freedom (i.e., the freedom to choose). In the beginning is then variability and difference rather than solidarity or — the solidarity is supplied only by this essential variability.

In the hedonist world the identification of the innate — of the ultimate limit — with that idea from which dissent is unthinkable converts it into some thing which cannot be altered through choice and will. Because the innate is presumed to exist independently of the freedom of man it can only coincide with him by existing as an external object. Otherness must then appear as the universal fact, the fact which constrains all speakers regardless of their differences. Such a fact is death. The facticity of Otherness renders it unalterable and because it cannot be altered, it ought be disregarded even though it is an innate limitation. It is this very unalterability that requires disregarding because engagement with the unalterable will only produce passivity and cynicism. What is first — for human purposes — is freedom, and the ideal of an innate or original limit can only be conceived as a limitation upon freedom.

Consider Locke's attack on the notion of innate ideas. It amounts to a contention that man cannot be intermediate or centred between the things above and below because there is nothing Other than man that is higher than he. While Locke permits the stratification of differences between the things that coincide with man, man is not stratified *vis-à-vis* the whole. It is interpersonal stratification that provides the original limit. The denial of anything innate is a denial of the stratification of man *vis-à-vis* what is Other than man because anything Other than man would be innate. Stratification is then conceived as social only in the sense that it pertains to the level at which things coincide with man.

When alterity is withdrawn — which is to say, when original stratification is denied — Otherness can only be conceived as nothing, and so rank and distinction are treated as a result of interior, enigmatic processes that differentiate one man from an other. The denial of the innate occurring as it does in conjunction with the affirmation of the firstness of denying — of freedom — means that diversification is primary. Since the source of diversification cannot reside in anything common (because what is common is only the most concrete limitation) it must be located in the enigmatic and unshareable. The only thing men have in common is the concrete, factual limitation of their mortality. The original differences which are generated among men must result from factors which coincide with these differences but which differ from the conduct in which they are realized as the private differs from the public.

If the existence of ideas is to be accredited, we must look for their traces in the form of human ratification that is speech. Words should be 'present' which make reference to such notions. Locke calls such 'making reference' assent. To argue for such notions in the absence of assent is 'hardly intelligible'.

> It seeming to be near a contradiction to say, that there are truths imprinted on the soul, which it perceives or understands not: imprinting, if it signify anything, being nothing else but the making certain truths to be perceived.[1]

While we all share the fact of death, the variability of our speeches means that there is no idea (fact) to which we assent in the same way. Yet, because man can choose to deny any speech, the *fact* of such (initial) choosing appears to have the same solidity as the fact of death. Because the commonality of our freedom to choose issues in different actions (speaking practices), we ought to direct ourselves between choice and speech, to the way in which speech is grounded in interiority. That is, by taking our bearings from the difference between an immutable existence such as the (common) fact of death and the variability of our speeches we can understand how our speeches make reference to ideas (unlike death) which are different for each of us. The denial of innate ideas affirms as original, *multis* or manyness and only denies solidarity. *That* there is something innate cannot be denied without the act of denial becoming what it is.

To say that there is no innate idea is to say that the words men use do not show such an original content for all men: that any common contents that are displayed through speech are contents that only come to enter the mind over time. Men's words display no thing in common, as, e.g., the fact of death is common, and so they are limited by nothing Other than their variability. The difference between life and death comprehended as the first thing — the thing that is mortality — frames the question of What Is-Not because the source of *this* thing is not the same kind of thing (it is no-thing) and thus, is not amenable to our 'conceptualization' (discourse).

The test of innateness is then sociological given a particular conception of 'social'. Social means that all men agree with one another or have in common; social means prevalent and universal; social means agreement. This idea of social grounds the use of the rule itself, for being in the mind *is* being present to man, and to deny innate ideas is to deny that there is any content (universally) present to man; it is to deny that there is original agreement; it is to deny that words are limited by anything more than motion. Existence is then subordinated to the rule of agreement or to convention, and the truth—just as man's nature—is conceived as essentially historical or relative to the speaking practices of a majority of the species in any one place and at any one time. A speech speaks about what exists only when it can be arrested and protected from motion. The image of such tranquillity is the common fact such as death. Speeches ought be organized in such a way as to induce men to assent to them with the same certainty that they assent to the fact of death. Locke's formulation of the innate idea as that idea which is prior to speech (which cannot *be* because it is not appropriated in a name) guarantees that it shall not exist (where 'exist' means to enter into the communal discourse) because his conception of this discourse formulates it as an exchange of determinant names. Anything Other than usage (which is what he means by 'innate') simply does not exist. What Is is defined sociologically as that which can be named and anything Other is to be accredited as an ineffable limit the common perception of which is grounded in its radical concreteness. Discourse has only to concede the abstract constraint of the Otherness of the physical or the temporal, but in no sense needs what is Other as anything more than a reminder of the requirement to make a difference between speech (life) and nature (death).

Locke then says that he will admit that an idea exists (i.e., is within communal discourse) when he finds its re-cognition in the word (when he finds it in the communal discourse); given this plan there is no innate idea because it is impossible to find a word before the communal discourse (that is, there is no idea that exists independently of the communal discourse). Men only cause themselves pain when—as instances of that discourse—they seek to comprehend that which is outside it and which is essentially inexplicable.

Whereas for Socrates original sociality makes reference to the alterity that while leaving its traces in words can never be completely appropriated to words themselves, hedonism formulates such alterity as the particularity and privacy of an original interiority that is essentially divisive. That is, any one expression of alterity is alien to any other because alterity manifests itself a-socially. The complete and concrete historicization of Otherness particularizes Being in a way that transforms it into the essentially inexplicable. Hedonism urges men to disregard any source of their divisiveness that cannot be named on the grounds that their continuous involvement in such a question will only perpetuate these divisions. That which divides one man from an other is sustained when men seek to address that which divides man from What Is Other because Other means that which cannot be named and the attempt to name the unnameable is what divides one man from an other. This attempt is divisive because it can never result in an agreement that is unproblematic enough to silence all dispute.

What is outside the communal discourse — what is absent from it — are those ideas which cannot be appropriated (that cannot be discerned as 'objects' to which all assent). This realm is divested of mystery in so far as it can be appropriated as a common object. Such a realm is inexplicable because its reception by any one man cannot be explicated as a presencing to which all can assent. Since Being is formulated as that which is absent from the discourse of man and yet, as that whose absence leaves its traces in the words and fears of men, Being is present but unavailable. Being is present in the sense that its work shows in the lives of men but it is absent in the sense that it is not available as an object for man. This mysterious presencing of Being which leads to the hedonist injunction to treat it as absent is what is intended by its inexplicability. Being is inexplicable because it cannot be shared, i.e., it cannot be entertained as a common object (it cannot be assigned a name to which all assent).

III

The only source of unity for man is his mortality, it is the fact of his limitation by death. Community is equivalent to the speechlessness of death. Yet, if the original differences between men cannot provide a surrogate for community, it seems as if man must ever hover between the twin silences of death and disorder. Hedonism needs to invent a genuine community around this very fearfulness: community is only possible on the grounds of the achievement of a limitation which on the one hand reproduces the facticity of death by providing a standard of speech with apparency and solidity, and on the other hand, through this re-producing, by managing to collect the differences as a unity. This very genuine interest of hedonism to re-collect the communal occurs on the grounds of its simplification of the problem of unity and difference as reflected in its denial of alterity as any thing Other than the facticity of corporeal limitation.

The difference between the commonness of the idea of death and the particularity and dispersiveness of our ideas recommends that we use the image of the facticity of death as the standard which our speech seeks to achieve in its practices. In relation to discourse then, Otherness can only be comprehended as the contingent source of particularity: alterity is necessarily linked to contingent differences between speakers in a way which requires the bifurcation of thinking and speaking (of 'internal' and 'external').

If the genuinely innate or Other (than man) is withdrawn, in so far as Other exists it exists among the things that coincide with man. What the things at this level have in common is that they vary or differ. If the difference and *multis* is original and if the practices that realize *multis* are not complete and self-evident, there must be something Other than such realization. Yet, such things cannot be Other than man since Other than man there is nothing. Such a thing that coincides with the thing(s) that appear can only be Other than such things by not being apparent. The private or the interior refers to the thing(s) that is co-present with the thing(s) that appears but which differs by being hidden.

What this variability means is that mind is an object for its owner in a way that is unsharable. In the effort to describe themselves men are ultimately rendered inarticulate in a way which partially isolates them by guaranteeing the essential impossibility of their being able to treat their several minds as one mind entertained and apprehended in common. While each mind is a repository for its owner that is complete and sufficient unto itself, this repository cannot be shared. There is then a permanent and essential disjunction between the interior and the public which makes every speech an interdeterminant and problematic display of private contents. Being surfaces for man in his mind and its manifestation is essentially particular and local. It is this particularization of Being that ascribes priority to interiority and which renders interiority fundamentally inexplicable to any body separated from the site at which it presences. This is why the conception of the primacy of interiority is essentially divisive: interiority re-formulates Otherness as a residual conception.

Since there is nothing Other than what coincides with man, any notion of Otherness or innateness must make reference to such things. There are the things that appear to man and to which he can affix determinant names. The things which appear to man as Other appear as innate not because they are Good but because they constitute unalterable limitations upon him. When the innate is seen as such a limitation it is conceived as inert and because Other means other than the variable, that which is common must unify the species by being an apparent and evident object for all observers. Only very simple, concrete 'facts' can be so apprehended. Thus, Other can only mean the most concrete constraint, i.e., that which is Other than these original variations because it is the most common limitation. The inertness of this common limitation or 'Other' is identical with its simplicity, apparency and self-evidence. This means that the only living Other on the human level is the person from which one happens to be contrasted, i.e., the other person.

The revocation of the conception of Other as Other-than-man translates Other into the common exigencies which constrain and limit man. From the point of view of man, all of the things that coincide with him which he cannot control then become Other to him, the most important being those things which are other persons. Otherness is formulated — socially — as the other person because alterity is identified with the unalterable and the unalterable interpersonal limit for man is his not being the whole (it is his perspectiviality). The unalterability of death is then reproduced in the recognition of the difference between one and an other as fundamental. Where the concrete common limitation of death recognizably collects all men, such a limitation provides no communal grounds: when the solidity of this limitation is reproduced in the apprehension of original perspectiviality as itself the fundamental interpersonal limitation, an opportunity for community is provided. Although hedonist philosophy as exegesis cannot alter this limitation, it can utilize it as a resource for achieving unity.

The innate as the inert recommends the firstness of speech: the denial of innate ideas is the rejection of anything outside speech, of anything more than matter. The denial is then an acceptance of nature but only as inert matter. Man *is* in so far as he transforms, creates and makes, and so it is the nature of man to be the labourer. Nature is withdrawn from speech and reformulated as that matter or material upon which speech operates — that external and oppressive material which only acquires relevance in its making, i.e., in its being used.

The inertness of the innate points to its lifelessness. The innate is lifeless. To associate with the innate is deadly. Man who lives in the shadow of death must work to transform this relationship. While he cannot alter the inert, he can officially disregard it. Man must work to re-achieve his freedom from what is lifeless by creating a kind of life among the things that coincide with him and the creation of a life among these things requires disregarding anything Other than him-self. Man's labour then appears as a commitment to reconcile and order the things on his level in such a way as to ensure their continuous survival as a collection of coincidences. Man's labour will then be a commitment to a method of collecting and relating the things that appear, a commitment which requires re-formulating the innate as the inert.

That which is Other than man is conceived as lifeless when it is not formulated as essentially implicated in the practice of discourse. For Socrates, the life-giving-power of Other is embodied in the testimony which speech gives as it displays its essential and positive dependence upon the difference between it-self and that of which it is an appearance. The conception of life as what is necessary and Good makes of the work of re-achieving the difference between the necessary and the inessential the work of life. This work — as conversation — is animated by a notion of the innate as the life-giving power of what is Good and indispensable and by the continuous Desire to re-achieve this difference between the innate and the derived. In contrast, the labour of hedonism as the method of exegetical labour is animated by a notion of the innate as the inert and deadly and by a continuous impulse to suppress the difference between the innate and the derived.

It is not a simplification to say that any conception of the innate as lifeless (which means as not needing to be continuously re-achieved) guarantees a simple conception of language as speech, because the need to fix and secure the determination of words is considered to be an exigency of life. In beginning with this conception of the requiredness of simple speech, hedonism not only idealizes the simple speaker (the common man, the primitive), but it commits it-self to a notion of individual differences as first since unity is formulated as abstract and lifeless.

To the questions: Why does man labour? Why does man speak? What is the good of labour? What is the good of speech? Hedonism cannot suggest an answer that draws upon the Socratic desire for the Good since the Good recommends a comprehensive and positive unity towards which speech aspires as a continuous feature of discourse itself and hedonism has elected to make its original unity inert or virginal. Because the hedonistic origin is silent or speechless, Locke's speaker labours as a moving away from this origin (from silence). The question of the good of hedonist speech then points back to the evil of speechlessness, and the rejection of the natural origin (which parallels the denial of innate ideas) is a rejection of the ultimate silence.

Inert nature as a symbol of the undifferentiation of oblivion (of the nothingness that exists before humanity — before infusion of value through labour) is the silence that can only be overcome through labour which punctuates that silence as a collection of discrete identities and names achieved through appropriation.

Man acquires value through labour because labour appropriates to man that which belongs to him by nature. That which belongs to man by nature is that which he requires to sustain his self as a discrete identity because such requirements constitute the property of man. The property of man refers not to the 'understanding' which is formulated as differentiating man from beast, but to the things which man needs to freely exercise this capacity which the 'understanding' describes. These *things* are conditions for the employment of the understanding and such things naturally and justly belong to a man.

If a man's property is his person, his absolute right is to create and sustain his personhood because the creation of personhood is what differentiated him from nature (it is what gives him dominion over nature). Such differentiation is good because it delivers men from the oblivion of nature. But this goodness is grounded in the idea of nature as silence or undifferentiation and consequently goodness can only be formulated in terms of its success in enabling men to forget or to move away from the original limit or rationality of the social (which is accomplished by conceiving of the origin as limitless, irrational and a-social).

Nature or inertness is conceived as static material and the only source of differentness lies in the labour that is movement. Movement or making confers value and man's natural right is to move (to move away) from the evil of undifferentiation. So when Locke says 'The exceeding of the bounds of [a man's] just property not lying in the largeness of his possession, but the perishing of anything uselessly in it . . . '[2] we see the evil to lie in uselessness or spoilage. Accumulation is rational *per se* because it uses (speaks) that which is inert and promises to lie fallow. Spoilage is a metaphor for the consequences of silence and points again to the moral requiredness of creating and sustaining personhood. It is *use* that creates value and spoilage refers to the silence that promises to ensue if men do not labour. Spoilage points to the obliteration of death from which speech labours to free itself.

But if all speaking is a triumph over death (over waste, over oblivion), given such a conquest (given a society of speakers) how do we differentiate between valuable and invaluable speeches? Or, how do we decide given a collection of useful speeches between their goodness and badness? Or do we celebrate any speech as good merely because of its accomplishment? Differences in rationality must still preserve the value of usage by reinterpreting the notion of spoilage or waste as a resistance to sociability. The evil of spoiled speech — of speech that cannot be used by an alter — is that it does not labour under the constraint of making itself present and available, i.e., useful to alter. The rational man is the sociable speaker or the speaker who resists the impulse to make useless speech. The sociability of the rational man parallels the exegete's repudiation of self-interest. The good of speech is its utility because only such speech will prevent the collective from recapitulating nature — from dying, from spoiling, from remaining inert, from unproductivity. Yet useful speech has to be sufficiently simple to permit all members to accept the speech as a whole without participation in its use. This is to say then that the spoilage principle which grounds the ideas of labouring itself also permits the exegete to discriminate between speeches; spoilage then becomes reformulated as the evil to which all speaking ought to orient, i.e., the necessity of speech to make itself available as material for judicial review and decision. Another way of saying this is that the good speech is the speech that can be used.

The collective then recapitulates the development of personhood: the collective is a person. Like the person the collective recoils from death through the labour of speech which appropriates to it its identity as a person. Both the individual person and the collective as a person triumph over nature through speech: the silence of nature is reflected in the inertness of oblivion for both person and city and the identity of both person and city is appropriated through speech.

The collective demands simple speech because — given nothing innate, either as difference or likeness — there are no innate differences between speakers and hence all speakers are equal. Similarly there are no innate likenesses, and hence the solution to community resides in the actual practices by which persons come together. Equality is then enforced by the conception of our original state as an array of persons who may, could and will come into contact, at first inert and then transformed by showing to one another our potentiality as objects. The original equality of speakers justifies the eventual differences between speeches in terms whether these different speeches are responsible to the universality implied by the original equality. The good speech as the simple speech is the universally comprehensible speech, the speech to which the species could orient. Since the denial of innate differences is authorized by an ideal of the a-social man as the common man — as the typical species member — good speech is that which he can comprehend. He is the speaker who brings together — who personifies — the essential equality between the parts of the species before positions are achieved.

The notion of original equality is dissolved by the differential appropriation that is speech, but the differences between speeches are grounded in the degree to which they are responsible to this principle of original equality. The rational speaker — as exegete — is one who carefully explicates the notion of original equality through the denial of any authority external to speech (such as innate ideas) and through his commitment to organize speech under the auspices of the requirement to prepare talk for judicial review.

If man needs the labour of method, what belongs to man by nature are the conditions which he requires to exercise the method. Although method is good in itself and these conditions are mere means to that end, the necessity of these conditions is seen in the fact that without them the speechlessness of death and disorder is inevitable. The conditions are then good because they are absolutely necessary for the exercise of method. Method is good because in organizing the application and enforcement of rule it enables men to survive by establishing agreement concerning the things that appear at the level of the coincidental. What is sacrificed for this survival is any concern with the essential.

IV

To confirm innateness is to seek to ascertain whether or not there are certain speeches which can make a difference as indubitable as the difference between life and death. Hedonism says that the differences between opinions lack such solidity. Hedonism worries that the social will disintegrate into a jungle in the absence of such an opinion (or rule). Yet, hedonism's fear is shaped by the rule of its standard of solidity, a standard which hedonism does not treat as another opinion. The solid speech must be universal since Locke's notion of innateness presupposes collective assent (the unthinkability of dissent). The collective character of such assent recommends to Locke the fixity of the idea to which the speech answers as a common (empirical) characteristic of the species. In other words the innate idea is conterminous with the species, it is a 'fact' for the species. In this formulation firstness (what is by nature first) is translated into descriptive universality, i.e., into the common empirical condition. What is first is not a necessity but an exigency. The requirement of commonality (of being entertained as common) alters the character of the criterion of presence because when presence is decided through the inspection of usage (of speech), the necessity of what is common is not an analytic necessity (an absolute that we require) but is, rather, that which happens to appear everywhere. What appears everywhere is what is everywhere named. The common is not the Good but a descriptive exigency. Since discourse cannot produce one thing that everywhere appears in a name, man is free to make his own limits. Locke's notion of presence and of the observational relationship between man and his mind is meant to exclude that which is absent from Locke's own beginning; Locke then begins with speech by starting with the words men emit to him, and since words are used circumstantially Locke *must* begin with convention (or usage). His test of innateness requires that he find the speech which is in universal use through the species (which shows the 'existence' of an idea because it is observed by all) and yet, by using such a criterion of usage as his standard Locke guarantees the absence of the idea because no word is universal (except words which refer to limitations so concrete that they are beyond the power of discourse to apprehend them). Furthermore, when the usage is itself formulated for the species (for anyone who uses words), the species as such a typical user is not a conception of a rational actor but only of a concrete organism (of a 'heap'). The species does not conjure up an image of the good society but rather, the universe of speakers, a universe founded by a limitation of membership to those who speak and so, to those who *appear* alive. The hedonistic version of society then limits it to a collection itself limited by the common conditions or exigencies of survival rather than by a conception of what is necessary and good.

Locke provides no analytic notion of innateness as there is in Rationalism because no corresponding word is universal. The range of the species as symbolized by universality refers to the prevalence of usage which cuts across analytic differences between good and bad speech leading to the conclusion that it is not all rational men who constitute Locke's original population but anyone who appears to be a man. This produces the hedonistic tolerance exemplified by Locke, i.e., anyone in the species is admitted into the city because the criterion of rationality is transformed to stand for the most common and inclusive characteristics of speakers (characteristics which are intended to re-present the solidity of the difference between life and death). Adequate speech is then necessarily formulated in terms of a standard of universality rather than of Rationality and the city becomes synonymous with the method that maximizes the intelligibility of speech for all users of words.

The idea is enunciated in its manifestation in the words of men. The idea has power. It causes men to speak it and therefore it exists. To say that there are no innate ideas is to say that there is no source of power outside (or before) speech and that it is only through the activity of speaking that men create limits; that there are no original limits but rather, that speech in its very occurrence generates its limits for itself to which it seeks to comply. The original limit has been formulated as that which discourse cannot touch. The very idea of innate ideas is an achievement of mature speech; as soon as speech begins speaking it loses its innocence and speech which tries to speak about innocence always speaks from the standpoint of maturity. If the existence of an idea is confirmed through reflection upon its presence, the history of ideas as existences is the history of their coming-to-be in time as objects of consciousness. Differences between men are then differences in time — in experience — where experience symbolizes moments in the history of the soul at which ideas are viewed as presences (are articulated in words).

When Locke says that if there were 'mature and original impressions' they 'should appear fairest and cleanest' to naturals (to children and idiots) because they are least 'corrected by custom' (by speech) he can only say this because his understanding of innateness as immutable facticity converts it into that which is so concrete that it does not require reflection. *If* ideas are as concretely accessible as the difference between life and death, the innate idea as the paradigm of such accessibility should be present to the most concrete observer. Yet the most concrete observer is not equipped to assess any thing — even the most concrete presence — and so his failure to use a name only confirms his speechlessness, and not the 'absence' of an idea.

It is primitives — children and idiots — whose public behaviour can be expected to be most concordant with the private, i.e., it is safest to assume in their case that deliberation and reflection would not intervene to disturb or render problematic the (assumed) self-evidence of behaviour (of speech). In other words, it is only man's intention to deceive, aggrandize, or to appear as other than he is, that complicates speech and thus, that produces discrepancies between what appears and what is. These discrepancies between the private and the public result from the fact of original differences among men and the continuous segregation of private and public which is used resourcefully to further perpetuate such differences. Children and idiots are primitive precisely because they are as they appear and this only because they have not been adequately socialized. When hedonism crystallizes into its exegetical form, its required assumption of the discrepancy between private and public poses for it the particular problem of method as its solution to this issue.

Such a view of language says that it is the essence of speech to be simple and that its simplicity consists in the way it describes the private contents entertained by mind. Speech becomes complex and enigmatic when discordances appear and such discordances appear increasingly as a result of man's desire to differentiate himself from his fellows.

The argument against the original commitment of man, i.e., against the innate idea, is itself based upon a conception of the species that includes all men (universality) because the idea of 'man' describes what all men have in common instead of formulating 'man' in terms of an end or aim (such as rationality) which is intended to bring out his best. Because man is formulated concretely and empirically, rather than analytically, theoreticity must be initially withdrawn from any formulation of him since theoreticity is understood as the source of man's inexplicability to his fellows, and any allusion to its presence threatens to deny the claim of man's original commonness. Man is required to be seen as originally concrete instead of deliberative. Man is originally speechless (brutish) and becomes social through his capacity to manufacture speech. In other words, if the excessive concreteness of the formulation of man excludes theoreticity as a feature of such a formulation (if it denies the stratification inherent in man's intermediate status *vis-à-vis* alterity) men are originally similar as instances of their common speechlessness; and if theoreticity is an acknowledgment of the essential implication of speech with alterity (a concession that there is something Other than speech and speechlessness), then men *must* be seen as equal since the only factors that differentiate them are features of their differential overcoming of speechlessness. The differences that appear can only be organized around the difference between speech and speechlessness, a difference that is always concrete. Yet, if men are not originally theoretic (if that is not their nature) then they are not equipped by virtue of the hedonist formulation itself to handle the complex understandings which Locke initially requires of them as (even) simple-minded observers and reporters of their minds. They could not accept the difference between speech and speechlessness as a real difference unless they had wrested it from some thing Other than either speech or speechlessness, for how could the word and the idea have become an intelligible contrast for them?

If commitment and original nature is everywhere revoked as a feature of the formulation of man, the standard of adequate (rational) speech that is developed must be sufficiently simple to unify men conceived as originally different only in terms of concrete characteristics. Since originally uncommitted men (brutes) became committed through *praxis* to their possessions, the only ground for their unity aside from self-interest (to further their possessions) is the desire for peace which enables them to continue and to protect the results of their appropriation. Yet such uncommitted men are constructed to have no original capacity even to re-cognize their interests let alone to act upon them. Unification can only be achieved externally when men come to acquire the theoreticity which they originally lacked. The emergence of the 'social' is then concurrent with the growth of theoreticity and man's nature is best understood as growth and development — as the achievement of the *praxis* of history — rather than as his origin and ground.

That men cannot be seen as originally theoretic as a solution to the hedonist fear of alterity requires that they be seen as originally equal (converting the idea of sociality into the idea of similarity), while the only criterion for warranting the adequacy of speech (presence) requires the very theoreticity that was originally withdrawn.

Naturalness as an icon of the concrete or 'pre-theoretical' is understood empirically as inexperience — as that which is prior to experience — and is formulated as that which mysteriously and externally precedes speech; it is formulated as speechlessness. Nature loses its weight as a constraint persisting within language because language is re-described as the speech that is responsible only to its making and that which is outside speech is either speechlessness as mind or as concrete and immutable nature. Speech mediates the relation between inside and outside by assimilating Other to discourse as the deliberation that concretely ignites it. The notion of 'outside' is then formulated as 'before being made' or as the virginal. Nature as 'outside' man is then truly inert, empty, nothing: this is to say that while the traces of nature are accredited as inexplicable features of interior life, such inexplicability only confirms the inert externality of nature until it can be transformed into a common object.

Locke's denial of innate ideas is developed under the auspices of a conception of the innate (the natural, the first) as that which *ought* to be assented to because it cannot be dissented from. Given *this* conception, Locke's inspection of usage reveals that the capacity to dissent is, first, there is no idea from which the practice of dissent cannot be imagined, and so the 'relativity' of every ought (that it can be dissented from) as a pronouncement upon the conventionality of all authority actually asserts that what is first is freedom (the capacity of the free mind to dissent). It is this first freedom which creates the need for certain common exigencies to ensure order; yet the idea of the firstness of freedom is itself created by a decisive understanding of notions of unity and difference.

The hedonist is intimidated by the heterogeneity of ways which shows the inexorable presence of dissent within the species of speeches and thus, his denial (his notion of what ought be authoritative) is controlled by and takes its bearings from the diverse practices of the multitude. Because the hedonist recognizes that his denial of the innateness of *this* idea would lead to cynicism, the denial of innate ideas is really the assertion of the innateness of the idea of the free mind (the mind which is free to convert speechlessness into speech).

If freedom (the mind, the human) is first, alterity can only be conceived as the negativity of randomness. The problem of unity is then formulated as the social order problem — the problem reconciling free minds — in such a way as to induce them to assent to that rule from which they are (theoretically) free to dissent. The ideal community (the social) is formulated as the typical understanding necessary to solve this problem: to accept the authoritativeness of the reformulation of language as speech as a solution to the social-order problem which the hedonist conception of the firstness of differences it-self generates. Hedonism denies the innate only under the condition of its acceptance of the innateness of freedom, while such an affirmation still testifies to that which is Other than what is affirmed or denied, to the truly innate which is Other than action.

To deny innate ideas is to deny what is Other than man, or it is to deny that man is originally limited by the positive and friendly instead of by the facticity of the corporeal. The Socratic conception of the end of man as his positive place within the whole — as the intermediate one — in equating place with end or aim says that the fate (*moira*) of man is the work of re-achieving a strong sense of his place. Socrates connects place and fate through the idea of work which re-achieves the original intermediacy of man as man's work or fate. In contrast, because hedonism denies anything positive Other than man, fate and place are segregated.

Man's place can never be a genuine topic because — strictly speaking — man has no place but only a position among other men.

The differences between men then describe how the parts *of the species* differ from each other and since each of these men has only a place in relation to other men, the place of *a man* is his position. Hedonism poses for itself the problem of how to understand the Being of man (what man *is*) if the idea of man has no place aside from its status as a summary of the different positions of men. Since men *are* different (their positions are transient and perspectivial), hedonism must attempt to take its bearings from a formulation of man which locates him before difference, before he is attached to a place (a position). If men are only differences, the Being of man must be formulated as what is common to all men — to the aggregate of men as a species — before they achieve places (positions). Since positions are different, what man is cannot be equivalent to any one position; since positions are achieved, what man is must be imagined as prior to such achievement. What man *is* is his origin not as the ground or foundation of the place of man *vis-à-vis* alterity, but as that which all *men* have in common as a species of parts.

The ideal man (what man is) as the common man is necessarily the a-social or pre-suppositionless man, the simple or uncorrupted man, a vision of which permits the species of men to see what it (what man) is.

The common man is the simple speech which is uncorrupted by reflection. In lieu of the essentiality of different speeches, each presenting a different disjunction of itself to its 'interior' referent, it is the hedonist philosopher's task to invent a version of the common speech as that speech which is as it appears. Such a speech would have the solidity of a fact and it would satisfy the communal need for exigencies of survival, exigencies that re-collect differences by establishing a rule to which all could orient.

V

We shall note how the hedonist conception of difference generates the need for an exegetical standard of re-unity personified in the figure of the common man. Locke formulates man as an observer who relates to the contents of his mind descriptively, i.e., ideas are those contents 'which a man observes and is conscious to himself he had in his mind.'[3] Locke begins with the difference between man and his mind as the *original* difference as if this difference has no source in unity. This difference repudiates the identity of public and private which is attributed to the common man as the ideal a-social observer and is re-achieved in maturity. Maturity — this difference — is then corrupt *vis-à-vis* the innocence of no-difference between private and public which is the Lockean formulation of the ideal observer. Instead of being identical with theoreticity, maturity is corrupt, and yet Locke begins with maturity. Since this difference between private and public is eradicated as a feature of the ascent towards hedonistic theoreticity, there is an essential disjunction between what is necessary to life (maturity) and what is necessary to theory (innocence). This tension can be detected in the hedonist notion of the artfulness or the 'pain' involved in theorizing. In this way, the segregation of private from public as an original difference based as it is upon a decisive conception of alterity, only reflects again the segregation of life from theory.

Thus, he begins with the difference between man and his mind as the *original* difference as if this difference has no source in unity. Although original sociality is denied in lieu of the requirement to repudiate man's original theoreticity, man is conceived originally as an observer. What kind of an observer can man be if he has no capacity for theorizing, if he is a-social? The idea of man as an a-social observer should not strike modern ears as strange: presumably, man's relationship with his mind is self-evident (it is self-sufficient and self-explicating) so that man requires nothing other than what appears before his eyes. This is to say that the original and primary observational relationship of a man to his mind is complete and its completeness resides in its a-sociality. Whereas a man relates to his own idea as an unalterable fact, such facticity is contingent upon the rule by which its character is established as an identity. A common fact expresses the theorist's re-collection of all such observations as one unalterable idea which he — as the collective — can re-present as necessary.

Locke's task is to 'observe and describe' what is in the minds of men (what is present and observable to them) and that which *is* present to them must be made present to *him*. That is, the contents of their minds can only be apprehended by Locke as a content of his mind (the relationship between man and his ideas itself becomes an idea in the mind of Locke as a man) which requires that *they* re-present their ideas in such a way as to make them (their ideas) into one idea for Locke. The difference with which he begins requires that both he and they share something in common — some resource, standard, or rule — which permits them to transform their ideas into material for him — into an idea about which he (the theorist) can speak. The idea in Locke's mind to which he as an observer relates then re-presents his consolidation of the disperse relations of other men-as-observers to the diverse ideas in their minds, a consolidation which he ratifies in his depiction of the common idea as a fact that 'exists'. The theorist is differentiated from other men because the ruling idea in his mind is the idea of their interactions with their minds.

Relations between men differ from the observational relationship that is interiority because What Is Other to the observer differs in each case. Alterity varies because its limitation to the things that appear with man accentuates its dependence upon the rule of man. One's mind is familiar to him as an observer in the way which an other's mind is not. One needs access to the other's mind in order to decide upon the adequacy of the name to the idea entertained, whereas one is not separated from the contents of his own mind. Another way of saying this is that discoursing cannot make a difference as immutable as the difference between life and death because discourse occurs between speakers who cannot produce a oneness in their speech as immutable as the fact of death. The innate limit which humans need respect is the concrete difference between life and death *vis-à-vis* this limit. Discourse appears as the attempt to make differences as incorrigible as the difference between life and death. But, no speaker can compel another to treat his speech as incorrigible and immutable because what one speaker speaks *about* can never presence to an other with the same immutability as the difference between life and death. What one speaks about is an idea in his mind and ideas are not innate (they do not have the immutable limiting character of common facts) because they (as products of choice, of seeing) are made — are achievements. To see a common fact — like the difference between life and death — is to see that which precedes and is not the result of discourse. Since ideas are always 'entertained' by observers (those who observe their minds) the only common fact (the only limit that is innate) must be that which observation cannot alter. If Other is that which observation cannot alter, discourse needs to be as indifferent to Other as Other is (seen to be) to discourse. Yet, while discourse does not need to suffer Other as a requirement to which it is continuously responsible it does acknowledge Other as that which it is not. In this way, hedonist speech can labour to create ideas which aim to re-produce and to resemble the facticity of the original difference between life and death. In its more despairing moments when hedonism (i.e., existentialism) re-cognizes the *descriptive* impossibility of such re-producing, it acknowledges its indifference to all difference (except the original difference) as a *reflexive* antedote to the illusion (the multitude) that speech makes a difference.

Because Other as that which precedes discourse is the most common and incorrigible fact, there is no way to relate Other to discourse, i.e., if Other appears within discourse as an idea it would presence as that which could appear otherwise to an Other observer. Yet if Other is segregated from discourse the question of how it presences as the common limit must be addressed. Other must be the overpowering which leaves men speechless and so discourse apprehends Other in its moments of inarticulateness (as, e.g., metaphysics). Men come to develop 'ideas' of Other that are, strictly speaking, copies and images (misdirected attempts to name the unnameable).

Men ought not to treat their speechlessness as an occasion for rethinking Otherness so that its difference can become a topic for discourse to re-achieve. Rather, that which causes speechlessness ought be left alone because dwelling upon it will only perpetuate silence. Interiority symbolizes man's place between speechlessness and speech and men must begin with a notion of Other (of Other-as-speechlessness) as a re-presentation of the silence that temporally precedes speech. Other as speechlessness or non-speech (Other than speech) is re-presented as the grounds of speech only in the way that thinking is seen to precede doing. Interiority symbolizes the work (of deliberating and deciding) which speech shows. Other is then domesticated through its limitation to the speaker: any thing Other must be disregarded.

Hedonism cannot permit Otherness to be anything Other than interiority. If it permitted a strong notion of Other, it would never overcome speechlessness (differences). If Otherness is formulated as the silence of interiority, the speech which 'follows' it can always be reconciled to it as a copy of an original if someone manages the reconciliation who has an interest in *this* relationship itself. Different speeches must be reconciled in order to produce the adequate or true speech. If all men are essentially observers of their minds all men are fundamentally limited by the interests of ownership. The hedonist theorist as an exegete is the safeguard against the possible divisiveness of ownership. As opposed to the majority, the theorist, as one who leads through his interpreting, is ruled by an interest in the contents of their several relationships to their minds, and thus he is alone in his collective interest in the communal relationship to *its* mind. As a solution to the problem of death and disorder, hedonism generates the exegete as its paradigmatic theorist.

The exegete is expected to exemplify statesmanship in his teaching by counselling men into proper ways of speaking in order to conform to the requirements of an adequate observational relationship between the community and its interior life. He himself seeks to exemplify a form of speech that is sufficiently comprehensive and simple to permit all speakers to respect it in their practices. Exegesis will protect men because the originally a-social (speechless) species could be irrevocably divided (locked within their own certainties) without the theorist's intervention. Yet it is exegesis in its hedonist impulse which in its creation of this original a-sociality produced the very problem to which its program is an attempted solution. Where hedonism generates exegetical labour as the method for solving its problem, such a solution accepts the hedonist formulation of the problem as its limits.

The resource which permits men to socialize appears at first to be the understanding:

> Since it is the understanding that sets man above the rest of sensible beings and gives him all the advantage and dominion which he has over them; it is certainly a subject even for its nobleness worth our labour to enquire into.[4]

The essence of man — that which man is — is formulated in terms of the limits of man, the contrast between man and beast. The anticipation of this contrast grounds the idea of man-as-man and in this sense the power of man lies in his understanding. Power is used as a metaphor for that condition which creates man as an essent autonomous and distinct from other beings. If the essence of man is the understanding, we have already seen that the understanding itself — as the relationship between man and his ideas — only becomes available as a topic for man through speech. It is through speech that man will prosecute his inquiry into his essence — the understanding — and the task of the theorist is to labour in such an enterprise. But this is made difficult because 'the understanding, like the eye, whilst it makes us see and perceive all other things, takes no notice of itself and it requires art and pain to set it at a distance and make it its own object.'[5]

It is the nature of man to forget his source of power, to forget that from which he derives his authority. Because man understands naturally, it requires an unnatural or artful turn to make understanding itself a topic. Because the majority are corrupt (are mature), the artful suspension of this maturity in the service of exegetical innocence is required. The innocence of exegesis makes reference to its dedication to a standard of interpretation that adequately reconciles differences. This should be the task of the exegete: to clarify and inventory the source of our natural involvements so as to guarantee the continuous and efficacious dominion of man as a being. He as no other man might take the effort and the pain to understand his understanding so as to protect the relationship between ordinary men and things external to them. The warrant for exegesis is to survey and inspect the work of making speech in order to ensure the continuation of such sociability. This warrant is then grounded in the conception of the exegete as the artful one, i.e., the one who will act or labour unnaturally — who will take the unnatural turn — in order to protect the natural conversation. In this sense, nature as typified by the routine relationships between men and their ideas actually requires assistance from that which is unnatural, and therefore exegesis warrants itself as the first art because it is needed to protect nature. Because it will protect the 'natural attitude' by describing it, its warrant shall only be grounded in the claim to complete what nature necessarily leaves incomplete. Exegesis will leave nature as it is and will abstain from teaching (from conversation) in order to provide nature with a record of its history that it can use in its very creation of that history. Without such a record men will not be properly organized. Exegesis will be successful when it can be oriented to within the natural discourse as itself an item of nature. Exegesis is compelled into being by the hedonist formulation of the fundamental injustice of nature and by the conception of exegetical labour as the adequate method for meeting the exigencies of survival.

It is man's intermediacy that compels him to work, i.e., his being different from God *is* his need to work. Yet, man's difference — expressed in the notion of Otherness — means that his labour has its own positive and distinctive character. The Socratic version of man's intermediacy says that man's work is an imitation of the Gods in so far as it is ruled by a Desire, as Socrates says, to 'please the Gods', but man does not seek to copy the gods. What man is is Other than divine.

In contrast, hedonism understands intermediacy as a privation and so, it must understand labour as an attempt to re-produce divinity. The intermediacy of man is firmly conceded in the re-cognition of mortality. It is in this recognition that man raises the problem of reason as the need for justifying his activity since his inevitable extinction means that he need account for the purpose or place of his conduct.

Yet the requirement to discursively formulate a *logos* only recapitulates this intermediacy since the defeasibility of any speech (his essential perspectiviality) only again confirms man's mortality (his intermediacy) as his self-conception of not being the whole. Perspectiviality is then the interpersonal icon of intermediacy, that intermediacy first grasped in the re-cognition of death. In contrast, the Socratic conception of intermediacy uses such (re)cognitions — of mortality, perspectiviality — as occasions for showing the work of intermediacy itself, i.e., as other opinions conceded and interrogated through discourse and not as indicators of a fundamental imperfection that requires surpassing.

Hedonist man begins with the re-cognition of his fundamental privation or incompleteness *vis-à-vis* Other, and so, begins under the burden of needing to copy that to which he is not adequate. He then seeks to overcome mortality by achieving a completeness in speech that eradicates perspectiviality by constituting itself as an opinion the apparency and self-evidence of which — given adequate 'technical' preparation — resists dissent. He faces the problem of adjusting the desire for immortality to interaction in a way which succeeds only by reviewing and assimilating to it-self (by possessing) all opinion in order to construct the complete speech. Possessive speech is the human (discursive) icon of the completeness of which man is originally deprived, and his labour requires of him the attempt to formulate and control any exemplification of (concrete) alterity.

The labour of hedonism is then necessarily exegetical, directed as it is to the interpretation of the 'point of view' of alter, a task which frames its judgmental problem (its problem of method) because this difference is first and essential (the difference between interpreter and subject as an icon of original *multis*). Hedonism generates exegetical labour intended to result in the cumulation of 'property' which is the ultimate comprehensible — complete — opinion as the exegetical version of the just speech.

If the self-interest of the hedonist actor makes him unqualified to consummate the just speech, the reflexive face of such an actor (as exegete) who commands a vision of the exigencies of survival — of the conditions necessary for the preservation of alternative points of view — is turned towards the possibility of achieving a surrogate immortality through statesmanlike speech. It is in this sense that the statesman is 'called' (the vocation of exegesis) by the injustice of nature, and it is in this sense that he disregards innateness as his condition for re-achieving a surrogate justice because of the apparent elusivity and intangibility of Real Justice. The exegete will defend the productive conversation by describing the way in which the understanding organizes itself as an orderly and rational achievement and such a description will record the history of the understanding as it occurs in actuality. This description will then serve as a statutory formulation of the limits of the understanding — of what the understanding is — to which members can always orient and make reference whenever their work becomes problematic. This inventory will then provide a stable point of reference for men to consult in the face of problems which intermittently threaten their connection to things and such a point of reference will be grounded in the painful but disinterested contemplation of the organization of the understanding now re-called as the empirical limits of understanding itself. Since the disinterested description of the understanding is furnished by addressing how the understanding is actually accomplished as a self-organizing achievement, the limits or essence of the understanding will be grounded in a conception of the capacities of man when those capacities are re-read into the understanding on the basis of what it does rather than what it could do. Limit is grounded in the empirical formulation of possibility as natural history. The exegetical speech must be as trustworthy as any of the facts of nature, even though such speech is produced unnaturally or artfully.

Locke then perpetuates the Baconian programme of collecting natural histories, because his formulation of the soul becomes a natural history of the typical understanding now resurrected as a standard which symbolizes the limits of the understanding as a normative order to which ordinary members can make periodic reference in resolving intermittent problems that result from their overstepping (through ignorance) the limit.

VI

If the understanding is what sets men apart from nature (and if the understanding is 'understood' through the labour that eventuates in its works), then the understanding is the source of the identity — which each man creates and appropriates. The rules of the understanding reformulate the limits of appropriation; if appropriation acquires value only in so far as it respects the demand for simplicity and clarity entailed by the hedonist formulation, the rules of the understanding must then re-describe the conditions of intelligible and simple speech as successful speech. The rules of the understanding must be anchored in a descriptivist conception of what is required to work out solutions to the problem of interaction. These 'conditions' of successful speech can be understood as exigencies of concrete interaction and exegesis is concerned with preserving the exigencies of successful (peaceful) interaction rather than with re-achieving the necessity of what is good.

> God having designed man for a social creature . . . it was further necessary that he should be able to use these sounds as signs of internal conceptions: and to make them stand as marks for the ideas within his own mind, whereby they might be known to others, and the thoughts of men's minds be conveyed from one to another.[6]

This need for exchange will determine the criterion of good speech. Since words 'stand for' internal conceptions and nothing else, men must understand their speech as being taken in this way. Such an understanding should rule the production of speech itself.

> The ends of language in our discourse with others being chiefly these three: First, to make known one man's thoughts or ideas to another; secondly, to do it with as much ease and quickness as possible: and finally, thereby to convey the knowledge of things.[7]

Locke's notion of adequate discourse is organized around standards of parsimony and economy: the reliability and economy of such discourse conveys an altogether different conception from dialectic, as hedonism treats conversation as a commercial transaction. Consequently language is seen as abused when:

> men have names in their mouths without any determinant ideas in their minds whereof they are the signs,
>
> they apply the common received names of any language to ideas, to which the common use of that language does not apply then . . .
>
> they apply them very unsteadily . . . .[8]

The second abuse is crucial for it establishes ordinary usage as the control upon speech and then, it even provides the test for determining whether abuse such as the first exists. The test is universality of agreement since the first abuse cannot be determined in a way that is free of language.

> It is not enough that men have ideas, determined ideas, for which they make these signs stand: but they must also take care to apply their words as near as may be to such ideas as common use has annexed them to. For words . . . be no man's private possession, but the common measure of commerce and communication, it is not for anyone at pleasure to change the stamp they are current in, nor alter the ideas they are affixed to.[9]

It is shown in one's responsibility to speech which is a responsibility to the city: man ought to be responsible to 'commerce and communication' and to the requirement of displaying this responsibility through his speech. Man's speech must be grounded in some prior descriptive knowledge of common speech — of common usage — for that knowledge becomes the order to which his speech is oriented and by which it is limited.

Therefore in discussing 'truth' and 'falsehood' Locke can say: 'When a man is said to have a false idea it is for no other reason, but that his agrees not with the ideas which each of those names are the signs of in other men . . . '[10] thus leading him to accept the description of practice as a mandate for theorizing, instead of seeing this very conception of truth and falsity — of the rule of ordinary usage — as the problem. When Locke announces his criticalness in the following way: 'nothing can be so dangerous as principles taken up without questioning or examination',[11] we must then hear this within the limits of the kind of interrogation which he has in mind, an examination that will conduct its review with full respect for the simple clarity and parsimony that the most conventional speech exemplifies; we can then question whether the concept of criticalness in hedonism is as critical as it supposes.

> If men will not be at pains to declare the meaning of their words, and definitions of their terms are not to be had, yet this is the least that one can be expected, that, in all discourses wherein one man pretends to instruct or convince another, he should use the same words constantly in the same sense. If this were done (which nobody can refuse without great disingenuity), many of the books extant might be spared many of the controversies and dispute would be at an end; several of those great volumes, swollen with ambiguous words, now used in one sense, and by and by in another, would shrink into another very narrow compass; and many of the philosophers' (to mention no other) as well as poets' works, might be contained in a nutshell.[12]

It is hard to reconcile the command to be critical with the subordination to conventional usage, for on the one hand Locke urges relentless questioning, and on the other, he counsels us to avoid creating dispute and controversy with eccentric speech. He treats extraordinary speech as motivated, as intentional, rather than as a display of the incompleteness of speech, and thus, as a 'social problem' or a matter to be remedied or reformed through legislation. Eccentric speech is a-social because it sustains conversation — it sustains 'controversy' and 'dispute' — instead of terminating speech in the tranquillity of complacent silence. Further, if dispute is to be avoided, it must still be recognized that men relinquish their opinions reluctantly. The hedonist ideal of rational speech cannot be articulated completely in the actions of men even though this ideal was derived from the descriptive study of such actions.

> Since, therefore, it is unavoidable to the greatest part of men, if not all, to have several opinions, without certain and indubitable proofs of their truth; and it carries too great an imputation of ignorance, lightness, or folly for men to quit and renounce their former tenets presently upon the offer of an argument which they cannot immediately answer, and so the insufficiency of: it would, me thinks, become all men to maintain peace, and the common offices of humanity, and friendship, in the diversity of opinion, since we cannot reasonably expect that anyone should readily and obsequiously quit his own opinion, and embrace ours, with a blind resignation to an authority which the understanding of man acknowledges not.[13]

This permanent and essential disjunction is the way in which essential incompleteness in the relationship between aspiration and satisfaction becomes articulated in speech. Given this inexorable disjunction which was the very reason for and source of the hedonist programme in the first place — the original disagreement of man — we must remain in a state of permanent restlessness and pain, with tolerance and peaceableness becoming the only sources of order to which we can appeal.

Good speech (true speech) must be agreeable speech, speech that re-presents the ideas to which it answers in a way that conforms to the same re-presentations of others. The good speaker must be able to speak in a way that describes the universal observational relationship between men and their ideas. The speech of the good speaker must then be controlled by his interest in re-presenting not merely his particular relationship, but the universal communal relationship to ideas. The good speaker is essentially a re-presentative who differs from the ordinary member through his commitment to re-presentative speaking.

Whereas the hedonistic conception of original a-sociality produces the essential restlessness and competitive appropriative activities of hedonist society, the good speaker will supervise the reconciliation of such differences through re-presentative speech, speech which re-presents the most prevalent and unanimous collective relationship to ideas. Such re-presentative speaking thus requires the empirical study of practices because its reconciliation is grounded in its claim of fidelity to the collective practice.

If the good speech was a mere summary, however, the reason for making it would only be clerical. It must re-construct the many speeches under the auspices of a format that can re-situate the great range of speeches in terms of categories that are sufficiently common and concrete to be invariant across all speeches. Such rules must be sufficiently common to elicit assent from all men to their credibility as limits, even though specific speeches might fail to articulate with this standard in particular cases. This is to say that the limits themselves must be assented to as the only rational rule for grounding re-presentative speech and re-presentative speech itself must be accredited as the only speech capable of organizing the collective. Good speech — the speech of exegesis — is then that speech which administers and re-presents the collectivity of speeches as a tacit but official reminder of the limits which speech ought not to transgress. Good speech preserves the common-speaking practice of the species instead of questioning that practice (which would ultimately be a questioning of the *social* character of the species as a community). Whereas exegesis seeks to preserve the practice, Socrates asks for the good or aim of the practice; Socrates asks what is exegesis practising (rehearsing) *for*?

Exegesis then, represents the multitude in the highest sense, by organizing its speeches into an interaction. In this way, such re-presentation intends itself as statesmanship, i.e., as speech which exemplifies rigour in order to preserve the 'point of view' of that which it re-presents and describes. It is only by exemplifying rigour that exegesis can arrest the injustice which the hedonist vision pictures.

The injustice conjured up by hedonism as its fearful point of departure occurs under the auspices of its recognition that the Socratic conception of Otherness only excites and continues conversation where the 'solution' of silence (of concrete agreement between different apprehensions of Being) is required. Hedonism simplifies the dialogue into Being not because Being *is* simple, but because its image of pleasure, pain, success, failure, man and species requires such a simplification.

Because hedonism sees sociality as agreement, men are not originally social because they do not universally agree. The 'social' can only become an external method for inducing men to agree to agree — to accept the minimum limitation necessary to recognize and to sustain their mutual accumulations of property. As a maxim, such a city exemplifies rational methods of communication. To hedonism, the city (the social) is a solution to the problem of order which they see themselves as inheriting in the Socratic conception of the city as conversation (in the Socratic notion of original sociality). Hedonism understands the evil of this inheritance to reside in the Socratic conception of rationality (of the conversation of friends) because such a conception provides no standard for addressing (for eliciting agreement from) those who are enemies (external to it) and thus can never eventuate in the 'works' and solutions which require collective action. Because such 'works' require universal agreement, Socratic conversation can only liquidate itself — it is powerless to preserve its own course as itself a 'work' in the history of productive men. The simplification of speech, the concretizations of language, Otherness, nature and the social, re-present acknowledgments by modern men of the need to de-limit the boundaries of the community of speakers in terms of a policy with which all of its members can be urged to agree on the grounds of the compelling image of communality to which the policy is intended to answer. The power of this image lies in its promise to preserve the conversations of men as memorable works in the history of the race — as works that testify to the triumph of art over nature as a realization of the organizing capacities of the race itself.

Perhaps we can now begin to comprehend the conception of pain in hedonism that compels men to simplify their speech: the pain represents the fear of oblivion and anonymity which is seen as extinguishing the Socratic conversation in the minds of men because of its failure to leave its traces in concrete works for which only a radical simplification of speech could provide. The death from which hedonism recoils in the form of its fear of not being re-membered or preserved compels the project to radically transform its conception of language in order to guarantee its own continuity through the concrete remains of the works which it promises to leave behind.

CHAPTER III

Exegesis

I

If hedonism takes as its point of departure a notion of the essentiality of original and unalterable limitation, what this means deeply is that in the beginning there is injustice. It is man's fate to live among things some of which are unalterable. These things among which man lives — as a feature of their essential unalterability — are indifferent to him. Man then lives among some things that are indifferent to him, and because of this indifference, things that intervene in his life without respect for his wishes and intentions. Man ought to seek to organize in order to minimize the extent of the influence of such unalterable and indifferent things.

According to hedonism, the essential unalterable thing is Being. Whether Being is a metaphor for an abstract creative God who withdraws after his work, or for the incorrigible common fact of mortality, it is — as Epicurus says — that which ought not to concern man because it is indifferent to him. Epicurus' advice that men ought to observe piety but 'leave the Gods alone' counsels them to formulate the innate as the inert. A continuous involvement in the question of the innate as reflected in the work of raising the question 'what is first?' can only appear to the hedonist as an impossible — because inevitable — source of contention among men. The sterile and unyielding character of the innate can only mean that it will never give man ground for re-achieving the difference between itself and man since it can only appear differently to different men. It will never co-operate with man because it is basically unfriendly to his efforts to re-collect it. This variability means that Being can never be observed or entertained as a common object and so, it can never be a source of solidarity for the speeches of men. Being can never be an integral part of discourse.

The disparity between man and Being — the indifference of Being to man and the requirement for man to reciprocate this indifference as an exigency of his survival — means that man recognizes his limitation by what is Other and thus, that he recognizes this essential difference. Yet this difference is recognized as finally and absolutely appropriated in a way which is itself unalterable and to which discourse is not adequate. Rather than revive this difference in its work, discourse understands its survival as contingent upon the suppression of this difference as a condition for the creation of agreement in speech. The conditions which constitute the survival of discourse are those contingencies to which exegetical labour seeks to comply as grounds for the continuation of its interaction.

The unalterability of Being is reflected in man's limitation by the whole, in man's being only a part. Being a part means — for hedonist man — being one man among many (and does not refer to the place of man *vis-à-vis* the whole). The limitation of one man by other men is the hedonist vision of man's essential limitation by Being. Thus, hedonism sees the difference between one and an other to be the unalterable and essential icon of the difference between man and Being. If this limitation of one by an other is as unalterable as death, it is nevertheless true that other men — unlike the Gods — are not presumed to be indifferent to one. The competitive and possessive practices of enigmatic hedonist actors guarantee their reciprocal concerns.

Exegesis advises men to address Being through the discourse of man. It shares with Socrates the idea of mediating the relationship to the Gods through discourse. However, the exegetical conception of discourse formulates the beginning as a collection of different perspectives. Exegesis formulates every interlocutor as committed to the hedonist maxim of desiring to appropriate the whole — of working under the auspices of an essential uneasiness with his perspectiviality — reflected in the practice of seeking to cumulate and possess that knowledge which would close the gap between men. Conversation is an exchange of opinions between participants who in being ruled by their recognition of fundamental perspectiviality seek to assimilate all opposition to themselves. Hedonism begins with the difference between one and the other as if it was essential, instead of starting with the difference between man and that which grounds him. If to begin with man and his surroundings is to begin with the intermediacy of man, for then hedonist man's 'surroundings' are other men — others like him — resulting in the implication that man is first.

The original injustice grasped by hedonism as an acknowledgment of man's mortality is then realized in its concession of the unalterable and primary character of man's limitation. This limitation refers to man's not being able to appropriate the whole. Whereas Socrates sees this very limitation as the occasion for man's work, as the ground and incentive for his continuous effort to re-achieve this limit as an end or place that belongs to him as man, as what he is, hedonism sees this limitation as the source of a fundamental gap between men which must be resolved. Hedonism requires of itself that it work to interpret the point of view of that which differs — of the other man, the material — as its way of closing this gap, as its way of re-achieving the unity of which man is originally deprived. Since interpretation always leaves an enigmatic residue or trace, this completion can only be surrogate.

Exegesis seeks to possessively appropriate the place of alter to its own as its way of overcoming the original limitation expressed in the fact of any one man's exclusion from being the whole, from being all men. Whereas the difference between one and an other is used by Socrates to preserve what we each are as an exemplification (a common exemplification) of man's limitation by the whole, the exegetical dream of unity understands this apartness as an impediment to speech rather than as a resource for conversation. The hedonist conception of this very difference as the problem to be resolved generates the requiredness of the labour of interpretation and exegesis, the need for the cumulation and possession of the 'property' of interpretations, an accumulation so complete and total as to render reserve impossible.

II

If exegetical labour is required to reconcile differences, it is only needed as a solution to *that* problem because of the hedonist conception of alterity as reflected in its denial of genuine innateness.

Locke asks about the grounds of our action and conceives it as an uneasiness:

> This uneasiness we may call ... desire: which is an uneasiness of the mind for want of some absent good.[1]
>
> Good and evil, present and absent, it is true, work upon the mind. But that which immediately determines the will ... is the uneasiness of desire fixed on some absent good: either negative, as indolence to one in pain: or positive, as enjoyment of pleasure.[2]

Locke had originally construed a world in which the Good as the necessary, absolute and essential, would be absent because he understood the traces of alterity to show itself in the pain and restlessness of man that requires reduction. In these passages Locke speaks concretely of the absent good — as if it was the 'goods' that men conventionally covet, and yet we hear in his talk the residues of his concern with the Otherness that he has eliminated.

Because any positive ground for action was originally revoked from this world, man can only be 'agitated' into action through inequities in the possession of 'goods'. The absence of alterity which his formulation required as a condition for initial agreement (and for the simplification of speech) leaves its traces in the various concrete disjunctions between aspirations and fulfilment where the objects of such strivings are possessions. Hedonist men are possessed by possessions and the dialectic between want and satisfaction organizes their lives as meaningful courses of action. Hedonist men are essentially restless, continually on the move, because their images of tranquillity and completion are symbolized by possession and the society has been constructed to produce essential inequities in possessions and thus, to be essentially incomplete. Inequities are inexorable because the objects of possession are inextricably tied to circumstance and accident. The original stratification of man *vis-à-vis* Other which hedonism withdraws is re-presented in the conventional differences and inequities between men because the place (or end) of man *is* the position of man within the society of men.

Hedonist speech parallels and is organized around this

conception of completion and aspiration, and the possessiveness of speech — the disarticulations between want and satisfaction — is mirrored in its radical simplification that produces the type of segregation between words and things (between speech and ideas, between public and private) that must itself resist every attempt at completion (at fulfilment).

Locke's conception of our 'want for some absent good' is a version of the problem which has exercised students of Locke, e.g., how what is held in common becomes possessed individually? First, what is held in common is not something positive (such as a duty *to* something) but is a privation or a lack. That is, the hedonist notion of original equality makes reference to the fact that *what* men have in common is *that* they are in a similar position *vis-à-vis* the void. What men have in common is their propensity to recoil. What men have originally in common is that they are without a place because they are without a position.

Second, men are then motivated by the void. This is to say that the actions of men are grounded in what-is-not (in Not-Being) because the possibility of the void incites them to speak, to move. Yet the void is not comprehended from within language itself as a point of reference or control upon rational speech because the void does not delineate the contrast between Being and nothing that is itself understood within language as no-thing; instead it comes to stand for that 'thing' that is absent from language.

Thus in answer to the question of how this propensity becomes articulated in different possessions, hedonism posits the innate restlessness of men as their common desire to attain what they lack. What men lack is what is absent where this absent 'object' is not formulated as the alterity that hedonism itself withdrew but as the 'goods or possessions' that men want. Absence does not depict the Otherness of a common object — an object which they concertedly entertain and share — but rather, it points to that which any one man does not own. Absence is comprehended possessively as some thing from which one is excluded.

That men are driven by the desire for an absent good means under these conditions that men are exercised by what they are not and the idea of what man *is* or *is not* is settled hedonistically. Since man is not originally limited, what he *is* is the capacity to become anything, and what he is not at any time is that which he has not yet become. What is absent is merely what man is not — his not-yet; as of any present, man is essentially incomplete or unfulfilled *vis-à-vis* the possibility of what he could become. This possibility is what he is not; it is the absence that compels him to continue.

The lack of an original limit upon man means that his incompleteness is not essential because there is nothing permanently and irrevocably external to him such as the traces of Being which continually resist his appropriation. What man is not is not Other to him but merely different; it is that which he could. become given an alternative arrangement of conditions and circumstances (given an alternative city, given a 'utopia'). In so far as man appropriates these conditions he becomes what he is not and so what he is, fundamentally, is growth, *praxis*, and appropriation.

Because there is no original limit upon man, the essence of man — what man is — cannot be grounded in any comprehensive delimitation of man from what is Other than man, for what is Other than man has no positive content. Hedonist man cannot 'imitate the Gods' as Socrates says, because the Gods point only to a void. Thus, the idea of 'man' loses all analytic weight for there is no rational way to comprehend the end of man through a formulation of the essent *vis-à-vis* which is Other to it. Given the absence of this Otherness we can understand hedonistic restlessness, for what one is controlled by the conventional circumstances that separate one position from another.

To be compelled by the absent object is then a way of speaking about man's grip in the control of difference: it is a way of pointing to man's fearfulness lest he fail to become what he is not (fails to achieve what he does not yet possess). Contentment — as a feeling of relative satisfaction — is expressed in the figure of man whose possessions are sufficiently exhaustive to enable him to treat what he is as well summarized by what he has (such a man has enough). Thus even hedonistic calm is a result of triumph, possession and appropriation, since it symbolizes a man's conception of his completion as sufficient only by comparison to what he lacks, i.e., that he has assimilated all difference to himself and so, *is* (because he has).

The right to address the differences symbolized by inequities and possessions is what the 'social' protects. The social protects the free exercise of this right to appropriate possessions in order to complete the essential disjunction between what one is not (the completeness that one wants to be) and what one is (the incomplete and accidental circumstantiality of one). Democracy as an example of exegetical labour makes reference to the method which guarantees the preservation of interactional exigencies.

The absent object can only be formulated as that which is excluded from one because there has never been a common object for all aside from the collective (universal) apprehension of the common and equal privation. What is lacked in common is not an object but the conditions that would allow us to overcome this lack — conditions that would permit all to exercise the collective right to accomplish such an overcoming. What is possessed in common is the right to move — the right to defend our differentiated selves and thus, what we lack is the complete fulfilment of this very right.

The absent object can only be the peace — the conditions — that will guarantee and enforce our right to labour and appropriate. The Good that is absent is the diminution of restlessness. The absence of such conditions results from the fact that while language belongs to us in common, we receive it (interpret it) differently because of the inexplicability of the presencing of Being for interiority, and our task is to re-member the commonness of language (by re-membering the a-social speaker). Only by remembering in this way our common possession of language will we be able to protect our own interior lives. Yet we do not protect the *contents* of such interiority for these contents must be collectively ratified: what we protect is our *right to entertain* such contents, our right(s) to apprehend Being. Hedonism then permits us to protect our right to have secrets, and provided that we comprehend such secrecy as inexplicable and as extraneous to the communal discourse, we can cultivate its realm as an irreducible mystery, as the ultimate province and source of all of our accomplishments. Remembering the commonness of language points to the peace-ableness of our interior life as the only precinct free from motion and restlessness. This is to say that the right-to-privacy makes method necessary and so, this right serves simultaneously to enslave man to method. It is the notion of a fundamental right as freedom from substantive commitment that is itself the source of the domination of method. It is the fact that communality is only understood as the concrete temporality of the body that produces the notion of Otherness as interiority where that very interiority can never become accessible to discourse as the kind of thing which is the body. If discourse is essentially incomplete it is because the difference between life and death as a concrete fact furnishes the standard of completion. Because interiority is the contingent source of speech standing as 'ground' to 'result', interiority is only accessible through speech itself and yet must always remain enigmatic as that which speech only partially re-presents.

The absent common object becomes the secret reserve in which Being presences in the severalness of the different minds of men, and the inexplicability of that region becomes the unexplicated agency of differentiation the exercise of which must ultimately be protected. Such protection requires limiting this reserve as a sacred province whose mysteries are not to be addressed. The simplification of speech is such a safeguarding solution since it uses the secret precinct of interiority as a descriptive resource and as an image of communality to which men ought universally orient. We are only at home — at rest — in our 'private' world because man's commitment to the social is a commitment to motion as an end. Tranquillity can only be envisaged as privacy and thus, as a-social. There is no way of comprehending tranquillity within the motion of speech and labour. What is really absent and desired is, then, a firm and positive conception of the place of man as a conception that will not perish.

Our innate restlessness is a function of the essential divisibility of this world and of our fundamental and irrevocable lack of access to the other sacred provinces of interior life from which we are essentially separated. We are required to respect this difference in order to exercise our right to control our other provinces. However, our restlessness is a feature of this inexorable difference that on the one hand, limits our acquisitiveness and on the other, legitimizes our own control of our property. Restlessness is then a feature of the dialectic between imperialism and nationalism, between possessiveness and autonomy, between private and public, between self and other: rules of rational communication ensure that we remain uneasily within such limits, i.e., that we respect them for egocentric reasons even while desiring to overstep them. If death is the first thing for hedonism, this is because life is seen as a thing. Such a view of this difference is responsive to the most deadly requirements.

Our appropriations are limited only by our respect for the right of appropriation itself and this respect is grounded in the belief that we are universally entitled to supervise our interior lives because such management is the source of appropriation itself. Our appropriative activities are then unlimited since the only limitation we recognize is the right to appropriation itself. The respect for interiority actually protects appropriation: it enjoins us to disregard alterity by seeing the mind as the unique site for the presencing of Being.

Respect and tolerance are hedonist metaphors that formulate the dialectical involvement as an invasion of privacy: hedonist respect means the simplification of conversation and the cessation of interrogation. Hedonist respect protects appropriation by treating the *aporia* of dialectic as a subversion of the communal discourse because dialectic refuses to accept the myth of the a-social presencing of Being in interiority.

The uneasiness of hedonism makes reference to the fact that its strivings are unlimited because the conception of respect is not a limit. Respect for the sacredness of interiority actually destroys the Socratic conversation through its radical simplification of speech, a simplification grounded in a particular construal of the alterity of Being that equates it with the a-social and the inexplicable. The notion of original a-sociality guarantees that if the object of such striving — as goods which promise to protect the continuation of striving itself — are appropriated by others they will be irrevocably denied to self. *Laissez-faire* means 'leave speech alone' and the very pain and restlessness which hedonism was concerned to address originally through its revocation of Otherness is permanently and essentially imported into its world as the fundamental incompleteness that grounds all action and which resists all efforts to exorcize it.

III

The conception of the unalterability of Being means that Being is revoked as a living force that impregnates and leaves its trace in every speech. The first relevant difference for man is his limitation by Being only in the sense that man is deprived of being the whole, where such a 'whole' stands for the collection of men. The original perspectiviality of man limits man's dream since the Good or end can only be the achievement of a unity which preserves this original perspectiviality. Thus, the revocation of the strong sense of Being results in the stipulation of a right to privacy as the basic right and it is the duty to preserve this right that generates the need for a rule to which one is required to submit, resulting in the actual qualification of that very right. If unconditional loyalty to the rule of method is originally designed to protect one's being as one's right to privacy, such loyalty itself requires a simplification in the very conception of Being which it is designed to protect.

Exegesis then accepts as its point of departure its relationship to the point of view from which it is estranged. This point of departure limits the exegetical conception of a problem by requiring the interpretation of this point of view as its method of reconciling the difference. The point of view of exegesis stands to hedonism as 'reflexivity' stands to common sense.

The difference between exegisis and hedonism is an icon of the difference between philosophy and common sense. This difference resides in the exegetical concern with community, tradition, with the fate of alter, and with the continuation of interaction. Unlike common sense, exegesis is concerned with the exigencies of survival, with the just speech. Nevertheless, this concern which exegesis uses to differentiate itself from common sense similarly binds them together, for exegesis accepts the common-sense (hedonist) conception of difference and unity as its point of departure.

Common sense has no notion of the requirements or of the exigencies. Common sense is indifferent to whatever is necessary for community and for the survival of the tradition. Because of this indifference, common sense is essentially barren since the continuation of its premises would be self-liquidating; it would lead to the silence of indefinite motion. It is the very communality of exegesis that succeeds in arresting motion. Wherever philosophy emerges, it identifies itself in contrast to common sense, which it distinguishes as the repetitive ritualism of unreflective practice.

Philosophy needs common sense as that limitation upon it-self in contrast to which it *is*. In fact, philosophy is different by virtue of its concern with this difference whereas philosophy's version of what it is different from — of common sense — is its version of the repetitive, ritualistic speech that is indifferent to the question of *its* difference and to the question of any difference which it makes. Unlike common sense philosophy is, then, concerned with the status of its speech, with justifying its speech as speech that makes a difference. Philosophy orients to what it conceives of common sense as being indifferent to, to the imperative of producing speech that can be justified because the need to justify speech is treated as an exigency which must be met in order for the species to continue. In its exegetical form, philosophy conceives of its ideal speaker as a statesman, as one who speaks under the auspices of the need to create justifiable speech, and thus, as one who seeks to re-present the interest of all speakers (of the species).

If the interest of the statesman is defended and justified *vis-à-vis* the contrast with the injustice of nature (of *multis*, of common sense), it is nevertheless true that the aim of statesmanship (exegesis) is different from the aim of dialectic in the way that the philosophic and Socratic conceptions of justice differ. Socrates finds the statesman just like the multitude against which he contrasts himself and in the sense that the statesman *qua* exegete starts with the difference (the difference between philosophy and common sense, between exegesis and self-interest), Socrates attempts to show the inessentiality of *that* difference in contrast to the Real difference between exegesis, common sense and that which is Other. Socrates must then resist the exegetical conception of it-self as a solution to hedonism that affirms its essential difference, and he must show his resistance by ironically reformulating this opinion.

The difference between exegesis and hedonism — between philosophy and common sense — is one of degree whereas the difference between whether either of these is or is not is one of kind. This difference between a difference in degree and a difference in kind says that the capacity to distinguish philosophy from common sense should not conceal the essential difference between distinguishing and not, by pretending that it is the difference between philosophy and common sense that is essential rather than the difference between What Is and What Is-Not. In its turn, exegesis must resist such a reformulation on the grounds of the injustice and tyranny of Socrates. In terms of the exegetical conception of it-self, it is compelled into being by the a-sociality of common sense which is fundamentally different from its own solution.

If the identity of exegesis depends upon how it asserts its contrast from common sense, it is still true that the exegetical standard of the just speech requires a display of equity towards the 'point of view' of common sense against which it contrasts itself.

Exegesis can only show its statesmanship by interpreting common sense. Exegesis has to show proper tolerance and respect for the point of view of the material which it formulates if it is to act justly under the auspices of its own conception of the exigencies of community. If exegetical prudence is to be reflected in the 'reflexive' grasp of its own perspectiviality within the whole, exegesis must require of itself civility towards the different perspective and opinion of its material. In terms of its own requirements, exegesis needs to renounce the impulse to tyrannize its material by ignoring what properly belongs to it, while on the other hand, exegesis cannot accept the perspective of its material without losing its own identity. Exegesis must then take the third way of describing the material as if it (exegesis) was uncommitted to anything other than the judicial way of mutual arbitration.

If exegesis speaks under the auspices of a standard of statesmanship and of the civility which provides for its interest in the point of view of its material, it is nevertheless contrasted in this way from the typical hedonist actor which it conceives itself as describing. That is, there must be a difference between the point of view of exegesis and the point of view which it assigns to its material. Exegesis not only seeks to exemplify statesmanship, but it is attempting such an exemplification through its interpretation of an actor that it conceives as systematically disregarding the very maxim of statesmanship and civility which it (exegesis) upholds. This is to say that the essence of the exegetical version of the common-sense actor resides in his disregard of the exigencies of interaction.

Exegesis must then resist returning this a-social indifference (which it ascribes to its subject) towards its subject, for it needs to develop and describe that point of view. It is this necessity which exegesis demands of itself. Yet the difference between the exegete and his subject, which exegesis itself produces, not only threatens to keep them apart divided against themselves, but diminishes the importance of any thing Other than *this* difference, including the notion of that in terms of which this difference originates. Because this difference is conceived as original, exegetical labour continuously orients to the cultivation of methods for reconciling the difference as its own criterion of success.

IV

Philosophy then lives uneasily with the need to interpret that which it elects to see as its original and unalterable limitation. The philosophic self-conception of the intermediacy of man says that man is deprived of the ability of being all-seeing, and so he needs to bring to view how that from which he is excluded — the other — sees. Exegetical man then needs to describe, to interpret and to explain, because he needs to assimilate and to possess the whole.

Because exegesis wants to substitute for what it sees itself as lacking — for what is missing — by accumulating and possessing, it cannot give that which it interprets the opportunity to be anything more than what it (exegesis) is not, and so exegesis does not give its material the opportunity to be anything great and valuable. Exegesis does not allow that which is different to be anything more than different, or to participate in any unity which transcends itself and the other as the limits.

The exegetical desire to explain — to domesticate the other — organizes itself as a reluctance to allow the other its place — its voice — because it equates other's having a voice with its own loss, and so as an expression of enmity. Exegetical hatred towards the point of view which it seeks to interpret appears incommensurate with its need to interpret that point of view until we recognize the essential co-existence of interpretation and rage. Interpretation is hatred in so far as it invents words for what it fears as different and it only fears the difference because of what it understands as its speechlessness. Exegesis can only feel hatred for difference because it must understand difference as speechlessness. Exegesis comprehends the invitation which difference presents only as an invitation to describe and domesticate it. This is what is often spoken of as the exegetical impulse towards criticism.

Exegetical rage takes the form of criticism as interpreting and explaining, and so as leaving secure and undisturbed that speech with which it starts in any essential way (even though exegesis will exercise *techné* in its organization and preparation of this speech for interpretation). In contrast, Socrates eschews interpretation in order to formulate and by radically disturbing the surfaces of that with which he begins, he attempts to re-collect that which can best be heard in the speech (rather than to 'describe' and 'explain' that which appears as the speech).

Exegesis expresses hatred for difference in so far as its

interpretation subjects difference to the limitation of being interpreted, of being subjected to general conditions which control and produce it. Exegesis shows its hatred because in its attempt to possess what is different — to describe, to interpret, to explain — it shows its impulse to keep the different in its place as that which cannot achieve something greater than it (exegesis) has. Yet, in the same way exegesis guarantees its rage towards what is different because of the impossibility of total possession. In its recognition of man's intermediacy, exegesis concedes the unalterable difference between itself and what is different, and so in its turn, exegesis acknowledges the inevitability of its own failure.

Exegesis then produces its own rage, its own failure, by erecting as its impossible task the work of possessive interpretation. At its heart exegetical interpretation domesticates the different by showing how its 'point of view' is realized as a result of conditions which it shares with exegesis itself. In this way, exegesis seeks to describe the cause of the different as instances of a unity in which both exegesis and the different participate. To say that exegesis suffocates alter by describing or interpreting it is to say that its version of what alter is requires alter to accept being whatever the equation of its essence and interpretation describes.

To describe the 'point of view' of the different as a realization of causes is to seek to show how what is different is ruled. The influences which exegesis identifies as ruling the different are influences assumed to be shared by exegesis and the different because they are features common to their environment and as such features, they point to the limits of community in the commonality of the species. In focusing upon the difference between itself and the different as the essential difference, exegesis disregards the difference between what is common (between itself and the different) and what is necessary (what is Good, needed).

In disregarding this difference, exegesis answers the question 'what is first?' by saying that what is common is first. Because exegesis equates success and failure with the commonality and disunity of itself and the different (common sense), it disregards the difference between commonality as a limitation and that which limits such limitation. That is, exegesis will disregard the difference between being ruled (limited) by what is good and by what coincides with one. If alter is limited by interpretation itself to *be* whatever interpretation requires it to be, this distinguishes exegesis from Socrates in the sense that interpretation requires alter to be only what it can appear as and nothing better, whereas Socrates requires alter to aspire to be that which they both value as good. Unlike exegesis, Socrates works on his material so as to provide it with the opportunity to exemplify what is good. In this sense, while both Socrates and exegesis commit violence on their material — submit their material to their own requirements — it is only Socrates that attempts to bring out the best of the material.

We might recall the opening exchange between Socrates and Thrasymachus in *The Republic* where the Socratic notion of the just speech as serving the interest of its subject matter is developed. In so far as the theorist rules his material (his subject) the just rule ought to be done 'with a view to what is good and proper for the subject for whom he practises his art'. Theorizing formulates 'what is good for its subject — the interest of the weaker party, not of the stronger'.

Theorizing produces formulations of its material — of its subject — as if that subject was oriented to and ruled by what is good and proper. It is in the interest of the subject — the weaker party — to be formulated as if it oriented to what is good. It is in the interest of all men to raise the question 'what is first?' and 'strength' and 'weakness' refer to whether or not this truth is known. The strong party — the one who knows this truth — speaks to those who do not as if they could; their speech is heard for this possibility.

Given this truth, the strong man can only be ironic; instead of letting weakness stand, he must actively work to transform the speeches of weak men in order to revive in them the interests of life — of the possibility of strength. In contrast, exegesis lets weakness stand: to paraphrase a philosopher, it is only 'productive about weakness' (which means that *it* can only speak weakly).

To strengthen the speech is to revive it to participate in the conversation about that which is essential and necessary. Since the weak man begins by burying the difference between the essential and the inessential, his speech must be used to revive that difference. The theorist serves the interests of his subject matter by strengthening the speech: by using the speech to make a difference that is strong. In contrast, exegetical statesmanship conceives of its task as fulfilled when it can represent through comprehensive interpretation the interests of weakness.

V

It is often said of the Greeks that they pictured the earth as the centre of the world. In order to supply a rational foundation for this opinion, exegesis thinks it necessary to locate evidence that — from the point of view of the opinion — could have counted as adequate grounds. Such evidence would be *evident* or adequate support for someone producing the opinion. This requirement leads exegesis to formulate the ground as part of the knowledge available to the typical actor subscribing to the opinion. Because it is always necessary for exegesis that the 'context' describes what is evident to the speaker, i.e., what is evidence for the opinion (because the point of view of the speaker is first), what is so evident must be one of the things that coincides with the speaker by appearing to him. Even if the context is conceived as an unalterable limitation upon the speaker, this unalterability can only be apparent because such a context can always *appear* otherwise. The context then is not an innate ground or foundation but only one of the things that can vary. The context through which exegesis inevitably formulates its notion of ground is then always an other way of describing the point of view of the speaker. The context is designed to describe the empirical limitation upon the opinion — the conjoint limitation of time, information and circumstance — which happens to combine in the production of the opinion. Exegesis shows that the opinion for the earth's centrality is a realization of certain requirements limited to that situation and circumstances, and thus it must formulate the speaker (its material) as one acting only and exclusively under the auspices of the need to conform to such requirements. Exegesis requires itself to assume as secure the point of view of its material as its only resource for interpreting that point of view because 'interpretation' is basically passive.

Interpretation is passive in so far as it does not seek to learn from that which it interprets except in the technical sense — to acquire information or to gain access to a 'viewpoint'. That is, interpretation does not treat the other as saying something that it (interpretation) does not — in the first instance — comprehend. Comprehension is secure for interpretation in the sense that whatever alter says is said within a shared context the parameters of which are secure. Socrates himself does not disregard the social origin of inquiry but this context is not for him a determinate 'thing' appropriatable to speech. While exegesis might accredit the enigmatic appearance of speech it never accepts a version of the 'context' which organizes speech as anything but secure, as itself available for, and possessible by, interpretation.

Socrates does not assume that the other opinion is as it appears, because then the other opinion will only appear to be saying inadequately what Socrates says well. That is, the idea of difference between one and an other always creates the temptation to begin with the other as an inarticulate version of one. Exegesis never succeeds in resisting this temptation because it always treats alter's otherness as an attempt to say what it (exegesis) means: exegesis always assumes the self-evidence of the origin in *this* sense, that the assertive use of language is shared and that it must be assumed to guarantee an eventual just decision.

In contrast, Socrates asks himself how whatever alter appears to be saying can be re-collected as something worth saying. Like exegesis, Socrates assumes that the speech occurs as an instance of 'action oriented to an order and governed thereby in its course' and so, like exegesis, he seeks to resuscitate that order. Yet, unlike exegesis, Socrates will invent an order to satisfy the requirement of making the speech affirm its good, and so his formulation is itself ordered by this requirement. In contrast, exegesis will not permit itself to show loyalty to any requirement that compels it to abandon what gives it its initial security.

Socrates, then, attempts to learn from the opinion by assuming an initial insecurity despite and in the face of the intelligibility of what the opinion speaks. Co-existing among the crevices of the intelligible speech is its Desire to make reference to that order or aim which only Socrates can re-collect because it is necessary rather than only apparent. Unlike exegetical passivity, Socrates is compelled into action, he is compelled to work to hear the speech's Good.

VI

Assume it as a 'fact' that the Greek world was 'closed' and that it was organized around a version of the 'earth' as the 'centre'. For exegesis, this beginning is not in question: Greek speech makes reference to the centrality of an earth surrounded by its 'secondary' environment of planets and stars and the use of such notions is secured as that 'opinion' for which a metaphysic is to be retrieved. If exegesis begins with its very particular conception of how speech is to be taken, it begins with its particular formulation of the speaker.

Even the best of exegesis begins with a preorganized exegetical understanding of the opinion to be reformulated. Earth, air, water, fire, circularity, planets and all of the other notions variously used by the Greeks are understood as words which make reference to determinant things, and the task of exegesis is seen as one of rationalizing such descriptive accounts (where the referents of such notions are treated as secure and unproblematic) in order to place them as credible displays of local requirements of rationality. The opinion with which exegesis begins is treated as the opinion of, e.g., Locke's primitive, in the sense that the opinion is as it appears. While there may be a variety of technical problems at this level, they will be settled under the auspices of an understanding of the descriptive intent of the opinion. The technical problem(s) will pertain to how the opinion as understood is organized and collected. Exegesis often regards its most challenging work to begin at the point when after securing this opinion, it seeks to formulate the 'ground' or influences which cause the opinion to come into being.

In this sense, exegesis does not treat the speech as the beginning of a conversation — as a display of the work involved in raising the question of what is first — because the speaker is not treated as an interlocutor. Instead, the test is to understand *why* his 'world view' compelled him to centre the earth as the point around which the planets move, and not to re-formulate that very notion with which we begin — the centring of earth — as a metaphoric way of speaking about some thing Other. That is, the speaker himself would say that he needs to be seen as showing what is required in asking what is first, what is required both of discourse and that after which it quests. Planetary speech is such an occasion not because it results from some metaphysic (because that secures the idea of the self-evidence of the talk and of the meaning of 'metaphysics'), but because it shows the work of questing.

Exegesis begins with the security of knowing what it means to speak — the usage with which it begins is to be explicated and re-described but not re-formulated. The idea of Greek speech about the planets as an attempt to depict the planets (to describe them) then meets *our* (modern) requirements of treating usage as self-evident. The work of exegesis is addressed to the technical excavation of this usage in such a way as to reveal its source in other usage which stands to it as the 'normative' relates to the actual. Yet, Socrates tries to teach us that the difference between these uses is inessential. Thus, if exegesis shows its respect for Greek speech by attempting to re-lay its grounds in 'metaphysics' (in 'culture'), it can only do so at the expense of that culture itself, by not reviving the essential difference and hence, the relation between 'culture' and the Good, the difference displayed in the Goodness of Greekness.

What occurs is that Greek science is rationalized as a moment of its culture in a way which preserves *our* idea of both science and culture, i.e., in a way which preserves our notion of Greek science as science and our idea of the Greek way of seeing. Exegesis then reasserts this critical impulse which it sought to surpass by formulating Greek culture (metaphysics) in terms of its capacity to generate a different (modern) science. The Greek is judged in terms of his causal efficacy in generating science as he knows it. In this sense, even the most careful explication (description) of Greek 'science' rests upon the understanding that as a physics it was 'reassuring to people who could not comprehend the possibility of the earth being just another planet' and that the resistances to the new astronomy (Copernicus, Bruno, Kepler *et al.*) was due to a certain 'view' of movement and of the relationship between earth and the planets. If Greek science was not 'common sensical' it was only because Greek culture (metaphysics) created no options to its own science: it was Greek culture that was common sensical *vis-à-vis* our understanding of the greater range of possibilities for differentiation. In this way Greek culture as a whole is evaluated in terms of its capacity to generate the kind of science that *we* (moderns) need, and because of its 'failure' it can only appear inarticulate and pre-historical to us. This is to say that, even the most rigorous exegesis preserves a notion that Greek science *was science*, that it was responsive to descriptive impulses to depict 'objects' that we can retrospectively understand as 'objects' of science (though 'primitive' in form). Exegesis preserves the understanding that Greek culture centred the earth among the planets and closed the world rather than opened it through infinitization. We might agree; but only when we begin to grasp the meaning of 'centring' and 'closing' in such a way as to allow us to revive the sense of this talk as a metaphoric display of the impulse to theorize (and not as talk about planets at all).

If, as exegesis claims, physics displays a 'way of seeing', physics does not stand to its 'way of seeing' as one of two parts in a relationship. This is already a Newtonian rather than a Greek 'way of seeing'. Only a modern would ask for the relationship between these 'two' parts. It is only exegesis that could see Greek physics as part of a whole in *that* sense. Greek physics *is* a way of seeing: it is an invitation for us to 'see' its 'way of seeing' through the particulars it speaks about. This reminds us that Greek physics speaks about the 'things it sees' as a way of arousing us to see the originals of which the things seen are inferior imitations. The relationship between the earth and the planets is then an occasion for us to re-collect the originals of which 'earth' and 'planet' are icons. This is to say that what the Greek speaks about is not what his words name, for the topic of Greek thought is always that which causes *both* the words and that which they name to be; the topic is that which is Other to both the name and the things that are named (that which cannot be named as an Other thing).

The Greek then asks: how can I speak about the things in a way that is true to that which is not-a-thing? By starting with the need for that which is not-a-thing he speaks about the things that he sees in a way that fulfils this need. The need is first: it is essential and required. It limits, prefigures, and grounds his talk about the things seen. Though the need *is* a need to talk about the things seen, such talk fulfils the requirements of what is needed. It is not Greek to see Greek physics and astronomy as science at all rather than as a way of making reference to the essentials (where these essentials are never the things that are seen).

We might understand so-called Greek astronomy as a story invented to satisfy the need for what is absolute and essential. It has to recreate a sense of the friendliness of the whole — of what is Other to man — as a positive limitation upon the life of man. That which is Other than man must be part of his life as that which he aspires to re-achieve in his discourse as an end which he seeks to fulfil in speech. The centrality of the earth means the centrality of man only in the sense that man must take his bearings from life and that 'life' imposes — by its very nature — its own rational limitation. Just as the centrality of the earth points to the need to accept life (language) as all there is, so the 'closure' of the Greek world makes reference to the necessity of discoursing under the auspices of this need (of the need to re-create speech as conversation).

The centrality of man means that man is intermediate —

centred — between the divine and the bestial. Man takes his bearings from the divine and the bestial in the sense that what he *is* is neither God nor beast. He must speak in a way that preserves this difference. But man is not a 'residual category' either, for what he is positively as a man is one who discourses under the auspices of his intermediacy. Man's intermediacy (his centrality) is his Desire to re-achieve through discourse what he is as the difference between his speech and that which is Other to it. This Desire limits man in so far as he acts under its auspices; in ruling his speech it 'closes' his world. The world of man is closed to anything Other than the desire to re-achieve this difference.

Modern science understands the Greek notion of the centrality of man as an assertion of the divinity or primacy of man. The modern understands 'centre' as the stationary or tranquil source of motion (which for the Greek confuses the necessary distinction between *arché* and speech). Speech *is* the centre in the sense that it is originated as a moment in the Otherness which sustains it. But this is not a mere dispute over names because the intermediacy of speech does not mean that it is a flawed and imperfect attempt to consummate the perfect discourse (the description which only God can make). Speech is centred at the place where the difference between language and nothing comes to be and the end of discourse is to revive this difference. There is nothing Other to this difference, for this difference *is* what is Other to speech. If speech is not the origin, neither is it segregated from what originates it (the essential) and so, its 'centrality' means that it takes its place (its end) seriously and not that it stands to its inexplicable origin as an incomplete description relates to a perfect description.

There are a number of alternatives to the Greek version of centrality of man. By understanding centre as the 'one' which originates the motion of speech, the origin is segregated as an inexplicable source that has no living relation to discourse (aside from creating it). Despite the variations on this theme the story is the same: when centre is reformulated as 'origin' and origin is itself understood not as *arché* (as a continuous 'need' unfolding its requiredness upon discourse), but as a concrete origin radically different from the 'things' that it creates, the strength of centrality as a *living* restraint diminishes to produce a God so remote and inexplicable that he actually frees discourse from any limitation. In effect, the famous conjunction of Christianity and science decentred discourse (freed it from any constraint) while preserving a notion of an origin that could remain ineffable and inaccessible to discourse itself. In this way both man and God (both discourse and Other) were guaranteed their places by being kept apart.

In this view, the Greek notion of *arché* is concretized to represent the source of motion as that One which is it-self beyond motion. Such an immutable One is distinguished by its 'infinite powers', i.e., by his power to multiply. *He* is the centre because he is power and unlimited fertility. The centre is withdrawn from discourse and attributed to an inexplicable creator in an attribution which at once de-centres discourse (frees it) while assigning abstract responsibility to a version of a creator as causal power personified. Discourse then shows its responsibility to such an externalized 'power' by intermittently acknowledging its presence as a name (faith) which it is free to disregard in its concrete practices as long as its acknowledgment abstractly affirms the 'power' of that which is named to limit discourse itself. The inexplicability of what is truly central (the 'power') can be used as grounds for disregarding any question of centrality within discourse itself. This corruption of the so-called pagan notion of origin actually guarantees nihilism.

To say that man is central is to acknowledge the immutability of Other as a constraint upon speech itself. By identifying the immutable with the non-human — by segregating discourse from its requirements — both tranquillity and motion can be preserved and change can be accounted for as a feature of the infinite power of this externalized source. To make earth the centre was seen as supposing an absolute point of view (a standard) which only appeared to restrict man's need to make differences. Man's restlessness has to be preserved and rationalized as it-self a product of the infinite powers of the source, and this could only be accomplished by treating everything beyond man (beyond discourse) as that to which his powers were not adequate. The externalization of Other guaranteed that speech would be free of any duty to convert Otherness into its continuous human topic because man and Other were segregated from each other as the perfect power (non-life) stands to the imperfect result (life). Speech could only make a difference by disregarding the question of origin as that which human discourse was not 'adequate' to comprehend, where such disregard took the form of positively affirming the *name* of that to which it was not adequate.

The modern denial of the centrality of man which is often

understood as a rejection of Greek particularism and egocentrism is then a removal of Otherness from life (from discourse) that succeeds in identifying alterity with ineffability. The relationship between speech and the whole cannot be reconciled positively in discourse-itself, but always remains 'incomplete' in the absence of the assignment of a name to that which is Other. Naming (faith) completes the relationship which the Greek reconciled through conversation (through analysis, through formulating) because the reconciliatory character of the Greek notion of conversation could never be grasped by the modern.

Like Christianity, exegesis is concerned with the problem of origin, of man's originality rather than with his centrality. While it is absurd to call man original since only God is truly original, the relevant dimension of manliness makes reference to the absence of true or divine originality as itself a kind of surrogate originality. In other words, man starts by being imperfect and incomplete rather than by being understood as positively central or intermediate as he is within the Greek tradition. This is reflected in the exegetical notion of intermediacy as lacking complete and total access. To say that man is positively intermediate or central is to say that he formulates for himself through the activity of theorizing his intermediacy as a feature of the work of reviving a sense of What Is and What Is-Not as his limit and source, i.e., as a constraint for this work. Intermediacy requires not working to overcome What Is lacked — as in exegetical accumulation — but the strength of ironic discourse as an affirmation of the place of man instead of the (exegetical) attempt to say everything.

VII

Perhaps the first requirement for the survival of interaction as conceived by exegesis is the preservation of the point of view of the interlocutor (the material). The exegetical notion of a friendly treatment reflects the idea that labour need be invested in settling the problem of the ownership of opinions prior to other work. Unlike the work of Socrates the labour of exegesis must absolutely renounce the ironic mode of relating to opinions because justice first requires a decision on the problem of property rights to opinions.

Like Socrates, exegesis recognizes the intermediacy of man, but this intermediacy makes reference not to man's discourse in the service of what is innate but to his being excluded from possessing complete control over the things which coincide with him. Exegetical man is not ironic towards all opinions and committed to the work of conversation because he believes in the correctness of some one opinion and thus, he believes that conversation must be terminated at some point if we only had control over everything (he still aspires to divinity). Exegetical man's moderation towards any one opinion is only a function of his recognition of being part of the whole in the limited sense that he is deprived of the point of view which commands all of the possibilities. Exegetical civility towards the point of view of its material — its tolerance — displays the exegetical self-conception of intermediacy only in the sense that deliberation and prudence is necessary to reach a decision about the correct opinion and not because irony is built into the nature of man. As far as exegesis is concerned, irony is incommensurate with the serious problem of the ownership of speech and opinions. The notion of the 'pagan Greek' always displays itself as a 'serious' exegetical rejection of irony and of the work of theorizing.

The moderation of exegesis renounces commitment on the grounds of the intermediacy of man, which says that man's perspectiviality shows any opinion to be merely one of *multis*, merely one among the plurality of alternatives. Commitment must be secured by creating a conversation which will test the opinion against its alternatives. Exegesis is dedicated to suffering the resistance of interlocutors which it creates for itself as a test of its strength, of the adequacy and evidence of its opinion. Exegetical prudence is directed towards creating and supervising this conversation as the measure of its strength. The possessiveness of exegesis is shown in its very attempt to conduct a comprehensive inventory of opposition to it — of all points of view — as features which enter into and constitute the essence of its opinion as an opinion that is correct and worth believing.

In contrast, Socrates regularly engages in the test of opinions as an attempt to strengthen the opinion. Socrates asks if we are willing to endure such tests. He asks if we can tolerate the 'test' that seeks to strengthen our speech. Socrates also tests his speech by creating resistance for it, also by re-creating the interlocutor as an occasion for re-achieving the speech itself. Socrates tests his speech by seeing whether it is strong enough to re-achieve itself so as to display the difference between itself and its source. Strong speech can endure such a test and in so far as speech is strong, it re-achieves this difference by giving its interlocutor (its material, its alter, its difference) an opportunity to share in such a re-achievement. Socratic speech becomes strong not by diminishing its material (by interpreting it) but by actively strengthening it.

If both the exegetical and Socratic commitment to the intermediacy of man issue in different conceptions of the work required by such a place for man, they nevertheless both understand the work of man as the work of imitating Other, of imitating what is first. Yet, if the exegetical just speech imitates Other by seeking to reproduce what is first, Socratic justice aspires to imitate the Gods by pleasing them rather than by attempting to achieve surrogate divinity. Because what is first is the Desire to re-achieve the difference between what is essential and inessential, dialectical *mimesis* continuously seeks to re-achieve this difference in its discourse. The exegetical failure to understand the difference between man and God as that which needs re-achieving — as what Other is — leads to the concealment of this very difference in the practice of discourse that seeks to produce a surrogate divinity expressed in the tranquillity of some opinion which appears correct because it has silenced opposition or the *multis* of opinions. In this way, exegesis produces a notion of justice as its particular solution to the problem of hedonism.

CHAPTER IV

Justice

I

At the beginning of the *Parmenides* Socrates challenges Zeno's denial of plurality (of difference):

> If anyone sets out to show about things of this kind — sticks and stones and so on — that the same thing is many and one, we shall say that what he is proving is that something is many and one, and not that unity is many or that plurality is one; he is not telling us anything wonderful but only what we should all admit.

Of course things can be seen in different ways (to say this is not so wonderful), but the notions we have of things cannot be unlike themselves for they must always be limited by that which is unlike them. It is not so wonderful to acknowledge that the 'things' with which we have routine commerce can sometimes be seen as this and sometimes as that: yet, that which grounds our seeing in any case must be steadfast and different from what is unlike it. Certainly what *we* call crimes, *they* might call piety (and indeed, many spend considerable energy describing how this is possible), but to say this is not so wonderful. On the other hand what we call crime can never be unlike it-self, what we call by the name of crime must always be true to it-self in the sense that the name must answer to the requirement that the idea which it names is not unlike it-self (that it is not different than crime because what it *is* is crime). This would hold likewise for what *they* call crime and for what *we* call piety. To say that the idea must not be unlike it-self is to say that what the idea expresses *is* its limitation by what is unlike it. This is the point at which the theorist dwells, at this limitation: and even though the idea is diffused like a ray of light through many different things, the theorist only examines these differences in order to re-assert the limit(s) of the idea by what is unlike it.

Socrates can then deny plurality only in the sense that these differences are 'not so wonderful' while yet accrediting that they are the place(s) to begin. Socrates can then begin with the multitudinousness of 'things' always remembering that this multitudinousness points to a notion of limit and measure which must be preserved. We might say then, that Socrates takes as his topic limitation, measure and necessity even while he co-exists within the realm of the indefinite, the multitudinous, and the capricious. In such a move, Socrates seeks to revive for us a proper sense of wonder by discouraging us from treating multitudinousness as a wonderful thing.

All of Socrates' predecessors were exercised by the relationship between limit and multitudinousness, between unity and difference, between justice and injustice. They were all concerned to prepare the just speech — the speech that would retrieve for multitudinousness its just place as a reminder of the justice of the limit. The just speech would set out to tell us something wonderful — it would tell us in what sense unity could be understood as many and in what sense plurality could be understood as One.

The thinkers that preceded Socrates were concerned to revive a sense of the limitation upon multitudinousness. The idea of retribution first spoken by Anaximander announces the way in which injustice — the injustice which is the obliteration of the notion of limit — is corrected in discourse. Because our speaking tends to cover over the essential limit in the way that the expression of wonder at multitudinousness deforms the notion of measure and proportion, we need to continuously re-collect what is essential. What is essential is the idea of limitation which itself limits any notion of multitudinousness. To re-collect what is essential is 'truly wonderful'. The pre-Socratics in their various ways through the metaphors of water, air, fire, number, rarefaction and condensation, and the opposites of hot and cold, wet and dry attempted to prepare the speech that would do justice to the multitudinousness of things (the 'motion' of things); they attempted this not by treating multitudinousness as wonderful but by locating a place for it in the order of Being. The just speech would do justice to multitudinousness by using it as an occasion to re-achieve the Reason of What Is (of language) as that indivisible unity which consolidates our seeing of multitudinousness as itself an expression of the limitation of What Is. Retribution would be secured by re-formulating multitudinousness in such a way as to re-assert the requiredness of unity and indivisibility.

The just speech will be the speech that answers to these requirements, the requirements of life. Because such a speech always begins in the midst of the notion of multitudinousness, the road of retribution (theorizing) requires reserve and patience. It requires the reserve that comes from knowing that retribution is secured only through the reformulation of multitudinousness itself; it requires the patience that comes with moderating the impulse to either annihilate multitudinousness or to withdraw from it. To say that we must spend our life reflecting upon life means that the requirements of unity and indivisibility are our topic; as retribution, our discourse continuously revives as its topic the question of the restoration of justice, i.e., of the revival of these requirements. To know one self is to be commanded by the requirements of life as the continuous effort to re-achieve the just speech.

The just speech is the speech that revives unity in discourse. This is the speech that re-collects the difference between what is essential and inessential and in such a gathering, points to the place or end of discourse. Socrates tells Zeno that the difference between a thing seen in one way and a thing seen in another is inessential: in contrast what is essential is the difference between what a thing is seen as and the conception which enables the seeing of a thing as any thing. The theorist dwells at the point or place of this difference — the difference between the origin and result of seeing — by using the result(s) to revive this difference. The conception which enables the seeing of the thing as the thing that it is is itself unlike the thing that it enables in that the conception is not a thing. Since the conception is not a thing, it — unlike the thing — cannot be seen in any way whatsoever. Understanding the conception is decisively limited by what is unlike it because the conception is what it is in so far as it is not unlike itself. The limitation upon the conception is then essential. In contrast, what a thing is seen as is unlimited, i.e., it is not limited by anything essential to the thing, and so, it is contingent and coincidental rather than essential.

What is essential is to distinguish between originals and images so that the conceptions which ground discourse can be interrogated. Certainly Socrates might be seen as a theorist on one day and not on another; yet the idea of theorist ought not to be unlike itself from day to day. Although different 'readings' of Socrates are possible (one reading can be unlike an other), the idea of a reading ought not to be unlike itself. This is not to say that the idea of theorist or of a reading cannot change or differ: rather, that it cannot be unlike it-self means that it cannot be its opposite, whereas Socrates himself (or any thing) can be its opposite (Socrates lives and then dies, was short and grew taller, was sick and then well).

A conception always acquires its identity in terms of what it excludes, in terms of how it is limited by what is unlike it. All conceptions are then governed or ruled by a strong sense of limit and even where what the limit limits is not in view, the limit is an omnipresent topic and concern. In contrast, there seems to be no limit to the ways in which things may be sorted and transformed. Whereas things admit a promiscuous, indefinite expansion of correct usage, the ways in which notions are correctly formulated are limited.

The just speech is then the speech that is ruled by a sense of the need to limit multitudinousness. Such a speech can only be about notions or conceptions and it always begins with the conceptions employed by the multitude. But, because of its promiscuity the multitude can only speak of these conceptions as if they were unlimited, as if they were things. The theorist elicits from the multitude the recognition that conceptions rule speech, and that these conceptions are themselves ruled; the theorist attempts to re-collect the difference between limitation and multitudinousness by showing how *this* difference is essential relative to the differences in degree which multitudinous speaking makes.

II

The promiscuity of usage is linked to the basic analytic conception of multitudinousness. Since usage licenses validity, the unlimited and indefinitely expandable character of usage creates unlimited *multis* (what Plato referred to as the indefinite dyad). That usage is multitudinous means that it is essentially promiscuous and ungovernable (it is concrete, happenstance).

When conceptions are treated in a multitudinous way they are seen as unlimited (as a matter of opinion or usage). A conception is not seen as having an essential limit, a limit which is given as part of its Being, as part of its history and resonance. Instead, the conception is treated as a thing. Socrates tells Zeno that conceptions are different than things and that this essential difference is obscured when differences among the uses of a conception are treated as essential.

Yet, Socrates says that the essential difference can only be approached by beginning with the multitudinous uses. Starting with different uses of the conception — with the multitudinous treatment of the conception as a thing — Socrates seeks to revive the just speech by re-collecting the unitary limitation upon all uses as a necessary limitation.

The difference between true and false speaking is a difference between the limitation of multitudinousness in discourse and the indulgence of multitudinousness. The difference between true and false speaking is an inessential or concrete difference contingent upon what is coincidental rather than essential. Speech can be true and it can be false and whether it is depends upon whatsoever happens to be the case. Truth, however, cannot be false and falsity cannot be true: they are limited by their opposites. Yet, the possibility for a speech taken as true to be false and for a speech taken as false to be true seems unlimited, it seems to be limited by nothing essential to the speech. In contrast, to say that truth is limited by nothing essential is the most indulgent, nihilistic talk, because truth is an essent whose nature is limited by what is unlike it. To deny this by treating truth as a thing is to say that truth could be any thing.

The theorist is personified by the figure of the just man in so far as justice is understood analytically, i.e., as a concern with the question of limitation, measure and necessity rather than with exigencies of interaction and survival. The just man personifies the obsession with the question of limit and foundation: but as an obsession which can never be segregated from the work of raising the question itself, it always re-cognizes how this very work can only show it-self through its reformulation of the unjust. The enemy of the just man is not *multis per se*, but rather, the inability to distinguish the essential from the multitudinous, an inability which shows itself in not knowing this difference. The just man understands as part of the meaning of necessity, the essentiality of re-formulating the unjust as that upon which *it* works.

As the Desire for the necessary and essential, justness displays itself as a reformulation of the way in which *multis* is limited and governed. Through such formulative work, justice continuously reasserts it-self as the need to reject the opinion that there is anything Other than language (or, that there is any thing Other than What Is). The theorist as a just man is committed to the necessity of showing that opposition to What Is (to language) is unthinkable.

Socrates requires knowing the difference between speech (which can be this or that) and language (which cannot be unlike itself). Conceptions then mediate between speech and language. This is to say that while a conception such as truth is limited by what is unlike it, this fact — that a conception is so limited — is not itself so limited. Yet this fact that is not limited is not empirically unlimited or multitudinous: this suggests that an opposite to the limitation of the essent cannot be imagined, i.e., that it is essential for the essent to be limited by what is unlike it. The fact for which we cannot imagine opposition limits us to accept it not because it is indefinitely expandable but because opposition to it is unthinkable. We call the fact for which opposition is unthinkable, language. In the strongest sense, we cannot imagine a difference to language since all of our imaginings only confirm our subjectitude to language. Since Socrates requires our knowing the difference between speech and language, he requires us to know the difference between that which can be anything and that which can be either something or nothing.

What Is is not that which is thought or that which is talked about, but those requirements which must be accepted as the absolute ground of speaking and thinking. Since speech comes to life through its participation in What Is, the act of speaking only confirms its subjectitude (of speech to What Is). Because What Is as an absolute origin cannot be appropriated — its 'status' is to be enunciated and confirmed — it has to be eternal. We can never speak about What Is because *about* presupposes distance or difference between speech and What Is (as if speech was added on after What Is secured it-self); in contrast, our speech necessarily acknowledges and confirms What Is as its omnipresent shelter. To seek to *describe* What Is is the first great illusion because description presupposes the independence of speech from What Is. This 'illusion' results in treating What Is as if it could be segregated from speech (or, in treating speech as if it was some thing really different from What Is).

The difference between What Is and What Is-Not is drawn as a living distinction and so What Is-Not draws its life from and is sheltered by What Is. What **Is** is not limited by what is unlike it in the sense that What Is-Not is understood as its opposite, because What Is is necessary and absolute and has no opposition. Whereas multitudinous usage is unlimited in the sense of its capacity to be anything, and conceptions are essentially limited by what is unlike them, that conceptions are limited is a necessity for which opposition is unthinkable. Language is then different both from the multitudinousness of speech and the limitation of the essent in that — like speech — it cannot be limited by what is unlike it, but only because what is unlike it is unthinkable, whereas speech is unlimited because it can be anything. The unlimitedness of language means its absolute necessity, whereas the unlimitedness of speech refers to its contingent happenstantiality; in contrast, the conception is intermediate because it is necessary for the conception not to be unlimited either contingently like speech, or absolutely like language.

If there is no thing Other than language, there is not plurality because language (What Is) is necessary. The necessity of language does not recommend passive subordination to some conception of fate or circumstance: it means that a difference to language is unthinkable. This does not mean that men cannot — by converting language (What Is) into speech and by conceiving of things other than speech — empirically imagine a difference to language; rather, it means that a proper conception of language entails that it is impossible to imagine some thing Other to language. Because speech exists within language, all ideas including the idea of some thing Other than language occur as a confirmation of language itself.

Further, as there is no plurality there is also no change. What is said here holds eternally of all men, times and places and even if men did not recognize it, it is true nevertheless. The equality of men means that though they do not all know this, that they could come to re-collect this truth, that it is often covered-over and concealed by their speeches. In this way Parmenides had said that what men call plurality and change are differences, that the limitation of What Is by What Is-Not as a feature of language itself (as the meanıng of what it is to *be*) provides for its own recollectability in speech as the appearance of differences; but he says that these differences (which as occasions of discoursing are occasions to re-achieve the unity of language) do not change the essentially unchangeable character of What Is (of language).

Socrates knows this but his interlocutors often do not: the enemies of Socrates try to differentiate language (What Is) from what is Other to it and he continuously seeks to show how every such attempt only confirms what it attempts to deny. Socrates attempts to turn men towards this recognition which they essentially possess. Yet, because What Is is not a thing, this recognition can never be secured as it-self a thing; it must be continuously revived and re-achieved as the topic of a life. If What Is is a thing it could be secured once and for all. Its essential elusivity means that it needs men and that it grants meaning to men in this need.

But what is it to know this which both Parmenides and Socrates know? It is to know one's place or end. It is not a matter of opinion, for its flawlessness and perfection is something that is settled without doubt. It is 'taken for granted' but not silenced for it is to be revived in every speech. Discourse orients to reviving What Is as its topic; discourse will seek to reveal and to make transparent the perfection of What Is (it is perfect because it cannot be otherwise, it expresses the limit).

Discourse uses what is known (its acceptance of What Is) as a resource for re-collecting the resource it-self, where what is recollected (the What Is that is 'accepted') is not a thing. What Is is Good because if we are to achieve excellence it must be friendly to us — it must grant us the power to reveal it — where our very revelation of What Is constitutes and confirms our aspiration to explore our end. Discourse keeps What Is alive in the lives of men (in the speeches of men) and men keep themselves alive (and enliven their speeches) through their re-collection of the limitation of What Is.

If discourse needs What Is, What Is needs discourse. Discourse points to the place of essencing and man needs this place as the setting in which the work of exploring his end is re-achieved. If the topic of this exploration is the excellence of moral virtue, the conversation in which it occurs does not arise as an arrangement to protect us from our natures but as an incentive in terms of which the cultivation of our natures unfold. Discourse requires What Is to elevate itself and What Is requires discourse to continously re-achieve its presence. Man and God, speech and language, discourse and What Is are brought together through conversation, through the just speech which collects while preserving these distinctions. Where Socrates' predecessors show the needfulness of man for God, it is with Socrates himself that the argument of God's need for man (for discourse) is consummately prepared.

What the theorist knows and what the multitude forgets is the difference between the multitudinousness of usage and the necessity of language: *this* difference is essential *vis-à-vis* the inessential differences between multiple uses. The just speech which the theorist seeks to re-collect is the analysis of the conception in a way which resurrects its limitation by what is unlike it as a display of the work involved in differentiating usage from that which is necessary (in differentiating speech from language).

III

It appeared to the thinkers after Parmenides that his assertion that nothing could not be was a denial of the void (a denial which appeared to destroy the possibility of change and of theorizing, creating the inexorable consequence of silence). It appeared to these thinkers that a notion of the void was absolutely essential to any version of theorizing because change could not be intelligible and rationally accounted for without a strong notion of difference. Parmenides sees that the void as that thing which separates What Is from What Is-Not must be denied (unless of course What Is is seen as coming-to-be and What Is-Not is seen as that which it excludes or *from* which it comes as an other thing). But for Parmenides there is nothing Other than What Is and so the 'void' must be a feature of the very identity which it itself confirms in its belonging to What Is. The need for a *space* between What Is and What Is-Not is felt only when the unity, eternality and indivisibility of What Is is rejected (by thinking of What Is as requiring some thing outside of it-self, e.g., What Is-Not). Parmenides' rejection of the void is then a rejection of any thing Other than What Is.

The atomists felt that the denial of the void entailed that reality could not move. In other words, that What Is would have no weight (reality would have no weight) without a notion of some thing Other than What Is (other than 'one') because they felt that One (What Is) *comes to be* and since that which comes to be cannot come out of itself it must come out of some thing Other than itself (which means some thing that is nothing, i.e., What Is-Not, the void). Because the atomists conceived of What Is as an *achievement*, they required a notion of the beginning as a differentiating. The void and 'motion' became metaphors expressive of the need for a rational account of the achievement of What Is. The atomists asked: how can you have motion (life) if the void is not a thing, because motion means contact and interaction between things? The void, then, must be such a thing. The idea of life as motion (as making differences) is responsible to the atomistic requirement for seeing What Is as achieved rather than as eternal. For atomism, what is eternal is motion (life means the continuous making of differences) and such a requirement guarantees the inexorability of change. The reaction of atomists to Parmenides then anticipates the modern critique of re-collection as reactionary theorizing.

Given the achieved character of What Is, a notion of initial difference or plurality is required. That What Is comes-to-be as a differentiating means that it is motion (it participates in a relation), and since only things can relate, atomism requires reformulating What Is as the *movement* between things. What Is is not first because it is ruled by the laws of motion which are first. Man himself cannot comprehend anything other than the rule of motion and must accept necessity and chance. He accepts the necessity of an inexplicable relation of motion (speech) to some thing Other, and the chance (accident) of his being a man, i.e., that since he is not a god he cannot comprehend this relationship. The atomists understood such solutions as being responsive to their conception of life (of What Is) as a result of the rule of motion (of the interaction between different things or of different appearances of the same thing).

Parmenides' denial of the void was a rejection of the existence of unintelligibility — of that which is Other than life — as anything Other than life's conception of its limits. The void exists only as the self-limitation of life upon it-self and in this sense, to say that the void *is* is to say that What Is-Not is (i.e., what is not *has* not-being and so, it *is*). If What Is-Not is to have any character it must *be* that which is not. Parmenides' rejection of the void then intended to deny the rationality of any assertion of the existence of What Is-Not that equates What Is-Not with a nonentity segregated from language. In contrast, the Parmenidean void (as expressed in the metaphor 'What Is-Not') emphasizes the opposition between unity and what is Other to it symbolized in the declaration that unity *is* only where this opposition points to the source or ground of unity in its being Other than nothing. The void then makes reference to the opposition between unity and nothing as the essential ground of unity it-self; that unity requires its limitation by nothing as what it means to *be* (to be one). To be is to be Other than nothing and so, in so far as unity *is*, it is Other than nothing. The being of nothing (of the void) is then expressed as an unfolding out of unity it-self as the limitation and ground of what it is to be. Thus, in its very perdurance, the idea of unity (of life, of language) collects itself as that which is (essential) and so, *is* not nothing.

Parmenides alerts us to the requirement of life for collecting its own limitation as a feature of what life is: he then shows us how this difference grounds and sustains our various oppositions, that these oppositions upon which we routinely depend only become intelligible in terms of the essential difference between unity and nothing. Though all of the ideas, notions and conceptions which we routinely and regularly employ as opposites *appear* to be differences, the difference between these opposites ought not to be taken as the essential difference: the relationship of these opposites reveal that they belong together as members (or parts) of unity and as such, each notion (each party to the opposition) is always an icon of the difference between What Is and What Is-Not — a difference which it translates and covers over in the distinction between itself and its opposite. Though these notions are always used as if they acquire their identity through contrast to their opposites, the contrast itself is only a solution to the problem of the relationship between What Is and What Is-Not that grounds and prefigures the contrast.

Another way of putting this is: in so far as any notion is a part of unity, its contrast (essentially) is with the limitation upon unity that is dispersion or manyness (nothing, the void) — and not with its opposite. Because opposites themselves are icons of unity, the relationship between opposites does not depict the movement of theorizing, i.e., theorizing requires the continuous re-achievement of the limitation of dispersion upon unity (of the relationship between What Is and What Is-Not, between Being and the void), a relationship that is covered over in speech which sees opposition as the difference. Thus, Parmenides taught Socrates to retrieve the essential difference which underlies opposition.

Parmenides could then say that plurality does not exist. Plurality results from treating opposition as difference. From this point of view, the opposite (or contrast) of unity is plurality. Parmenides could also conceive of plurality as a limitation upon unity except for him it would be the 'indefinite plurality' of dispersion (of the void). On the other hand, oppositional thinking sees plurality as a collection of unities, and so not as limitation at all but as unity multiplied (as a concrete difference of degree). Parmenides rejects this notion of plurality because it is no different from unity at all. Plurality in this sense does not exist because 'more than unity' does not exist, and though contrasts can be indefinitely multiplied, such fertility *is* (and so, is part of unity). The rational conception of plurality occurs as the comprehension of the limitation of dispersion (of What Is-Not) from Within unity it-self as its self-asserted limit. The conventional contrast of unity and plurality covers over the essential difference between unity and that which is not.

Parmenides' theorist searches notions in this spirit: that he will revive the life of the notion (he will draw attention to what gives the notion life) by re-collecting its limitation upon dispersiveness as a way of referencing what the notion means. What the notion means deeply is that as a part of unity it *is*, in so far as it limits What Is-Not, and so he uses the notion to re-achieve that difference. As he revives the life of the notion he uses the notion to revive the sense of life as the belonging-together of this difference (the difference as an indivisible unity which is to be accepted). The indivisibility of unity means that the notion essentially belongs to unity, always participating in the mutual limitation of unity and What Is-Not. The notion neither relates to unity as one unity to an other, or as a part relates to a harmonic totality, for in these cases the 'relationship' is pluralized. Rather, the notion relates to unity by recapitulating in the depths of its history the meaning of unity as the limitation of What Is-Not.

The indivisibility of What Is is a corollary of the denial of plurality and change; What Is cannot be divided. Because it is not a denominator that is reducible into component parts it is not a harmony or a totalization that can be re-presented by the relations among its parts. It is something more than its parts and of any harmony which the interaction of its parts achieve. There is no surrogate for What Is because it persists throughout all operations as the irreducible shelter of the operations themselves. Indivisibility means that from which we cannot separate, that which is always with us. The omnipresence of What Is means that we cannot re-present it in notions that are conceived as Other since every re-presentation is ruled by it. The indivisibility of What Is means that there is no-thing Other to it.

The indivisible character of What Is refers back to its absolute necessity, that exegetical neutrality or justice cannot be achieved in so far as it is grounded in the idea that the dividing of What Is is a making of differences that is done from a position different from or separate from What Is: that because exegetical neutrality assumes the possibility of being separate from What Is, it assumes something Other to What Is. In this sense, by always presupposing that What Is is limited by what is unlike it (where what is unlike it is conceived as What Is-Not), exegesis invariably treats the necessary and the absolute (e.g., Being) as if it was a thing. Even when exegesis treats Being as the historical or social context, or the mind, method, or point of view of an author or a setting, it necessarily conventionalizes the necessary by treating it as that which has an opposite and so, as that which can be different (as a thing).

Yet, if the indivisibility of What Is means that *it* is Other (that there is no thing Other to it), it cannot be the source or ground of indefinite multiplication. In the sense that no thing can be added to What Is, change does not exist because the things which men take to be additions are re-achievements of What Is in discourse. What Is is differentiated through re-collection rather than through change, and though the differences speech makes appear to re-present changes in the form of progressively evolving accretions to the secure and steadfast corpus of What Is, they are actually re-achievements of the unity of What Is under various conditions of discoursing. Change does not exist in this sense: that men cannot escape from What Is — can neither get outside it or leave it behind — no matter what fantasies and technological change they imagine of the future; that these requirements of life are the eternal and unchanging requirements. That they are unitary and indivisible means that life is One and that there is no thing Other to life, that plurality and change — other lives or life and non-life — do not exist. The implication of course is that we must accept life and speak under the auspices of such a requirement. To say that life must be accepted is to say that the necessity of language must be accepted (that opposition to language is unthinkable). Such an acceptance entails the indivisibility of What Is.

The re-collective character of theorizing is grounded in the denial of the void because this denial says that 'all is one', that there is no thing Other than One, that One includes the limitation of Other than One as what One means. Theorizing intends to re-collect this limitation.

Dialectical justice must then differentiate itself from exegetical neutrality through its own acceptance of the necessity of What Is and all that this acceptance entails. For Socrates this acceptance must be shown in the practice of formulating the limitations upon multitudinous speech in a way that revives conversation. Since the only speech that converses is the speech that points to what is necessary and absolute, multitudinous speech must be made transparent in its dependency upon conceptions, limitations and commitments that point progressively to what must first be accepted. The just speech shall reflect the difference between the inessential and the essential by beginning with the inessential different uses of the notion.

Real rather than exegetical justice is then always and essentially an erotic or sensuous activity in so far as it begins *in medias res* as a moment within that which it addresses. *In medias res* suggests that the continuous attachment between part and whole which is presupposed in the relationship of speech to Being continuously confirms the dependency of speech upon that which precedes it. That justice is erotic suggests that it is the *in medias res* character of speech which must necessarily qualify its neutrality, which in its turn recommends not a problem to be corrected but rather, that the achievement of justice (the just speech, the formulation) starts with multitudinous usage and occurs through the practical display of the work necessary to the making of a difference between the usage and what is essential.

IV

If Zeus is a metaphor for a language, the end or aim of language can be discerned in the myth of Zeus. In the *Theogony*, Zeus comes-to-be as an offspring of Cronus and given the goodness of language (of Zeus) we can understand the relationship between Zeus and Cronus as a dialectic between good and evil. The *Theogony* formulates the good of language not by describing how language comes-to-be (causally) out of nothing but as an account or justification of our need for language (a logos of the good of language) and of the implications of this need. The *Theogony* then tells us what our requirements are. We must ask what the myth begins to tell us about the practice of theorizing.

The myth ought tell us how theory needs a vision of the necessity of language and how in the absence of such a vision injustice will prevail. The necessity of language means that opposition to it is inthinkable, that the distinction between What Is and What Is-Not is governed by language it-self and is always made by a participating speaker rather than by a neutral arbiter.

Eros saves this notion from exegesis in the sense that the very necessity of language is testified to by a speaker, by one who participates within and is inescapably and essentially attached to that about which he speaks in a way which qualifies his every attempt to imagine himself as Other than what he speaks (to imagine himself as a-social, as independent of language, as presuppositionless).

Eros can 'overpower the prudent purpose of the mind' in so far as the speaker can imagine his otherness to language by succumbing to the pressure to think of language conventionally — as a thing — as speech, and so, to imagine something opposite to language. This susceptibility to imagine the firstness of speech must be regulated by conversing in a way that actually acknowledges the inescapable government of language.

The reign of Zeus is the reign of language. The myth re-collects the pre-Olympian 'period' as a vision of the dispersion of these requirements against which language acquires weight as the Good. Language reintegrates unmediated eros justly: the comprehension of the good of language which only occurs within the context of a vision of the evil of dispersion is personified in speech's struggle to imitate the gods — in its attempt to make the just speech.

> First of all, the void [chaos] came into being, next broad-bosomed Earth, the solid and eternal home of all, and Eros the most beautiful of the immortal gods, who in every man and every god softens the sinews and overpowers the prudent purpose of the mind.

This ought not be heard as a causal account. 'In the beginning' makes reference to What Is. Any weighty notion of What Is must include as its feature What Is-Not (the void), for *to be* is only comprehended in terms of the contrast of dispersion: eros makes a place for man as part of What Is (as the need of What Is for discourse). If there was only What Is (earth) there would be no sense of its limitation (void) so, really there would be nothing. If there was no place for eros there would be no grounds for differentiation and continuation (and we would have nothing to say). We need each of these three terms in order for our imaginings not to be incredible for we could not even talk about what their absence means: we need them so as not to be inarticulate.

What is required is a notion of What Is and What Is-Not (earth and void) that concedes their togetherness as a distinction sheltered by What Is: that while What Is absolutely requires a notion of the dispersion against which it *is*, that notion itself is drawn under the auspices of What Is.

What Is is indivisible and eternal, which is to say that there is no external limit upon it for it limits itself. Though there is no thing Other than What Is, What Is provides for its own sense of limitation — of what cannot be imagined — as the void. In this and only this sense the void exists as the comprehension of What Is-Not as it-self a moment of What Is: What Is both requires and gives life to the idea of What Is-Not as its limitation. What Is-Not (the void) is then not a thing, but it is: it is the limitation from which life takes its point of departure for comprehending its own requirements — the requirements of life. The void is then not death, but life's requirements for a notion of the limits upon life (life's version of this limitation), and as such, the void is both Other to life and generated by life itself as the limitation which is Other.

Eros is necessary as the desire for difference. The danger of this desire is that it will transgress the internality of What Is-Not to What Is by seeking to make What Is-Not external to or different from What Is. Desire must be channelled into the making of a difference between What Is and What Is-Not *within* the unity of What Is (which is to say that man must take his bearings from life and from the contrast between some thing and nothing which life provides as its own limitation); Desire must be prevented from continuously differentiating What Is-Not into a plurality of fantastic unities external to and independent of What Is. In this sense desire must be prevented from dispersing.

Eros is necessary for the bringing of What Is to presence in the life of man and yet it tends to 'overpower the prudent purpose of the mind' when it sees What Is-Not as What Is. On these occasions Desire (for a difference between What Is and What Is-Not) conjures up differences in surrogate forms of What Is-Not as a plurality of external things. This is to say that while speech must know the difference between What Is and What Is-Not as a requirement of life, eros threatens to 'overpower' this purpose by obliterating the difference. Eros must be guided to re-collect the Real difference (by continuously re-thinking the limitation upon life) and thus, must be diverted from inventing icons of What Is-Not in the form of unities externalized from life (from language).

In the beginning were chaos, earth and eros. Earth produced 'starry skies', the mountains and the waters 'without the passion of love'. Where this difference between What Is and What Is-Not is not sustained as life's limitation upon itself, the desire for difference will be consummated in unregulated making. Where the requirements of *anamnesis* are not vivid, change will be equated with the making of differences.

Unregulated making can only create indefinite plurality, the plurality which requires the desire for unity that had been revoked. Among all of the 'things' made must be some one thing that will reconcile these differences, and so earth must lay with one of her own products — sky — 'to cover her on all sides'.

Given the absence of a firm sense of indivisibility and unity, in the beginning is proliferation, multitudinousness (*multis*) and difference. The authority of paternity is lacking because the source of power is productivity it-self and productivity is always feminine. In the world of original *multis*, authority is maternal, never transcending making itself. If the producer is to arrest this continuous proliferation she can only do so incestuously with one of her offsprings because there is no notion of an origin that transcends productivity. The producer is then rendered obsolete because those whom she produces replace her in the chain of re-production and so, the authority of an origin is perpetuated only as the memory of the founder or initiator which diminishes as her fertility ceases. The absence of the authority of paternity means the absence of a continuous authority which transcends the particular re-productions of nature; the absence of paternity means the need for incest as a solution to the problem of order.

The absence of paternity is linked to the diminution of the proper sense of eros. As the acknowledgment of the firstness of language and of the *in medias res* character of speech, eros requires a vision of the necessity and absoluteness of language (of paternity). And yet, such a vision itself can only be confirmed in speech.

The absence of paternity reflected in the unregulated lusting of eros means that in the absence of a strong analytic sense of the necessary, what is done and produced will become what is necessary (or: what is necessary will not be what is Good or what is needed, but rather, it will be that which depends upon coincidence, chance and accident). Since what is produced could always have been otherwise, what is essential will always be that which is conventional: *arché*, origin and ground will be formulated as a thing.

In the dialectical world, it is paternity which provides speech with the sense of succession and continuity in the figure of discourse that continuously seeks to re-collect its place in the whole. In the absence of paternity, the sense of continuity is only provided as a relationship between successful creations having nothing in common above their being produced. In the absence of paternity, arbitration is necessary as the paternalism of exegetical justice is needed to replace a sense of genuine paternity. Exegesis then reformulates paternity as paternalism.

Where paternity is absent, authority is essentially unstable because competition answers to the temporal cycle of fertility. Though maternity persists as the ground of all subsequent productions, she must guarantee her replacement by her own offspring who themselves must be replaced by those whom they produce. Maternity must depend upon its offspring to intermittently reconcile the pluralism generated by the equation of fertility with authority. Maternity will then seek to 'produce' paternal authority it-self and thus, will turn to one of her offspring.

Sky can come to rule because he 'covers her on all sides'. The first icon of paternal authority is mathematics — sky is produced as such a surrogate (in the absence of a sense of genuine paternity) because he can cover; he is the inclusive. The first source of authority is the universalism of mathematics, and sky is required because of the divisiveness and particularism of fertility. Sky is produced by maternity not out of love, but from the need for the re-assertion of something beyond maternity, for without such a re-assertion maternity it-self promises to be forgotten.

The relationship between earth and sky — between maternity and her most inclusive offspring — suggests the relationship between nature and mathematics. Nature produces mathematics to preserve her but mathematics because of its very inclusiveness is unmindful of the particulars. Sky punishes particularity with such violence that nature herself is put in jeopardy. As the offspring of sky — of the loveless and abstract union of mathematics and nature — Cronus re-presents the rebellion of physics as the attempt to reassert the claim of the things — of the reliable and steadfast, of maternity.

The children of the union of nature and sky — the re-presentations of physics — are hybrids. They are monstrous products of the loveless union of nature and mathematics. The mathematization of nature deforms the particular. The children of sky can only re-assert their particularity in monstrous ways because in regressing to the pluralism of maternal fertility they revoke the only grounds of authority (mathematics); they can only re-assert the value of particularity itself and in so doing personify the destructiveness of the natural world which maternity herself had glimpsed and had tried to reconcile in her union with sky. The castration of sky by his children symbolizes the begetting of violence from violence in a relationship that does not teach. The monstrousness of the children of sky — of the generation of Cronus — means that they personify the accentuation of difference, of particularity in its most concrete form.

From the point of view of Reason, Desire expresses the requirement to continuously revive the authority of paternity as the contrast between What Is and What Is-Not within life itself. The generation of Cronus re-presents the attempt to revive paternity in a world in which fertility has the highest value, and the eros of the titans only means — that given the destruction of mathematics — they can find no grounds for authority outside of force itself. If differentiation is the highest good (because of the good of unregulated fertility), any solution to the problem of order must itself be produced and consequently will itself not be regulated. This is to say that any solution to the disorderliness of a world oriented to the good of fertility will as a solution be unregulated and fertile. What is required is a producer who accentuates and encapsulates in himself the values of monstrousness. Such a monster (Cronus) as the tyrant is granted authority because he personifies the monstrousness of the collective. If we recall Socrates' description of the tyrant as one whose dreams are unlimited seeking to consummate the incestuous act with his mother and to slay his father, we can understand the meaning of Cronus as a solution to the problem of order in the world of fertility in which paternity has been transformed by castration. Tyranny represents the source of order in the world which respects no constraint beyond becoming.

V

Books IV to VI present a list of the genealogy of the gods. This idea of listing adapts to the nature of the pre-Olympian world for where Becoming is itself the good, one can only list. Until man's desire for paternity is revived the world can only be described with a list: physics as the study of pre-Olympian nature by disregarding the question of paternity (in treating the limp authority of mathematics as a residue of paternity no longer deserving of respect) makes necessary the idea of the list. The list narrates the interaction between products — the alternation of generation and productive cycles, the ceaseless motion, coming-to-be and replacement of parts. Though the list will include Zeus, his appearance signifies the need to re-assert the essentiality of that which cannot be listed. Zeus personifies the need for paternity, for that which itself transcends the list. The list prepares for the story of Zeus' campaign to replace nature with wisdom through his re-achievement of the idea of paternity. Zeus' campaign will be organized around the need to reintegrate eros.

Man's place in nature generates Zeus as a requirement in that man's coming to understand his place is a coming to understand his requirements. God shows his necessity through his re-integration of man and nature; man's presence raises the question of the relationship between fertility and authority and in that sense man is intermediate between fertility and authority requiring a sense of paternity to be fertile and needing the sensuality of fertility to show his piety towards the paternal. God is good not because he makes the world (not because he is a supreme artist or craftsman) but because Reason requires the authoritativeness of paternity. Paternity creates authority by showing how a world without it is soulless, violent and monstrous.

Because the necessity of paternity can only be shown through the practice of discourse, fertility and paternity require each other. If the absence of paternity raises the spectre of a soulless world, the need to arrest multitudinous speech itself presupposes the fertility of multitudinousness as a beginning. Fertility (which makes reference to the necessary collaboration in the practice of theorizing expressed in the work of re-collecting unity from different uses) is essential to the very activity of re-achieving paternity.

In this sense, man must re-create — revive — the idea of paternity through his practices. He must find his place between the monstrous particularism of nature and the violent universalism of sky. As a descendent of nature man must re-assert the requirements of a genuine paternity against the solutions of either abstraction (mathematics) or particularism (physics): the enemy of man is the failure of maternity (of unregulated nature, of productivity) to understand any solution to its unregulated 'indefinite pluralism' that is not tyrannical. A paternity that is just rather than tyrannical must be re-achieved. Zeus is meant to signify the essential requirement of man — as neither man nor god he serves as an image of the requirements which must be envisaged. His 'campaign' will then narrate the presencing — the re-collecting — of such requirements.

Before Zeus, the idea of ruling (of paternity) had no weight and both sky and Cronus were concerned only with preserving their authority, with protecting their possessions. Such rulers do not teach: they transmit only the passion for self-preservation and possessiveness as ends of life. Authority must be re-achieved as an object of respect through just rule — ruling which includes as its essential feature a commitment to restore the collective's place in the whole.

The war between the children of Cronus and Zeus records the struggle to reconstitute the requirement of reason. Zeus marshals force against nature (the monsters) rationally, i.e., Zeus employs reason to bring reason into the world. Zeus sees the 'hundred-arms' and reminds them of their obligations, showing that knowledge can control force and violence through its capacity to make reference to the essentials. Zeus deals justly with his allies in speech, he tells them what they ought to hear. Zeus only triumphs because of the justness of his speech: he placates allies and organizes weapons which reason needs in its struggle with nature.

Zeus' campaign displays the way in which the Good of language is grounded in his capacity to create community. Such an effort is achieved through his restoration of respect for the authority of paternity. This respect is earned by Zeus' ability to embody justice in his speech. Zeus adjusts to the circumstances as required and such adjusting is just. This adjusting does not mean that Zeus is instrumental, that he is one who seeks to manipulate in order to preserve his authority as an end in itself, rather, Zeus recognizes that authority must be preserved if order is to prevail and that its preservation consists in its continuous exposure to the dialectic between What Is and What Is-Not. Zeus' just speech says to each man what he needs in order to remind men of their duty (but this duty is not to Zeus as much as it is to the vision of communality which Zeus as a symbol of paternity represents).

This is to say that the justness of Zeus resides in his relation to differences; he formulates for the different their essential need. Zeus seeks to teach what is essential or required to those who differ. His essentiality is neither based on his universalism nor monstrousness, but on his claim to personify that which needs to be respected. Yet he will earn their respect through his practices, for these practices will revive the sense of what is needed.

When Metis was about to give birth to Athena, Zeus deceived her with a trick and swallowed her and kept her in his belly. Zeus uses charms and tricks to consolidate reason and to prevent its dispersion because Zeus recognizes the need to maintain and solidify the unity of paternity. Zeus makes himself the father through cunning because such tricks are required constantly to arrest the inexorable tendency of reason to regress — to succumb to the temptation of unregulated eros to disperse — and thus to revive the monstrous pre-Olympian period world of nature (the world in which differences are Real).

Hesiod's pre-Olympian world conjures up an image of the truimph of the monstrous in the absence of respect for paternity. In this sense, when the difference between genuine and spurious paternity (the real difference between What Is and What Is-Not as a difference within life) is overpowered by eros — by the desire to make a difference that is apparent but not Real — What Is appears as What Is-Not. Theorizing as the continuous need to revive the Real difference continuously seeks to charm the monstrous as a feature of its very own work.

The just speech as the speech which accepts the necessity of the co-existence of paternity *and* maternity can only be achieved, on the one hand, by resisting the tendency of paternalism to concretize itself as an abstract disregard for the erotic character of justice, and on the other, by resisting the tendency of maternity to equate fertility — as the making of concrete differences (the multiplication of usage) — with what is good and what is necessary.

The just speech achieves in its discoursing a measured relationship between paternity and maternity. In seeking to revive the sense of What Is it prosecutes its endeavour through discourse in a way that is responsive to the erotic distinctions assembled by multitudinous speech without accepting such usage as What Is. The justness of the just speech consists in this: that its strong sense of what is necessary permits it to relate ironically and healthfully to what is inessential; that its knowing the difference between the essential and the inessential means knowing the place of the inessential as that which is itself necessary to what is essential. It is knowing this which gives the theorist the strength to resist the horrors of unregulated particularism and abstract universalism.

The monsters must be charmed: the monsters are both within and without. Just speech tricks and charms the monsters in order to consolidate and sustain respect for paternity. The theorist as one who imitates the gods is one who charms the monsters both within and without. The monsters are manyness, multitudinousness, multiplicity, disorder and dispersion, and theorizing is the conversation which seeks to charm *multis*. Yet, because of the essential difference between man and God — between the theorist and Zeus — the monsters can never be extinguished. The just speech is the speech that seeks to charm the monsters under the auspices of the recognition that they cannot be extinguished, that the monsters are as omnipresent as the language which shelters them. The just speech then imitates the Gods in a way that preserves the distinction between man and God.

VI

Then I hope you will agree to this. Every one of these individuals who make a living by teaching in private and whom the public are pleased to call sophists and to regard as their rivals, is teaching nothing else than the opinions and beliefs expressed by the public itself when it meets on any occasion; and that is what he calls wisdom. It is as if the keeper of some huge and powerful creature should make a study of its moods and desires, how it may best be approached and handled when it is most savage or gentle and what makes it so, the meaning of its various cries and the tones of voice that will soothe or provoke its anger; and having mastered all this by long familiarity, should call it wisdom, reduce it to a system, and set up a school. Not in the least knowing which of these humours and desires is good or bad, right or wrong, he will fit all these terms to the fancies of the great beast and call what it enjoys good and what vexes it bad. He has no other account to give of their meaning; for him any action will be 'just' and 'right' that is done under necessity, since he is too blind to tell how great is the real difference between must be and what ought to be. It would be a queer sort of education that such a person could offer, would it not?

It would indeed.

And is there anything to choose between him and one who thinks it is wisdom to have studied the moods and tastes of the assembled multitude, either in painting and music or in politics? Certainly, no one can go into such mixed company and submit to their judgment a poem or a work of art or some service he would render to the state, thus going out of his way to make the public his masters, without falling under the fatal necessity to give them whatever they like and do whatever they approve; but have you ever heard any argument which was not beneath contempt to show that what they admire is really beautiful or what they approve really good?

No; I do not expect to hear one.

Now, with all this in mind, recall that distinction we drew earlier, between beauty itself and the multiplicity of beautiful things. Is it conceivable that the multitude should ever believe in the existence of any real essence, as distinct from its many manifestations, or listen to anyone who asserts such a reality?

Assuredly not.

If that is so, the multitude can never be philosophical. Accordingly it is bound to disapprove of all who pursue wisdom; and so, of course, are those individuals who associate with the mob and set their hearts on pleasing it.

That is clear.

The philosopher is the custodian of the beast whereas the theorist tries to reorganize or teach. The beast is the multitude which 'can never be philosophical' and the theorist thus seeks to do the impossible, he seeks to tame the beast. The beast is within as well as without, and the corruption of the theorist's nature occurs when he comes under control of the multitude. The theorist is unable to tame the beast within. He cannot charm or trick his *multis*.

Though the theorist co-exists within the multitude he will differentiate himself through the way in which he charms his *multis*. The theorist shows reserve, for even within the motion of *multis* — within the disorder of speech — his very speaking intends to achieve tranquillity. In this creation of discourse which embodies no-thing, the theorist makes reference to the stillness that impregnates words; the theorist makes reference to the stillness of no-thing through speech.

Theorizing makes reference to no-thing as a speaking that is a restraining. The intensity of theoretic passion appears in its restrained and patient dwelling upon words, in its decisive holding-back from that to which the word assents — not in a spirit of scholasticism but through the desire to teach. The desire to hear no-thing requires the passion of reserve, of restrained holding-back, for it is only through such *intense* patience that the uncommon can be recollected in the crevices of the common.

The theorist teaches by resisting and counteracting, his charming is such a resisting. In this resistance he teaches: his resistance serves to preserve the autonomy of *multis* by refusing to allow *multis* to have it easy: he seeks to make *multis* strong by inviting *multis* to suffer the re-cognition of no-thing and in such an attempt, to teach *multis* What Is and What Is-Not as parts of What Is. The theorist's aim to bring No-thing to presence is served by his reserve: it is through this reserve that his speech's embodiment of no-thing can teach. Yet, *multis* is a beast, it cannot be philosophical. The theorist co-exists within the unphilosophical with the passion of restraint (he passionately restrains his impulse to withdraw from the multitude or to annihilate it).

To say that the theorist charms the monsters — the monstrousness of *multis* — is to say that he resists the impulse to treat the making of concrete differences as the end of speech. Whereas eroticism issues in the impulse towards concrete originality — to treat what one originates as a real difference, it also generates the desire to tyrannize all difference by assimilating it to self. Eroticism threatens to obliterate the idea of difference either through the vanities of originality or tyranny. In this sense the erotic man seeks to resolve the problem of the opposition of theorizing and *multis* through a radical indifference to *multis* that eventuates either in the segregation of self from *multis* or the assimilation of *multis* to self.

Multis itself cannot understand theorizing which does not seek to tyrannize difference, it must see such work as withdrawal. To *multis*, the monsters to be feared is also a divisiveness, but not the difference between genuine and spurious paternity; rather, these are the irreconcilable differences that are released by the spurious notion of paternity itself.

Theorizing requires *multis* as the opposition in terms of which it acquires weight. The idea of theorizing only makes sense when the differentness of *multis* is acknowledged as its contrast. In this sense Socrates tells Glaucon of the mandate of theorizing.

> Is it not also likely, indeed certain after what has been said, that a state can never be properly governed either by the uneducated who know nothing of truth or by men who are allowed to spend all their days in the pursuit of culture? The ignorant have no single mark before their eyes at which they must aim and all the conduct of their own lives and of affairs of state; and the others will not engage in action if they can help it, dreaming that, while still alive, they have been translated to the aisles of the blessed.
>
> Quite true.
>
> It is for us then, as founders of a commonwealth, to bring compulsion to bear on the noblest natures. They must be made

to climb the ascent of the vision of goodness, which we call the highest object of knowledge; and when they have looked upon it long enough they must not be allowed, as they now are, to remain on the height, refusing to come down again to the prisoners or to take any part in their labours and rewards, however much or little these may be worth.

Shall we not be doing them an injustice, if we force on them a worse life than they might have?

You have forgotten again, my friend, that the law is not concerned to make any one class especially happy, but to insure the welfare of the commonwealth as a whole. By persuasion or constraint it will unite the citizens in harmony, making them share whatever benefits each class can contribute to the common good; and its purpose in forming men of that spirit was not that he should be left to go his own way, but that they should be instrumental in binding the community into one. . . . You will see, then, Glaucon, that there will be no real injustice in compelling our philosophers to watch over and care for the other citizens.

Socrates is not recommending the return of theorists to labour camps or to community welfare programmes; he is pointing to the essentiality of theorizing to continuously reformulate *multis* in conversation. The theorist neither escapes nor seeks to annihilate *multis*, nor again to be its custodian. He co-exists with *multis* through his continuous formulation of multitudinous speech as a way of teaching by reviving the difference between spurious and genuine paternity. Theorizing reformulates the putative 'ignorance' of multitudinousness as it-self a kind of knowing which is licensed by requirements to resist formulating and to terminate conversation. The theorist is compelled not to perpetuate the stratification of theorist and *multis* but to use that difference as an occasion to revive the idea of Real or essential difference. If the theorist stands to the multitude as knowledge of genuine paternity stands to knowing spurious paternity, he also stands as one who knows the difference between What Is and What Is-Not stands to one who covers-over the difference by concretizing What Is and by externalizing What Is-Not.

If What Is co-exists with What Is-Not as its self-imposed limitation, the continuous revival of Being is the revival of this difference. Because What Is needs being revived it needs the formulating — the convening — of man; What Is is never possessed absolutely though it is omnipresent in the life of speech. The decisiveness of What Is is re-achieved in the presencing of its own limitation by What Is-Not as its own requirement. It is violent formulative work that continuously exposes this difference *as* What Is. Men misunderstand the nature of What Is when they think it appropriable in a final and absolute act, for what it means essentially is that it need be continuously and eternally re-enactable. What Is means: its continuous need to be re-achieved (this *need* is what What Is means). What Is means that discourse is continuously needed, that any deliberation or question about whether or not to speak is already segregated from the meaning of What Is, that it is already out of touch with its requirements. In this sense, What Is is not to be deliberated because it essentially requires re-enactment. Discourse authorized by a sense of the requiredness of What Is can never be (merely) repetitive, but only re-collective, because understanding What Is means accepting life (which includes the requirements of discoursing). *This* is what Socrates tries to tell Glaucon and how much deeper than the advice to which we are accustomed on the relation of practice to theory.

In terms of the acceptance of life, deliberation about 'going on' can only appear monstrous: as an attempt to deliberate upon the contrast between life and not-life it suppresses Real difference in the service of a difference that is spurious because it is only when life is not comprehended that a Real difference to it can be imagined by one who lives (and can we imagine anyone imagining, other than a one who lives?) Such imagining suppresses the Real difference within life as the difference that *is* life. In this respect, suicide is a fine metaphor for the failure of discourse to appreciate how its requiredness is laid down by life itself, its failure to appreciate how its requiredness is what life means. Because suicide sees What Is as static and secure it can only formulate speech as repetition: this is because suicide sees What Is-Not as some thing different from What Is rather than as a difference made by life itself.

The struggle between the theorist and the multitude is personified in the *work* of the just speech (the analysis). In that discourse the dialectic between limitation (the essent) and multitudinousness is worked out in a way that intends to re-centre the difference between what is necessary and what is inessential. The practice of this conversation continuously shows itself as the strength and reserve to resist multitudinous notions of origin, difference, fertility and justice through its work of reformulating these notions, where the work itself displays the difference between that upon which it works and that which makes its work possible.

It is the intermediacy of man — the essentiality of Other — that makes the work of justice continuous and required. Intermediacy gives to the just man his reserve and irony: he needs to be ironic in so far as he exists among the things through the practice of re-collecting their limitation. The irony of the just man means that he withdraws his loyalty from the view that the things are first: he dissents from the commitment to the firstness of speech. The irony of the just man — required by the injustice of the things among which he exists — consists in his practice of retrieving the limits upon this injustice as a way of pointing to the justice of that which is Other than the things.

If Other means the Desire for justice, justice it-self makes reference to that which can only be enacted in work. The work of enacting justice is the discourse in which opinions are re-formulated. Such Desire compels man only because man is grounded in and given by the difference between him-self and Other. The Desire for justice is conterminous with this difference, with this intermediacy: it compels man's irony as his necessary mode of existence among the things which are unjust. Man examines injustice's claim to be just not by discounting it but by showing the measure of its truth.

CHAPTER V

Work

I

Conversation re-presents the Socratic conception of work. As the work of discourse, conversation is necessary; it is a requirement of life (rather than an exigency of survival). This necessity — the requiredness of work — is itself given by the fact of man's intermediacy (by the difference between man and Other, by there being something Other than man) in the sense that man's intermediacy means that he is continuously required to re-achieve his place. The Socratic notion of work contrasts to the hedonist notion of labour as exegesis. The work of dialectic is grounded in the Desire for justice — the Desire to sustain the question 'what is first?' — just as exegetical labour is grounded in the image of interactional democracy as the method of guaranteeing the exigencies of success and survival.

For dialectic, the work which enters into man's discursive re-collection of his place requires reserve (a kind of moderation or *sophrosynê*). Adequate conversation must moderate the impulse to conceive of the appropriation of man's place as exhausted and terminated at any one point, by understanding, in contrast, the commitment to the work of reformulative activity as a continuous engagement. What must be moderated is the notion that the analysis of opinions can be dispensed with, that impulse to establish a direct communion with Being which is not mediated by the practice of re-formulating multitudinousness. Socratic work contrasts itself as conversation to the madness of unregulated abstraction that conceives of it-self as free from the conversation of opinions just as it contrasts itself to the madness of unregulated fertility.

Both of these madnesses share a commitment to disregarding conversation. In contrast to the way of Socrates are those madmen who speak as if their speech could not be Other than first. Such madnesses make reference to the course of action that organizes around the deliberation over, or description of, opinions, as its end or good instead of committing itself to re-formulative work. What Socratic moderation moderates is the impulse to argue, adjudicate and describe as if there was a Real (essential) difference between speech and that about which it speaks. Socratic moderation moderates the impulse of speech to assert its firstness as displayed in its possessive attachment to its opinions.

If the difference between Socratic moderation and these madnesses is reflected in the difference between irony and possessiveness (between formulating opposition and taking the extreme position of denying opposition), it is still certain that Socrates was not ironic towards his commitment to irony (he was not moderate towards his own moderation). This particular madness — the madness of Socrates — combines prudence and violence by taking an extreme position about man's intermediacy and work.

II

In the famous exchange with Thrasymachus, Socrates is accused in a peculiar way by the sophist, and the opinion which Thrasymachus expresses is worth considering because it says something very important about Socrates. Thrasymachus identifies Socratic questioning as a kind of malingering. Socrates always *asks* questions but does not *answer* them and because 'everyone knows' that questions are easier to ask than to answer, Socrates takes the easy way out. We use this opinion as an occasion to examine the work of Socrates as exemplified in the maieutic conception of questioning. The place to begin is at the opening of the exchange in the *Theaetetus*.

After a brief opening exchange, Theaetetus has trouble finding his feet. He threatens to withdraw with the following speech.

> But I assure you, Socrates, I have often attempted myself to study that problem, when I heard reports of the questions you asked. But I cannot persuade myself that I can give any

> satisfactory solution or that anyone has ever stated in my hearing the sort of answer you require. And yet I cannot get the question out of my mind.

To this Socrates responds

> My dear Theaetetus, that is because your mind is not empty or barren. You are suffering the pains of travail.

Socrates recognizes the pain of labouring. He also recognizes that Theaetetus is an exceptional lad, because he cannot get the question 'out of his mind'. Theaetetus needs to see that this kind of pain is different from failure, that it is a feature of the work of inquiry. Theaetetus is too preoccupied with success and failure — he has never 'heard anyone give a satisfactory answer' and he accepts this as his licence to resign from the conversation prematurely. When the youth's speech is challenged under the force of questioning his first impulse is to withdraw. Previously he had lived in harmony with speech but now the security of his relationship to his opinion is questioned. Theaetetus exemplifies the Socratic notion of 'common sense' as the 'idling' of speech, whereas Socrates requires that he create a difference — a tension — within his speech. Socrates is trying to arrest the 'holidaying' of language.

Theaetetus cannot imagine an answer as if the absence of an answer constitutes grounds for discontinuing work, as if he 'lacks' some thing — an answer — as a privation or imperfection. Theaetetus not only accepts the history of his experiences as binding (that he has never heard an answer), but he also accepts the idea of *an* answer as a criterion of successful speech. Theaetetus treats the tension of unresolved questions as failure, mistake, or imperfection because he thinks of good speech as that which creates answers, i.e., that which silences. Theaetetus cannot imagine silencing Socrates' speech because he subscribes to a notion of successful or complete speech that is divine rather than human, a notion of speech that is it-self segregated from language. Yet, Socrates only responds to Theaetetus' complaint that he 'cannot get the question out of my mind' as if what Theaetetus says *here* is essential. Despite all of his reservations and fears, Theaetetus is in the grip of the question; the question disturbs him. This is a good sign, for what it signifies is that Socrates is speaking to a person who cannot get the question out of his mind. Even though he cannot acknowledge an answer, he concedes the seriousness of the question. Perhaps the most serious questions are those for which answers cannot be imagined: perhaps the most important work is to address such questions. What Socrates wants Theaetetus to eventually see is that this omnipresence of the question *means* that it can never be terminated with the kind of 'answer' which Theaetetus feels he *lacks*. That to think of answers to such questions as 'lacking' is to misunderstand the *nature* of such questions (that they can never be 'gotten out of the mind').

It is exactly at the point that Socrates introduces his midwife story.

> How absurd of you, never to have heard that I am the son of the midwife, a fine buxom woman called Phaenarete!
>
> Theaetetus: I have heard that.
>
> Socrates: Have you also been told that I practise the same art?
>
> Theaetetus: No, never.
>
> Socrates: It is true though; only don't give away my secret. It is not known that I possess this skill; so the ignorant world describes me in other terms as an eccentric person who reduces people to hopeless perplexity. Have you been told that too?
>
> Theaetetus: I have.
>
> Socrates: Shall I tell you the reason?
>
> Theaetetus: Please do.
>
> Socrates: Consider then how it is with all midwives; that will help you to understand what I mean. I daresay you know that they never attend other women in childbirth, but only when they are too old for that.

The story is designed to mobilize Theaetetus' faith by pointing out first, that one cannot wait to produce an answer because that shows a possessive (i.e., passive) relationship to speech. One begins as a speaker not by laying his own grounds (by seeking to 'possess' his own beginning in words), but by re-achieving his beginning in his speaking. Theaetetus wants to ground his speech in a conception of a complete productive conversation (of total explication) the possibility of which he cannot imagine. Socrates' story will then have to contrast this impatience with his own maieutic reserve — the restraint of faithfulness. Further, his story will have to show Theaetetus the concreteness of his conception of speech and of answers and questions, i.e., that man is one who exists within the incompleteness of unresolved questions, suffering them as his manliness rather than as pain or failure. Perhaps that this milieu of unresolved questions is what the 'social' means. He will have to show Theaetetus that his 'pain' is only a symptom of his erotic attraction for the Good which is awakened in the youth by his teacher and which must be suffered as the first step in such a re-collecting.

Socrates must teach Theaetetus to comprehend what he treats (practically) as 'pain' — as a trouble to be relieved — as the *aporia*. In the practical sense, Socrates — the teacher — makes trouble — and Theaetetus must understand this as his first lesson; that the theorist must, in his speech, make trouble for him-self; that the theorist's speaking is a continuous creation of opposition for him-self within the speech it-self; that this opposition, this tension, symbolizes in the metaphor of the *aporia* the distance which the theorist has to create in his words as the dialectic between their surfaces and resonances. As a novice, Theaetetus needs a teacher to make such demands upon him and as a novice, Theaetetus can only see such a teacher as a source of trouble and his demands as 'pain'.

Socrates' story must show further that he (Socrates) was like Theaetetus, a learner, a one in pain, and that his present tranquillity is not the result of his possession of some correct answer, but rather shows that he has converted that pain into the re-cognition of its place within the human relationship to language. Socrates' tranquillity is not a consequence of his riches — of his accumulation or addition of new things to himself — but of his re-collection of the need to continuously re-achieve that self as an icon of his origin. Socrates must then show Theaetetus that the tranquillity and reserve of the theorist is not a result of his possessiveness or of his having many things in his possession, but results more from his poverty, i.e., that it is because he is not attached to any one thing that he re-collects the Good as the need for this continuous re-achievement. The problem, of course, with Theaetetus is that his possessiveness is directed towards his speech and not to this need, that his love is directed towards his opinions and not to that from which they devolve.

But why do midwives come from the ranks of those too old to bear children? Why must midwives be past the age of childbearing?

> Socrates: They say that it is because Artemis, the patroness of childbirth, is herself childless; and so, while she did not allow barren women to be midwives, because it is beyond the power of human nature to achieve skill without any experience, she assigned the privilege to women who were past childbearing, out of respect to their likeness to herself.

Midwives are recruited neither from the barren nor the productive, but from those who like Theaetetus laboured and produced and are now 'past childbearing'. While the productive (the member) are still in pain — in labour — the barren or the sterile have never laboured, they can have no respect for labour. The barren woman — like mathematics — is indifferent to what is different from her — productive — whereas the productive woman can only treat her labour as an other instance of work. The theorist must avoid the excesses of particularity and abstraction, he must personify the intermediate: the theorist must neither recapitulate nor disregard work (the practice, the 'concrete') and thus, must re-present the 'middle way', the way of midwifery. Socrates himself is past 'the age of childbearing' which means that he is no longer like Theaetetus, i.e., he is past the concern with possessing his opinions, past the stage of a possessive attitude towards speech. Yet, as a personification of the human, Socrates was productive, he was (is) a member. That is he begins with his sociality. Socrates is saying that he was once possessive towards his speech, that he had opinions. He is telling Theaetetus that *his* pain at the moment re-produces the pain experienced by all who begin to theorize. Socrates is then testifying that he is no God, that he studied physics and made speeches and can only now reintegrate those experiences as moments in the evolution of his soul. Socrates can then relate to Theaetetus' pain respectfully and gently for he too is a man and all men 'whose minds are not empty or barren' must proceed through the pain of labour, they all must experience the *aporia* when they begin to examine the good of their possessions (when they begin to ask what their possessions are for). This is to say that the commitment to theorizing is an achievement, that it begins as a convention within society and proceeds as a reformulation of this beginning.

There is a conception of natural limit here which differentiates the teacher from the student, the theorist from the member. These limits correspond to stages in the evolution of the soul. Theory is then linked to that which precedes it as the activity of re-collecting the Reason for the speech, a re-collection invited by the very speaking it-self. Theory is speech supervising itself by reviewing its place within the whole of a Rational conversation; this supervision is an administering, a managing, a disciplining. Speech supervises itself as it disciplines it-self. Is this not *sophrosyné* — self-control supervising it-self as a listening to it-self? Theaetetus must learn to supervise him-self. Yet this is not a temporal sequence: theory must continuously re-achieve its place between sterility and productivity.

Socrates tells Theaetetus that he cannot become a midwife overnight, that he must conceive through the pain of labour, and that this is a natural state (dialectic has no place for genius). His story must caution Theaetetus from the mania of erotic attachment to some image of completion that obliterates the differences between the stages in the history of the theoretic soul. There are natural and innate limits which must be respected. The teacher treats himself as a God who never suffered the *aporia* of possessive speech: the student treats himself as a genius who does not comprehend the sociality of the *aporia*. Gods and geniuses do not belong to dialectic, for they are creatures of art, of mathematics. The difference between teacher and learner must be preserved not as a privation but as a constructive limit upon their capacities. Thus it is the essence of theorizing as *maieutics* to respect the learner on the grounds that the teacher's commitment itself is an achievement, and to respect the teacher on the grounds that the learner can only begin to re-collect his place under the auspices of the supervision of one who has already begun to manage his movement away from possessiveness. Socrates then begins formulating the art of theorizing in order to preserve this difference for Theaetetus.

> Socrates: And it is more than likely, is it not, that no one can tell so well as a midwife whether women are pregnant or not?
>
> Theaetetus: Assuredly.
>
> Socrates: Moreover, with the drugs and incantations they administer, midwives can either bring on the pains of travail or

allay them at their will, make a difficult labour easy, and at an early stage cause a miscarriage if they so decide.

Theaetetus: True.

Socrates: Have you also observed that they are the cleverest matchmakers, having an unerring skill in selecting a pair whose marriage will produce the best children?

Theaetetus: I was not aware of that.

Socrates: Well, you may be sure they pride themselves on that more than on cutting the umbilical cord.

The midwife questions pregnancy and labour. Is this not what Thrasymachus and Callicles find offensive in Socrates? That he questions labour? Is this not what Thrasymachus finds easier than labour it-self — the questioning of labour? as if such questioning was not it-self work! Labour produces possessions that Socrates' questioning questions, but the result of Socrates' questioning is not itself a possession. Socrates is poor; he possesses nothing. Moreover, the midwife matches the learner to those conditions that will make him productive. The good teacher as a successful matchmaker matches the learner to those conditions that will first make him fertile, i.e., that will first arouse in him the desire to experience the painfulness of the preliminary steps in theorizing. Are these not the conditions metaphorically enumerated in *The Republic*? Youth must be protected from the evil of pandering, from being exposed to destructive influences or rhetoric. The good teacher will match the youth to those conditions which promise to bring out his best. The midwife knows that different natures require different conditions: he does not speak to all but only to those who promise to conceive, and yet he can arrange matches for those 'who have never conceived at all'. The midwife is just, but he can only talk to those whose fertility seems to him a possibility.

What of the conditions which the midwife arranges? Are these not the conditions of good talk, the conditions under which Rational conversation unfolds? And yet a feature of these very conditions is the commitment of the learner to the Rational conversation which the conditions nurture. Because Theaetetus' mind is gripped by the question and is 'in travail' he appears to be one so committed. He is promising, and yet Socrates cannot speak to everyone, for many are impatient or angry or brutish, and thus do not desire the Rational conversation because their minds are not 'in travail'. These others reflect enmity to Socrates and if they stay with him they shall re-collect what they are, they shall discover their barrenness. Those who are fearful of such a discovery should go else-where; he will even find them teachers. In fact is this not what the very conversation is about — to discover how far the interlocutor is prepared to go? Is this not the *topic* of the conversation — the secret topic — the testing of souls? Is the conversation not a way of preparing the interlocutor to understand the difference between barrenness and fertility — between having nothing to give and taking the risk of giving — as the first stage of the theoretic life?

The barren ones are unyielding in the sense that they do not give incentive or ground in their speech for its reformulability: they do not take the risk of work — of discourse — for they speak safely rather than invitingly. Socrates will teach the interlocutor that barrenness is a commitment and so, he will teach him the difference between barrenness and fertility; Socrates will also show the barren ones themselves what it is to be barren.

The friends of Socrates are those who take the risk of fertility, who undertake the work of exposing their talk to reformulability. The sterile ones do not speak in such a way as to invite the re-achievement of their authority, for they are indifferent to the *production* of their beginning. Whereas Artemis' childlessness is a positive feature of her divinity, these 'other teachers' are simply 'barren' humans, men who think they are divine. The students with whom Socrates cannot converse and these 'other teachers' deserve each other: neither of them can *experience* their authority as a re-achievement, in the first case because the authority is seen as residing in the product, and in the second case because the productive character of the authority is disregarded.

These students and teachers provide a glimpse of the soil on which enmity to Socrates grows: they think that the difference which Socratic speech makes between the authority and products of speech is not a real difference, they are indifferent to this difference. In contrast, Socrates and his friends think that making *this* difference makes a real difference between speech and that which is Other to it. The enemies of Socrates do not think that re-collection makes a difference because what it 'promises' is no-thing new, is no-thing different.

Socrates says that he — Socrates — is not productive because he has passed the stage of possessive speech.

> My art as a midwife for you is in general like theirs; the only difference is that my patients are men, not women, and my concern is not with the body but with the soul that is in travail of birth. And the highest point of my art is the power to prove by every test whether the offspring of a young man's thought is a false phantom or instinct with life and truth. I am so far like the midwife that I cannot myself give birth to wisdom; and the common reproach is true, that, though I question others, I can myself bring nothing to life because there is no wisdom in me.

Productivity is identified with fertility, generativity. Socrates' remark that he 'cannot give birth to wisdom' asserts that he is past the stage of possessiveness and of the possessive productive relationship to speech. To what can 'offspring' refer? Certainly not to speeches *per se* since Socrates is a tireless speaker. To what kind of relationship to speech does offspring make reference since it is that relationship that Socrates cannot produce? Socrates does not understand his speeches as offsprings, he does not understand his speeches as belonging to him, as his property or possession.

Socrates is fertile but he is not possessive. This is to say that he is neither a barren, unyielding speaker, nor a promiscuous one. His fertility is regulated by care for language rather than by possessiveness towards speech. Socrates cares about the relationship between his speech and language as an eternal relationship that must be continuously re-achieved through work. He cares about the infinite eternality of work rather than for the particular temporality of a product. Socrates cannot give 'birth to wisdom' because he is the child and not the father: he does not possess Being, but is in its grip as its subject. He does not seek command over his possessions, but shows care for what possesses him, and he shows that care in his regulated fertility — his taking the risk of discourse that is designed to express his gratitude.

One who is taught by Socrates to understand the difference between barrenness and fertility can still succumb to the destructive eros of unregulated fertility. Theaetetus must still control his monsters. Socrates will try to teach him to temper fertility — to combine violence with prudence — by exemplifying for and with him care for language rather than possessiveness towards speech. In showing Theaetetus the difference between multitudinousness and limit Socrates will seek to point to the difference between time and eternity.

In his capacity as theorist, Socrates does not intend his theorizing to stand as some thing to be possessed. Socratic theorizing invites its own re-formulation and so, while the fertile ones personify the practical understanding that action must be taken as their origin or point of departure, Socrates does not accept such limits. The Socratic invitation is communicated by his manner of speech, by the demand established by adequate speaking, the demand to concert in taking its measure. The invitational character of adequate speaking is its calling forth a response not as a query calls for a reply, but as Reason makes its demand and lays it down. Such speech 'invites' by compelling those who are prepared to heed it to attend to the dimensions of limitation, measure and justice.

Socrates' claim to be unproductive is then a claim not to be possessive towards his speech merely because it is 'his' in some concrete sense, it is his claim not to treat his speech as a thing which he possesses, but rather, as part of a relationship that possesses him. The relationship of parent to offspring is sensual in the same way that the lover of beautiful things differs from the lover of beauty. In *The Republic*, the lover of beautiful things is depicted as a lover of things and not of beauty, as the lover of parts and not of the whole. To truly love the offspring is to love the best in the offspring; it is to love the goodness from which the offspring is differentiated and with which it ought be re-united. To love the offspring is to love that which is Other than the offspring; it is to love the whole of which the offspring is a part. To love the offspring without respect for that from which he springs is just to want him as a possession, as a thing that is one's own.

Socrates' claim not to produce wisdom does not mean that he is not wise; rather, it means that what is truly 'wisdom' is not produced. Any wisdom which he appears to exemplify is not *his* but is something which he has inherited. Socrates might be wise but it is not *he* that 'gives birth to wisdom', for he has no authority — he is the accomplice and subject of Otherness (of the Gods). Socrates is past the stage of claiming to be so productive because he re-cognizes his indebtedness. Therefore, he is not possessive towards his speech for he knows that *he* is poor; he is not erotic or sensual towards the things that he *happens* to have because they are not his things (they do not belong to him).

To say that wisdom is not a possession is to say that it is not an acquired *techné* or goal. Wisdom is not some thing to be coveted; it is not a possession in that sense. Wisdom as knowing the requirements of life is the continuous need to practise these requirements; it is knowing how one is 'enjoined' (by the Gods) to practise these requirements. The fact that wisdom is never satisfactorily possessed though we *have* it tells us not what we lack but what wisdom is. Socrates *is* wise *and* he possesses no wisdom because having wisdom is re-cognizing its re-possessibility and *this* re-cognition (which is wisdom) has to be continuously re-achieved (as a requirement of life it is more than the particular life of Socrates).

The parent ought to love his offspring only as a moment in his love for the Good and not as an end in itself. One way of understanding the task of the midwife is as one who teaches the parent the meaning of his love by re-directing him to the whole of which the offspring is a part. This is the way in which the midwife makes demands upon the labourer.

Typically parents relate erotically to offspring because the offspring is seen as a result of parental labour and so, labour reproduces the parent in the offspring. Thus the parent's love for his offspring is a form of self-love, of taking pleasure in what is familiar and secure. The parent's love for his offspring is incestuous, i.e., the parent takes pleasure in his speech and this incestuousness is grounded in the love of parent for him self. The incestuous relationship of parent to offspring which characterizes all speaking is rooted in the notion of authority: whereas the midwife is no author and makes no claim to be first, the parent by virtue of his labour reproduces himself as the author and the ground of his speech.

Incestuousness is part of the meaning of life. That men take pleasure in what belongs to them is seen even when men attempt to reflect upon the source or reason of such pleasure; one never escapes from what is his, for the idea of life means that it is *mine*. And yet, life is not a property or possession of mine but rather, it is that which is inescapably 'my life'. Strictly speaking then, life's essential belonging-to-me means that I am part of, or a moment in, every move to reflect upon 'it'. To accept life is to accept the inseparability and indivisibility of life into a 'me' and an 'it'. Yet, the theorist must 'laugh at incest': because the theorist knows that life must be accepted, he laughs at the attempt of such speakers to 'divide' life or to create differences (differences themselves dependant upon the unity and indivisibility of life) between life and non-life. The theorist knows 'What Is' and 'What Is-Not' and he knows 'What Is-Not' as a moment of 'What Is'. He knows the incorrigibility of this difference as a difference sheltered by life itself. The theorist's 'laugh at incest' is his way of referencing the essential Otherness of life as the real difference, as the requirement of (accepting) life it-self for re-cognizing the need to continuously re-achieve this difference.

Socrates produces no wisdom. The midwife does not re-produce himself as the grounds and the authority of his speech because the midwife recognizes that his grounds have produced him.

> Heaven constrained to me to serve as a midwife, but has debarred me from giving birth. So of myself I have no sort of wisdom, nor has any discovery ever been born to me as the child of my soul.

What is the good of midwifery? If Socrates would produce an account — a logos — of midwifery in that way he would only recapitulate the possessive relationship to speech. Such an account would be sterile too, for it would suppress concern with its own production by deflecting attention to the product (account) it produces. Socrates' peculiar 'justification' of theorizing does not result in an offspring of his own for he is himself an offspring of Otherness and thus cannot claim any authority for himself. Socrates begins with the sociality of his conversation (with the acceptance of life) recognizing that his responsibility will become manifest as he and the learner come together (take the risk of speaking). Socrates will not lay his own grounds because that would only perpetuate the possessive relationship of speaker to speech: in trying to relay Theaetetus' grounds Socrates will bring the good of midwifery to light because his conversation with Theaetetus will itself exemplify a re-collecting of his faith.

The theorizing of Socrates is then inspired by the recognition of the prospect of evil. Theaetetus personifies evil in his reluctance to continue. This evil manifests itself in the resignation of speech — in the tendency of speech to stay with what is secure and familiar and in such a move to resist the ascent of the soul that is learning. This evil manifests itself in the impulse to limit speech to the same (to what can be appropriated, subjected and possessed), in the desire of men to ground themselves in their selves and to save these selves through a radical simplification of the idea of

Otherness. This evil is reflected in possessiveness and in the reluctance to question the Reason or Good of possessions. Such a failure can only lead to the justification of what is possessed as good because what is possessed is possessed by me.

The evil which Theaetetus' resignation symbolizes is this: he is resigned to the absence of an answer as the absence of a policy, rule, or standard. That this is felt as an absence suggests that it ought to be present. What ought to be present and is absent (what is 'lacking') is a standard; Socrates' teaching is 'incomplete' because it fails to provide what is *needed*— a policy. Why is a policy needed?

Without a rule, the words of speeches that would terminate the conversation cannot be detected because there is no policy for deciding upon an appropriate answer to silence the question. This is a 'lack', and a 'correction' is *needed.* Socratic speech will then make no difference because it supplies no rule for making differences, differences cannot be *produced.* Socratic speech is not productive; it has no criterion for producing differences; consequently, it is static, unchanging and never generates, i.e., it never produces any thing new (any new thing). Socratic speech can only re-collect.

The unproductive character of Socratic speech is linked to the lack of a rule: it never changes, it never *makes* a difference because it is repetitive, it moves endlessly about in circles. This movement must be arrested and what we require is a rule for arresting the 'motion' of Socratic speech so the 'real' differences can be produced and so that 'real' differences and change can be made (rather than motion). In terms of Socratic speech, the differences that are desired here are only instances of movement because the *real* difference is that which is shown in the (theoretic) understanding that any rule is always ruled, and this (real) difference (as Other) resists all appropriation and policy; *this* difference as what both initiates and resists the possessiveness of speech is what the theorist knows and accepts in his 'laugh'.

The enemies of Socrates also fight the evil of resignation, except that for them Socrates himself symbolizes this evil. By destroying the possessive community the midwife interferes with the pleasure of self-love. The midwife is conceived as the stranger — the alien — who renders the incestuous relationship insecure and whose detachment appears as a monstrous violation of the textures of intimacy and trust which bind men to their words.

These enemies formulate Socrates — the stranger — as the one who in laughing at incest questions possessiveness from the standpoint of poverty. Whereas Socrates treats productive speech as dispersion, as a moving away from the essent, they treat his questioning as the interference which deprives men of their possessions and leaves them nothing. Whereas Socrates defends the speech by inspecting it to see if it is real or a phantom (by staying with Being) they see this very defence as alien (as interfering with the pleasure of simplification), as the resentment of poverty which seeks to render all men naked.

Socrates then lays down the grounds for the classical version of theorizing: he will not take the kind of 'part' in the discussion which he is expected to take; he will 'relate' to the discussion but in an altogether different way and in such a departure he will provide a new warrant for theorizing.

The maieutics of Socrates comes to this: that he will examine what they are doing; that whereas they are rushing ahead, he will hold back. Socrates will examine their offsprings while 'they' who are the parents or genitors of these offsprings will tend to resist such an examination. Maieutics points to the tension between the theorist and member as a tension between the midwife and the parent.

The offspring is the speech, the parent is man. The parent — man — produces speech which he loves merely because it is his. The parent accepts his offsprings because he has made them. The parent then accepts the firstness of 'making' as his rule or policy. The parent is productive and fertile, generating many speeches through which he comes to see him self; the parent sees his self in the speeches he makes because they are his. The parent then likes what belongs to him or what is his and he does not see that what is really his is life — is that which is Other than his making in the sense that it can never be assimilated to his making, while yet every moment of the making conforms to its requirements. Thus the attitude of parent to offspring is a surrogate form of self-love grounded in something deeper than 'like likes like' but in a decisive attitude towards making, labouring and possession (as reflected in the need to reject 'What Is').

The parent feels close to his offspring, he feels an unmediated unity or oneness. This closeness of parent to offspring prevents the parent from questioning the offspring; if urged he might summon up an account of how he produced the offspring (he might re-produce an 'account' of his making), but he will never examine the Good or aim of such production itself (because such an examination is seen as interminable, as an 'infinite regress'). The parent might describe his work but he will never examine its Reason because any such examination will require him to re-cognize that the possession which his work realizes is not it-self a Rational ground for the labour — that there must be some thing Other than the work or its product and that this thing is not a thing for it cannot itself be commanded and possessed. This thing that is not-a-thing (this no-thing) leaves its trace in the silence of every suppressed question. The parent will never conduct his examination as a way of referencing this no-thing which *is*. The closeness of parent to offspring means that any such question would only appear strange to him; the relation between parent and offspring is so close that some questions shall always appear to be strange.

The fact that the midwife has no progeny frees him to inspect the offsprings of others in a way which they do not. They see him as strange, as alien, as impersonal, as monstrous: they truly see him as unproductive and as joyless for he refuses to celebrate their offspring, preferring instead to restrain *their* enthusiasm. His unproductiveness consists in this: that he celebrates no products, has no enthusiasms, makes no claims for him self, has no thing for him self; he is parasitic; living off their offspring, taking no risks, creating no thing for himself, never relaxing, never holidaying, never moving. He annuls their joys, dissents from their enthusiasms, declines their invitations to relax and conjoin intimately.

The midwife then lives off their labour for they fail to see his questioning as work and his poverty as good. If the midwife has an art it is essentially parasitic, it is a counterfeit art whose artfulness consists in undermining sociability. The art of the midwife dissolves the close relationship between man and his speech. The midwife perverts the product of labour, for instead of contributing to the development and articulation of possessions already secured, he quests after the source: the art of the midwife is a questing rather than a contributing. Midwifery is seen as the paradigmatic parasitic art, as perfecting destructiveness — scepticism — as a skill behind the disingenuous mask of irony. In this sense midwifery is anti-social, it is the artful *techné* of dissolving the social (the close relationship between man and his offspring); it is the subversive art.

III

Thrasymachus' offhanded remark that 'questions are easier to ask than to answer' seems to be based upon this traditional distrust of the midwife. Let us try to understand this distrust because it licenses an opinion of Socrates that is widespread — that his questioning is a shirking, an avoidance of work.

Why would questions be easier to ask than to answer?

Perhaps the asking of a question makes reference to its invention or creation: that it is easier to *invent* a question than to provide an answer because answers are not freely created, they are induced. It is easier to invent because invention is free from any limitation or restriction, whereas answering is to respond-to or to comply-with some external demand or limitation. Whereas answers must be responsible to the question that rules them and which organizes their coming-to-be, questions are preceded by nothing other than the capricious desire to be inventive. What conception of ease do we have here such that questions are easy because they are not constrained and are unlimited, whereas answers are difficult because they are 'responses'?

It might be said though that questions are constrained in so far as they are 'quests after' and in this sense they are limited by that after which they quest. The question is constrained by *what* it questions and Thrasymachus' opinion might reside in this recognition. That is, the question is easier to ask because that which it questions has already been laid before it as the complete work about which it asks. Asking as querying denies or dissents, it seeks to annul that which is complete. The difference between questions and answers, between asking and answering, reduces to the difference between denying and assenting. Questions are easier to ask than to answer means: it is easier to dissent than to complete (it is easier to destroy than to construct?), it is easier to take away than to give. This is the sense in which questioning is not productive because it makes no difference, whereas the 'answer' supplies a standard which — in terminating the quest — produces the 'solution' *as* the termination. The termination in its very act of terminating differentiates it-self from the interminable (no-thing) which precedes it.

Dissenting presupposes that from which it dissents whereas assent (positing) has to create or build from nothing. Dissent depends upon something before it as its ground whereas positing creates its own ground in its very work. Because positing undertakes its work in and by itself, it creates that from which questioning will dissent: questioning depends upon the courage of positing — of that form which it dissents — to live.

Answering or positing seeks to create in the face of the inexorable question which it will elicit because of the essential defeasibility of speech. Answering or positing is difficult because it works under the auspices of the risk of ridicule which its very work invites. In contrast, questioning shows no courage and takes no risk because it only seeks to demonstrate the incompleteness which the work of positing invites and makes possible. Questioning repeats and conserves whereas answering advances by making a difference.

Thus, Thrasymachus could understand Socrates much as Plotinus later understood the Gnostics: by treating rejection — dissent — as an end, as itself the Good, he achieves the identification of theory with scepticism. It is easy to dissent — it does not require the labour of committing one's self to possible dissent — because dissent only uses what has been done.

The theorist as the questioner is then contrasted to the man of action, the man who acts; the theorist is only a technician who shows his technical mastery of the various methods for dissenting from work which has been accomplished. The theorist as the 'critic' is best personified by the figure of Carneades who lectured in Rome for two consecutive days on the same subject, alternately demonstrating the validity of opposite arguments.

Questioning is easier than answering because of the essential incompleteness of speech. Because speech must always posit in the face of possible dissent (dissent which the very character of speech invites), to accept dissent as the Good is to be intimidated by the fear of scepticism. Questions are then easier to ask than to answer because asking is not limited by a communal impulse, the impulse to see 'making a difference' as making a change, as progressive. In an important sense, the 'what' after which the question quests can never be attained (complete satisfaction cannot be achieved) and so, the object of the quest is never actualized for review. Giving answers realizes objects for assessment whereas asking delays the creation of works. Answering which is responsible to a constructive interest in the face of the question is essentially a social action (an action that is responsible to the collective commitment to move, to change) whereas asking is responsible to nothing Other than itself. Answering as an icon of courage, commitment and creativity succeeds in bringing about something new — it punctuates silence — whereas asking introduces nothing into the world since its questing is only a denial (actually, a re-collecting) of something already here. The destructiveness of questioning resides in its impulse to take away, to impoverish, to annul what is prosperous and plentiful.

Peculiarly, Thrasymachus and Socrates both comprehend the danger of cynicism, but Thrasymachus identifies Socratic questioning with cynicism itself. Thrasymachus fails to see Socratic re-collecting as a positing — as a labouring — for he only sees it as parasitic and destructive. Thrasymachus' conception of questioning as parasitic dissent then fails to comprehend the spirit of Socratic questioning as a building and constructing, as a teaching. Thrasymachus and Socrates have radically different conceptions of critical speaking, for whereas Thrasymachus views it as denial and dissent, Socrates sees it as *sophrosyné*.

Furthermore, Thrasymachus understands maieutic irony as a celebration of dissent itself as the Good. The Socratic review of the possessions of men only teaches *that* they are possessive, leaving them with no-thing or with no-thing good to strive for. The greater ease of questioning in contrast to answering is a feature of the nihilistic character of Socratic irony.

The condemnation of Socrates is then intelligible: the 'critique' which questioning releases in the form of its withholding of assent — its denial and reserve — shows the aloofness of the alien, a refusal to join the city (which assent as assertion, as a joining, shows). The crucial issue then concerns the way in which Thrasymachus formulates questioning as anti-social (as alien to the city) rather than as an instance of the city itself. This understanding in turn depends upon his decisive conception of criticalness and of the a-social character of critical speech.

IV

If Thrasymachus views questioning — asking — as destroying the tranquillity of possession, we could also understand a view of the answer as that which terminates the quest. For Socrates it is the answer which is destructive because its realization as a possession that is achieved (as a definition, a solution) kills the desire released by the *aporia*. The maieutic conception of an answer does not formulate it as an action that completes wonderment but as a speech that co-responds to an order which licenses its quest to make the question that initiated it transparent. Answers then answer by answering-to the demand of the question and thus, are only further embodiments of the quest into the question. Maieutics answers to the demand to reveal the quest of which the question is an icon; maieutic answers are intended to re-present progressive stages in the revelation of that after which the question quests. The answer answers-to the demand to re-collect the difference which the question necessarily suppresses in its quest. The answer re-creates the resistance which is Other to the speech — as that which needs be consulted for the re-achievement of the rationality of the question. The answer answers-to the demand to re-introduce this resistance between the question and that after which it quests.

Maieutic answers exemplify disciplined speech because they are intended to answer to a standard of control which lays down and provides for their very possibility. Such answers are measured in that they co-respond to a measure, a conception of measured speech by which they are ruled. Whereas Thrasymachus' answers are meant to break the tie of (in) questing to language by seeking to complete an action that would terminate the quest, maieutic answers mock this restlessness by holding-back through the measured exercise of reserve and restraint. Maieutic answers answer-to the demand to measure the question — to take its measure — within language itself. The maieutic answer answers-to the demand to situate the (in) quest in a measured way, to measure the place of the (in) quest within language itself: the maieutic answer makes transparent the place of the inquest within language by resisting the impulse to break the tie to language. In this, the maieutic answer shows its reserve, its restraint, its criticalness.

The famous 'what is X?' questions of Socrates are not transient expressions of pain designed to elicit the completion of an answer. 'What is X?' 'What is the end of X?' 'What is the place of X?' all initiate the conversation into the place of X. The conversation quests after the difference which X makes. X makes a difference, it is different from the whole, and the task of the quest is to re-centre this difference. The task of the quest is to progressively re-centre the inarticulateness of appropriation as a reminder of the difference between speech and Other as that resistance which occurs as a moment of speech. The opinions with which the conversation begins all express an interest in re-discovering what belongs *with* X or what has a place *with* X as if X was the whole. This interest assumes the security of the place of X by thinking of X as the whole. This interest is expressed in the impulse to discover what X *is* as if X describes some determinant 'thing' in a way that is final and possessible. Maieutics does not dissent from the opinion that X has a place, but it wants to make that place transparent: maieutics desires to convert the conventional protection of X — articulated in the concern to discover what has a place *with* X — into a quest that seeks to place X, to discover that in terms of which X has a place.

What the midwife knows is that the placement of X is work which never eventuates in a product but which needs to be re-achieved in every instance. The discovery of X is then not a settling of what the essent is, but rather, is a continuous exercise in resurrecting the limitation upon X by what is unlike it and thus, only intends to achieve discursively the Real difference, that between X and what is Other to it, rather than the differences among the re-presentations taken to exemplify X. To find the end or place of X *as* the work of discoursing relates to the continuous need to re-create conversation concerning the limitation of X by what is unlike it. The idea that success in the placement of X is shown in one definitive action which realizes the work as a product does not grasp the midwife's understanding that the placement is a questing and conversing — a working — which is independent of its particular realization in a product. The midwife knows that the very idea of work given as it is by the difference between man and Other as a Desire for the positive re-assertion of this difference, means that theorizing never appropriates.

'What?' essences as a feature of man, for neither gods nor brutes question: 'What?' expresses the intermediate place of man and if it is because we are men that we quest, it is because we are not-Other than man that we quest. 'What?' essences because of 'What-Is-Not' and so, the quest presences through the Otherness which itself resists all attempts of the quest to appropriate it. The question presences only because of the requirements which it leaves behind and yet which shelter its words as that which cannot be appropriated.

Socrates will not appear as positive because his speech conforms to the status of man as intermediate between God and beast. Socratic speech will claim no authority for itself and will seek only to expose its authorization as that for which it speaks. Yet Socrates will only appear as 'negative' to one who ascribes primordial authority to man, for he *will* speak positively as a man — his speech will exemplify the end of man as the intermediate, as the questioner.

We might consider what it is to know the difference between God, man and brute in terms of the question of friendliness and enmity to Socrates. How is the necessity of questioning, of discourse, linked to man's intermediacy? Obviously, to know this difference is to know the intermediacy or centrality of man. This difference itself is a difference man makes; man makes the distinction between himself and what is above and below him. Or — the distinction between man and what is beyond him is made by man. We can say that this difference is necessary or essential for man; it is a difference alongside of which other differences are inessential. It is essential to know the difference *between* such differences.

If the difference between man and what is beyond him is absolute and necessary, this difference which man makes himself nevertheless *gives* to man the capacity to recollect or forget it. The necessity of this difference means that its omnipresence provides for its re-collectability in discourse. The centrality of man refers to his being subject to the Desire to re-achieve this difference (between man and God) in speech, where the re-achievement occurs as a violent re-formulation of how other differences are limited and grounded by that which is beyond their usage. That man questions because of what is Other than man means that this sense of necessity, of life, requires by its very nature the work of re-collecting it. Man questions — discourses — because his vision of Other is a vision of the Desire — the need — to discourse. Other *is* the Desire to provide for the co-existence of life and theory through discourse.

It is then the care of man for language (rather than his possessiveness towards speech) that signals his acknowledgment of his intermediacy. This intermediacy is not suffered as a privation (as an imperfection needing to be corrected), but as an icon of the perfect self-understanding and self-realization of the theorist — of the one who knows that his fate (his *moira*, place, end) is to work (to labour) under the auspices of the Desire to continuously re-achieve the question 'What is first?' or 'What is the end?' What such work means is that it needs continual and eternal re-achievement and not that it realizes itself in a thing or product. This care can only be shown in the practice of re-formulating *multis*.

The answer to 'What is X?' *explains* by re-situating its place within the whole, where such a placement takes the form of a continuous explication of the requirements of rationality to which it is forced to conform as a condition of its excellence. The 'requirements of rationality' to which the X is 'forced to conform as a condition of its excellence' are these: that if the X is Good (if it has an end or limit) it has a place *within* the whole, and so the X is not self-sufficient and complete, for it is essentially open to that which envelops and pervades it (to that which gives it life). To say that an X is Good is to show how it meets its requirements, how it satisfies its own conception of conditions of life that are themselves only formulated because of the requirements of the theoretical life. This placement occurs as a continuous explication of the X where that very explication is organized to display *its place* within the whole. Both the explication and the X which it explicates are the same in that they are placed within the whole, and yet they differ in the way in which the end or Good of the explication differs from the very X which the explication seeks to make explicit. It is through its formulation that the explication affirms its loyalty to the requirements of the theoretic life, requirements symbolized in the difference between that after which the original question quests and the theoretic version of the life and requirements of questing.

Sophrosyné points to the organization of this placement as a continuous explication: Socrates informs us that such continuous explication, such *sophrosyné*, is good (that *it* has a reason). Yet, when Socrates is invited to give an account or logos of this explication, he invents myths, tells likely stories, or merely says that he is enjoined (by the Gods) to proceed in such a way. If such 'continuous explication' cannot defend itself (if it cannot give its reason) it is perhaps no different from that which it questions.

Yet recall the maieutic conception of reason. The explication does not *give* a reason, but it proceeds in such a way as to display its comprehension of its status as a part within the whole. In this display, the explication defends reason. The rationality of the explication is seen in its speech which shows that it knows its place. The difficulty of distinguishing the philosopher from the sophist is only raised as a problem for one who wants a rule which the explication does not provide (because somewhere 'reasons must come to an end') and the one who demands such a policy is seeking to avoid doing the work — the analysis — which would constitute that reason as a conversational moment.

This is to say that the Reason of speech does not reside in the speech — in the words— nor is it a conventional result of Socratic usage (for then it would reside in *his* words). Reason is shown in the mix (see the *Philebus*) which is the conversation (the explication). If it is true that Socrates can transform any speech into conversation (if it is true in principle that there is nothing in the words of speeches that resists such a Desire) it is also true that many speakers refuse to converse. Socrates does not seek to *describe* rationality as a predicate of persons or of speeches because rationality resides in the 'mix' which is conversation (and even here it does not 'reside' in the way in which predicates reside). Those with whom Socrates cannot speak resist the demand to transform their speeches into conversation, and thus they could be said to be irrational because they show no interest in the place of speech within the whole; they show no interest in placing speech or in Reason. Does the absence of a rule mean that we are having trouble identifying such people? That we do not want to do the work of analysis? Is there some decision which we have to make for which we lack a criterion? The problem of policy only emerges when we *want* a policy, when we feel the *absence* of a rule, itself presupposing an ideal of complete explication. To feel weak in this way (deprived of or lacking a policy) is to refuse the challenge of acting (of analysing).

To understand Socrates we must place him: that is, we must come to terms with the reason why the good or end of speech resides in its interest to place speech itself. The heritage which Socrates has bequeathed to us is this: that man's attempt to re-collect the relationship between the 'X' and the whole (his placement of the X, his theorizing) is itself done from *his* place within the whole. In other words, man is originally *social* in the best sense. This is why maieutics remembers the social by remembering the intermediate status of man (of speech). Because of this, he is vulnerable to pressures to forget *his* place by thinking of himself as homeless, or as altogether free from the whole within which *he* seeks to place the X. That is, he is vulnerable to pressures to conceive of himself as a-social. Even the best exegesis does not show in its speech that it re-members its sociality. Because man's placement of the X must show his re-membrance of his place, it must be prudent: man's placement of the X must be organized in such a way as to keep alive and to invite attention to, the question of *his* place within the whole as the very topic of the conversation. Such organizing capacity is prudent; it is *sophrosyné*. This is why we can say that *sophrosyné* makes reference to the restraint which allows man to make sociality a conversational topic in such a way as to confirm this very speech as an instance of sociality.

V

In a sense, Socrates is seen as unproductive because he never leaves the essent. He stays with the idea by rejecting the impulse to fix it and to move on to 'new business'. Yet this kind of lingering over the essent is not scholastic (as we understand it) for it does not seek to circumscribe and characterize the multiple possibilities for speaking about the essent (it does not seek to arrest and tranquillize the many uses of the word in a harmony), but shows instead, the constant impulse to re-view (to bring to view, to re-centre) the foundation upon which the essent rises to light. This 'foundation' is not an other word or essent but a continuous and resonant conversation; and what the essent calls to mind is the need for conversation. Socrates has the patience to resist the impulse towards exegetical simplification. This patience is what Socrates understood as *sophrosyné* and is what moderns see as unproductive.

Sophrosyné as prudence is the topic of the *Charmides*. *Sophrosyné* is a difficult notion to grasp — probably the greatest exemplification of Greekness — and it lies at the centre of the Socratic world. *Sophrosyné* organizes the most crucial Socratic idea — the management of soul and conversation itself — of critical speaking, or speaking in a way that is critical. *Sophrosyné* locates the *public* character of the management of soul, thus evoking a sense of the Greek notion of reserve. It is only because we have come to understand prudence or reserve in altogether different ways that we fail to grasp the essentiality of *sophrosyné* as criticalness. This means that we are within the grip of an uncritical (un-Socratic) notion of critical speaking (a notion much like that of Thrasymachus which sees criticalness as denying and which would see *sophrosyné* as withdrawal). In the *Charmides* the conventional conception of *sophrosyné* as temperance is addressed by Socrates. *Sophrosyné* is interpreted as 'keeping to one's own' or 'minding one's business' and Socrates points out that this conception equates *sophrosyné* with the limitation of speech to what is safe. In this formulation the prudence of *sophrosyné* actually resides in its cynicism, i.e., it is a detachment of self from anything external to it as an attempt to safeguard its speech through a decisive limitation. Yet, *sophrosyné* is more than knowing one's speech is a part, for it is a way of showing this knowledge as a mode of mastering the relationship between the part and the whole. Although *sophrosyné* evokes a sense of limitation for Socrates, how it limits is altogether different.

Socratic speech is prudent not because it stays with itself or with what is safe and secure (for that is possessive), but because it seeks to take the measure of things. Whereas the conventional version understands prudence as the kind of management which enforces the self-sufficiency of speech by ensuring that speech does not seek to overstep itself by speaking about that 'to which it is not adequate', the Socratic limitation is prudent towards this very injunction. Socratic prudence seeks to take the measure of this relationship itself — between speech and that which 'is not adequate to it' — by reformulating 'that which is not adequate to speech' as alterity. It is prudent not to disregard alterity, but to take its measure. To take the measure of alterity requires discipline and restraint for its measure is not 'taken' through characterization and predication (in fact, it is not even an 'it' whose measure can be so taken). Since what is Other to Socrates is the whole in which *he* has a place, to take the measure of alterity is to acknowledge his speech as a measure of his place within the whole (which is 'to take the measure' of alterity).

The 'whole' is knowing the inseparability of life and speech, the indivisibility of life. The 'whole' is knowing the requirements of life as the need to continuously re-achieve the limit of life as the difference between these requirements (continuous re-achievement) and silence. To 'take the measure of Otherness' is to speak under the auspices of this need; and so *sophrosyné* pertains to the passionate affirmation of this need, the passionate protection of this difference as the limit. The whole *as* such a knowing is shown through the work of questioning, through the action of re-centring the limitation upon multitudinousness in so far as the practice of that re-centring shows it-self as knowledge of the difference between what is necessary and what is inessential.

To take the measure of alterity is to realize that one's very speech about anything *is* a measure of alterity. That is, one's speech does not measure alterity, but it is a measure of alterity. The prudent speaker is one who comprehends his speech as a measure of alterity, and so there are two forms in which *sophrosyné* is repudiated: either through the decisive disregard of alterity and the limitation of speech to what is secure (as Critias proposes in the *Charmides*), or through the attempt to predicate of, and to characterize alterity directly (as Aristotle, Plotinus and others later attempt). Both of these attempts are extreme for they do not seek to limit and moderate their speech in such a way as to show *its* place within the whole. In the first case, the whole is disregarded through a radical simplification which limits it to the speaker, and in the second case, the whole is seen as an other place, an other part. If in the first case the whole is simplified as a product, in the second case it is abstracted from the practice of formulating it. In neither case does the speaker acknowledge his place within the whole, for he forgets his sociality and thinks that he is first, that he is complete or is the whole.

The maieutic explication is intended to exemplify its involvement with *its* place (the place of speech). In so far as it exemplifies this involvement it displays its reason. This exemplification requires *sophrosyné* because its intention to re-create a concerted concern with the place of speech requires disregarding pressures to give a reason since *a* reason cannot be given but reasoning can be shown; and reasoning is shown in sustaining the conversation, whereas *a* reason merely terminates the quest. The maieutic conception of 'defending reason' means: to re-create the conversation into reason through the restraint of continuous explication, where this explication has to resist its own inexorable impulse to liquidate itself, i.e. it must renounce the goals of either simple speech, or of complete explication as possessions to be appropriated. The explication has to be an invitation because its rationality resides not in its reason (in its giving a reason) nor in its words, but in its evocation of the Good (or reason) of continuous explication as the highest (most desirable) form of concert and conversation. This is to say that maieutic explication after transcending the pressures toward simplicity, must resist the demand of exegesis for total explication; this is the irony of maieutic explication, for unlike vulgar description and sophisticated exegesis it uses its very explicative activity as a way of re-centring attention upon the place of speech within the whole by drawing it away from the words of speeches (even while it listens ever so carefully to those words).

Why does maieutics think that what is best is exemplified in the concerted continuous explication of the dialectical conversation? Socrates asks — do you want an other reason? That very question can only be a topic for the conversation from within the conversation itself as an instance of the conversation. That very quest(ion) is what the conversation is about: reason is defended not by giving an *answer* to that question but by submitting to the demands of the conversation itself. Thus, those who resist maieutics by desiring a policy for beginning will either be assimilated by maieutics as a moment of the conversation or will be urged to withdraw to 'other teachers' because maieutics will restrain itself in order to formulate their resistance rather than to solve it by supplying an answer.

Because maieutics identifies theorizing and life, it will make no 'space' for theorizing as 'non-life' — as an 'other' perspective for viewing life from within life it-self. Maieutics resists the demand of death for a policy or rule for assessing life as if such demands can escape from the requirements of life to which they essentially conform. Because maieutics will restrain it-self from 'taking the perspective' of such resistance — from dividing it-self from it-self as if it was two — it will never give satisfaction to resistance choosing instead to formulate and thus, to disregard what resistance *wants*. Unfulfilled resistance will linger on in enmity — either sputtering at the unresponsiveness and incompleteness of maieutics, or will move to 'other teachers'. *Maieutics will then teach resistance to make a move* for it will not allow it to protect it-self by living off life in the shelter of its illusions; maieutics will provoke resistance to reflect upon what it is.

Why does the maieutic conversation exemplify the Good society (the end or aim of the 'social')? What is the good of maieutic conversation? Socrates says — it is only through a commitment to maieutics that that question could be asked. That is, to ask this question seriously of maieutics — why is it good? — is to accept the invitation of maieutics to participate in the quest. The question does not then require an 'answer' to terminate the quest, and perhaps now should only conceive of it-self as needing to work for that after which it quests. Maieutics does not punish or accuse, for it does not seek to liquidate the 'X': its continuous explication is an invitation to re-collect the place of the X where the re-collecting displays *its* place in the whole to which it belongs with the X. The realization that speech is a measure of alterity means that every reason (answer) invites a question and the conversation is essentially eternal. The usual responses to this recognition are either cynicism (scepticism) which denies the authoritative claim of any speech just because it is a part, or hedonism which radically simplifies speech in order to ensure safety by enforcing a concrete standard of completion.

Socrates says that the fact that every reason (answer) invites a question does not mean that all answers are bad, only that all answers (reasons) are moments in the eternal conversation, each answer invigorates and sustains the conversation. The fact that all answers are incomplete means that they all invite questions. This does not mean that all answers are equal because they are certainly different in how they expose themselves to further questions (they differ in how *they* question). A good answer is that which exposes itself as a question: in this invitational character of good answers resides their 'reflexivity' because good answers put themselves into question. The good answer places itself within the quest; it enters and inserts itself into the place where the quest proceeds. A good answer re-organizes the quest through its formulative work. The incomplete character of the answer is not a problem to be corrected because it is the very resource which sustains the quest.

Any reason which Socrates can give to formulate the good of maieutics, just as any reason which Thrasymachus can give to formulate the good of justice, or Gorgias the good of rhetoric, is incomplete. The difference between these men does not reside in the formal features of their reasons as answers, but in this: that Socrates is the only one among the three whose answering is a questioning and who knows this. Socrates does not fault rhetoric for failing to have *a* reason, but for not showing concern in its speech with Reason. Thrasymachus and Gorgias believe their answers to be complete and so, they stand as men who attempt to extinguish the quest. Socrates' answers might be more intelligent or sophisticated 'reasons' but the rationality of his speech resides in this only in so far as the reason shows his concern with the place of speech. Socrates' obsession with Reason is not shown in his possession of *a* reason, but in his desire to sustain the quest into Reason (into the grounds or foundation of speech) while fully aware that his speech issues from his place within the whole (that his speech is an icon of these very grounds).

Sophrosyné is speech that takes the measure of alterity by comprehending it-self (speech) as an instance of the very alterity the measure of which it wants to take. The prudence of speech which so understands it-self is shown in its speaking in a way that is true to (this understanding) it-self. Such a display resides in its capacity to organize its answering as an asking. Such an organizing manifests itself in the desire to continuously explicate the place of the speeches which it organizes within the whole where the organizing itself has a place. It is in placing speeches that maieutics shows its reason; and it is in answer to the request to show its reason that maieutics places speeches. Whereas moderns understand *sophrosyné* (prudence) as withdrawal from conversation (from the risk of sociability) on the grounds that only the self is sufficiently safe and secure to justify one against the movement of fortuitous nature, maieutics sustains and creates conversation wherever it goes. The weight of *sophrosyné* is that it exemplifies rest-within-motion, that its conversing is itself tranquil, is a resting, that it exhibits patience and reserve within the motion of speech in its very attitude towards the words (in its very listening).

If maieutics explicated the reason of speeches without respect to the reason of *its* explication, it would degenerate into mere exegesis. Maieutics must keep alive the idea that its explication of speeches (its analysis) is its way of making reference to its place and so, maieutics must organize its speech about the place of other speeches as an invitation to put its own speech into question. If maieutics loses its head to exegesis it closes conversation. Similarly, if maieutics merely explicated the reason for *its* speech it would only be doing exegesis on it-self (which is still exegesis). Maieutics must keep alive the idea that it cannot explicate it-self because regardless of the totality of the explication, the whole cannot be appropriated without becoming an other place within the whole that licenses the appropriation and which resists its attempt to possess it.

Maieutics tries to get itself questioned: which is to say that it attempts to elicit work — it trys to revive the Desire to work, to labour (to converse), it seeks to invite analysis. In so far as maieutics seeks total explication (description, exegesis) it terminates the conversation by seeing itself as having to complete the work. The reserve of maieutics is shown in its strength in resisting the demands of exegesis because it knows that such a totalization would extinguish the conversation which it desires to sustain by concealing the work which enters into its speech. The speech of maieutics invites work by bringing to unconcealment *its own work* because it is only such unconcealment that invites analysis. Because maieutics must resist the desire to terminate work in silence, it requires the prudence of *sophrosyné* to withhold assent to this demand by speaking in an inviting way. Yet, what maieutics invites is not a mechanical question in return, but work, formulation and analysis: maieutics invites the reformulation of it-self, and is therefore ruled by a standard of discipline. The knowledge which maieutics has of its place is not its end because that is only to know difference (between the part and the whole); maieutics is ruled by a standard of the *relationship* between part and whole as a positive mode of reconciliation.

The relationship between speech and the whole is often seen as 'incomplete' because of the essential impossibility of a rule for overcoming partiality. That rule is envisaged as a complete speech, as a speech that transcends speech itself. In this move, the complete speech is comprehended as a speech that transcends conditions of speaking such that its attainment is impossible. Yet if such an attainment is impossible, we would always be 'lacking' a policy for reconciling differences. This empirical conception of speech and of wisdom concretizes our need by taking the absence of a standard (of a 'norm') as our limit. Maieutics says that what we need is that for which we cannot imagine Other: since *that* for which we cannot imagine Other is life (that which cannot be divided), the whole is reconciled by speaking under the auspices of such a need. What we need is not something that we lack, but that which we have: our need is to sustain and re-achieve what we have.

Yet, if we have what we need, why do we continue speaking? Maieutics says that our 'having' what we need is not a (empirical) possessing, for it is a 'having' that is a continuous re-achieving. That is, that the idea of our having what we need includes as the feature of having that it is not possessible and appropriatable at any one moment. The complete speech then includes as its feature its being *ours* — that we have it but not possessively. What is first as our need is then not our privation but what we have — our requirements, and so our having complete speech *is* our speaking.

From the standpoint of maieutics, the idea of wisdom as a goal or possession necessarily concretizes desire because 'complete' is formulated as the tranquillity of perfection in the form of a speech arrested from life. Speech must then be a method or medium for the acquisition of what is lacked, as the home of imperfection and 'incompleteness'. In contrast, maieutics begins with our continuous speech as our effort to re-assert and re-achieve our requirements, as our *having* complete speech. The 'incompleteness' of our speech only means: from the perspective of non-life (of death) speech *looks* imperfect. Maieutics says: our requirements completely say that there is nothing Other than these requirements, that living speech seeks to re-collect these requirements by continuously re-achieving the sense of opposition to life as a mode of meeting such requirements. Speech is 'incomplete' only from the standpoint of resistance to life since speech is (completely) sheltered by life in a way which makes its attempt to appropriate its origin (its indivisibility) *look* incomplete to one who does not accept this indivisibility.

Maieutics says that the requirements of life mean that it cannot be transgressed; that life cannot be transgressed is complete for this requirement means that the limit of life continuously re-asserts it-self *as life itself* (as the complete life), as what we have. Our speech revives this limitation of life upon itself as the opposition of speech. Speech then re-creates this opposition as its method of sustaining the heightened sense of life.

VI

The question 'What is the good of maieutics?' really asks: what is the good of the conversational ideal that rules maieutic speech? No answer can be given: nor can men be coerced to see the good of this image of sociality. Maieutics does not seek to answer this question with a reason: rather, it tries to induce men to participate in that about which they ask. Not all men will participate, but those who do will become friends. This friendship will be shown by their ceasing to expect an answer to the question, 'What is the good of maieutics?' because they will instead put their question into work; by sharing the maieutic moment they will begin to formulate.

The friends put maieutics into practice, they practise maieutics. We might ask: why are they practising maieutics? It is important to them, it is critical or central to them; without maieutics these men who practise it would not be men. But surely those who practise maieutics are already men. If they are already men and not desirous of becoming gods or beasts, they must want to become better men. These men practise maieutics to become better men. Beasts do not want to become better (they have no desire), and gods are already good (they are complete) and so, man is unique in his wanting to become better. Men practise maieutics for a reason that is Good — indeed there is no better reason (unless you ask: why become better? in which case you are a beast or a sophist who is practising the art of dissent as an end-in-itself).

Socrates can only speak to those who agree that they want to become better. Socrates cannot speak to everyone who looks like a man because many of these do not want to become better. Socrates will test in his talk with interlocutors whether they truly want to become better, to become friendly. The practice of maieutics will itself be such a test and maieutic conversation itself will be a covert topic of this practice because the conversation will ask of maieutics itself why it thinks that it will make men better? Yet the conversation will not seek a 'proof', for many men who want to be better still cannot *become* better. Maieutics will seek to show that whether or not men become better it is maieutics that is the only rational art for such a practice. Maieutics will teach men that it is *only through its practice* that the requirements of life will be respected and that any thing else is a simplification. Maieutics intends to teach that in their speech men estrange themselves from life, that they evade the requirements of life by simplification.

Maieutics will attempt to teach men respect for the whole by collaborating in the creation of an ironic attitude towards their possessions. Maieutics will try to teach men to exist ironically towards their possessions and the way in which maieutics will proceed is to refuse to allow the conversation itself to be possessed. Maieutic irony towards maieutics itself is enshrined in the Socratic critique of writing: it says that maieutics (and man) are, after all, parts of the whole and not the whole itself. The extension of maieutic irony to itself shows no self-hatred; rather, it shows that maieutics knows *its* place.

Maieutics is good because the conversational ideal which governs its speech — the ideal of the dialectical conversation — is respected as the art whose practice ought to make man better. That conversation idealizes an image of the social — of social discourse, of the convening (the convention) that is dialectic. Maieutics says that when it assimilates other speeches to its conversation in order to retrieve their place(s) within the whole, it finds without fail that such speech shows its requirements in such a way as to suppress or simplify the governance of these requirements by life itself. Maieutics conceives of its practice as an effort to teach these speeches to re-collect the sense of their limitation so as to re-centre the question of limitation itself as the topic of the conversation. Maieutics believes that such a re-centring will in its very accomplishment contrast these commitments to its own (which organizes the re-centring itself) as reminders of the requirements of life. In the showing of such implications, maieutics claims to 'teach' — to make men better — for it is assumed that men become better by learning to address the Reason (and place of) for their speech. If men treat such exposure as extraneous or tangential to their work, maieutics only assumes that they are not interested in reviving the sense of life in their works, that in subjecting life to the requirements of simplification, they choose to divest their works of life. Maieutics says that men teach and learn by understanding what stands under their speeches, that in the comprehension of the place of their speeches they prepare themselves to place or measure their speech. Maieutics believes that practice in measuring speeches is practice in measuring one-self — in placing one-self — because this is what education or becoming better means: it means learning to govern one-self.

The man who knows his place within the whole is the man who can govern the relationships between the elements of his soul. The relationship of speech to the whole is recapitulated in the relations between the words that comprise the speech. Analytically, justice makes reference to the ideal of proportion or order that governs these relations: to speak justly is to guard such relationships from the competing extremisms of sophistry, hedonism and exegesis. To guard these relationships is to keep the conversation alive and to protect it from extinction by the simple and the cynical. Maieutics defends reason by protecting conversation from terrorism.

These relations among the words are governed by a conception of justice — of order and proportion — which is unlike the mathematics of a calculus or of a concrete standard of exactitude. Because each word is impregnated with the resonances of a history (of alterity) of which it is a mere trace, the mathematization of such relationships would only integrate remains and traces. Irony makes reference to the speaker's comprehension of the essential historicity of the word — a historicity which does not make the word arbitrary, but which shows in its accomplishment the traces (the foundation) to which its resonances invite attention. Justice refers to the management of such resonances. Thus, while explication avoids exegesis (as if the history of the word is only named through other words), it is linked essentially and inseparably to the word as the occasion which invites the quest. Explication then, must show its responsibility to the word *by* addressing its historicity, and so the irony of explication is neither cynical nor surrealistic. Explication then knows the difference between beauty (exegesis as itself the good) and *its* Good (the Desire to place speech within the whole).

VII

The continuity between self and other — between the same and the different — which lies at the heart of maieutics is expressed in various ways in the stages in the ascent of the soul, in the continuities between teacher and student, in the relationships between the parts of the society, and in the organization of the arts. This continuity concedes both the togetherness and the difference of the same and the different as co-existences; the same and the different are parts of the whole. Men who think they are the whole (hedonists, men who think they are Gods) forget difference, they ignore their original and essential sociality. Men who think they are only different (cynics, men who think they are geniuses) forget unity, they ignore their original and essential sociality.

The maieutic conception of difference is grounded in the repudiation of empire — the desire to conquer the species, to institute a policy or rule — under the auspices of its understanding of *its* place as a part of the whole. What is unusual is that historically this recognition has either eventuated in the desire for empire, or in the withdrawal and resignation of pluralisitc tolerance. In contrast, maieutics makes a distinction between the city and the barbarians, and within the city, between those who are friendly to the conversation and those who are not; yet, maieutics does not seek empire. Every man in the city has a duty to be tested in the conversation: every man can come to the conversation but few will join. And while those who are not enjoined to join are not 'equal', they must still be cultivated since they represent a constant reminder of the trace of possessiveness which those within the conversation need to surpass.

The natural stages in the history of the soul reflected in the transition from possessiveness to poverty are exemplars of the maieutic paradigm of inquiry as conversation; these stages reflect the member's progressively articulated understanding of the analytic status of 'conversation' and of him-self as a 'conversationalist'.

Because maieutics demands of the interlocutor that he orient to the requirement(s) of life as the shelter of conversation, maieutics re-collects the interlocutor as one who exercises authority. The conversationalist is the author — the one who comes to his place, one who seeks to re-achieve the authority which he exercises in his speeches in the re-cognition of his limit as an icon of limitation itself. Maieutics constructs the different — whether interlocutor or text (materials) — *as if* it oriented to maieutics' conversational requirement of seeking to re-achieve the authority which it exercises; maieutics construes — constructs, constitutes, collects, creates — the different only and exclusively to meet its formulative demands, to orient to its formulative requirements.

The activity of such a construal is the maieutic method of displaying *its* re-achievement of *its* authority, for it is only through the maieutic violence (method) that maieutics invites its own re-formulation. The maieutic conception of conversation means: in showing its work (in doing analysis, in formulating) in the way it does (by re-creating usage to meet its own terms) maieutics invites these very 'terms' to be re-created as occasions which revive the question of the Otherness of life.

The theorist is one who formulates any collection of practices (any speech) as a conversation by asking for the possibility of the practice. This asking is a forceful violating or intervening which constructs the practice *as if* it orients to its possibility (to its status as conversation). In formulating the speech *as if* it was a conversation the formulative work puts its own possibility into question: in resisting the impulse to describe the practice the formulative work makes its own practice of formulating the 'answer' which invites questioning.

The relationship between theorist and practice whether exemplified in the co-existence of inquirer and materials or in the co-presence of two interlocutors is an expression of the dialectic between repetition and desire that characterizes the 'soul' of the theoretic actor. The theorist formulates the practice as a practice, as a method for displaying the source of his work as itself a conversational topic.

The theorist forces the practice to confront the formulative requirements which his practice demands and through such violence prepares his practice as that which revives the quest into the relationship between life and practice. The violence of the theorist is a method for inviting violence for it is only through the formulative work involved in the transformation of speeches that conversation is created.

The *aporia* symbolizes the theorist's recognition that that which he repeats must be grounded, that that which he practises must have an aim. The *elenchus* symbolizes the practice of retrieving that aim through the *anamnesis* (re-collection) which requires of other practices that they orient to the demand of re-collectability so as to invite attention to the (maieutic) aim of which this demand is a trace.

Maieutics seeks to remind men of their strength (*eudaemonia*), that to speak with authority — to find their place — they need to free themselves from what is external to them. Maieutics reminds men of their weakness — their passivity, their reluctance to do the work of analysing — on those occasions when speech construes what is Other to it in such ways as to guarantee its continuing passivity (its continuing subordination to convention and usage). Men estrange their speech from life and create their own source of intimidation, when they externalize life as that alien and oppressive 'Other' which exists outside their speech as an incorrigible obstacle.

VIII

We emphasize again, that the work of Socrates is directed towards preserving the co-existence of life and theory and we acknowledge that our claim intends to do such work itself by combining prudence and violence. This is to say that if the work of Socrates combines both prudence and violence, any work on the life of Socrates — any writing such as this — should do the same.

Socratic work exercises violence in restraining itself from accepting the democratic problem of interactional justice as primary. Socrates' prudence is shown in his re-cognition that man — the intermediate one — is required because of this very intermediacy to address truth through the conversation of opinions. Man must moderate his impulse to disregard opinions because he is the being for whom truth is only and essentially approachable through the conversation of opinions. We have entered our examination of the life of Socrates by re-creating a conversation of opinions about that life.

Yet, because the conversation of opinions is entered under the auspices of the theorist's dedication to the question 'What is first?' the work released by the Desire for justice must violate these opinions as a feature of its (ironic) use of them. We attempt to manage our relation to this conversation ironically by eschewing exegesis, by promoting re-formulative violence.

If the essence of man makes reference to his intermediacy, manliness requires the work which is the ironic re-formulation of opinions. Enmity to Socrates (to the work of ironic re-formulation) emerges as a possessive attachment to particular opinions and always in conjunction with a conception of the ironist as a thief or robber of opinions (of speech). Because Socrates needs to say that the identity of man reposes in his work (in his showing through his work his commitment to something Other) and not in particular opinions, enmity to Socrates is embodied in the idea of possessiveness and in the proprietary conception of speech as property rather than in particular opinions *per se*. While Socrates' tendency to take an extreme position on particular opinions is always moderated and thus, always *appears* moderate, it is always moderated by the violent single-mindedness of his commitment to what is absolute and essential.

This re-construction of the figure of Socrates has intended to provide for the conception of Socratic questioning as malingering and of Socratic work as anti-social. Socrates could be seen as anti-social because he proposed violence rather than accommodation.

Socratic talk as violence acquires its character to those who so formulate it on the grounds that it is not responsive to what the interlocutor wants (that it does violence to alter's wants). However, what the interlocutor as the enemy wants, is death. The fact that Socrates does violence on the wants of the multitude instead of taking his bearings from those wants — by serving or gratifying them — leads to his being formulated as violent. Socratic violence consists in its re-orienting to a version of what the interlocutor needs (instead of 'wants') which it itself re-achieves by re-collecting such requirements from his speech.

Inasmuch as maieutic violence consists in its refusal to come to terms with difference by preserving its wants (weakness, usage), it refuses to accept a member's problem as *its* problem; it refuses to accept his weakness and to be productive about it (it refuses to provide a 'solution' that re-produces his weakness or his reluctance to work). What maieutic violence violates then, is the conventional member's version of this sort of accommodation and preservation as quintessentially social.

Maieutic sociality consists in the resolve to speak from a conception of strength — of what is required and needed — rather than of weakness. Such resolve consists in the concentrated formulative work — the analysis — which in providing for the speech, orients the member to requirements (strength, essentials, the Good) and away from wants (weakness, the inessentials, the useful). The depiction of Socrates as a-social and as unresponsive to difference is only possible through a conception of sociality as accommodating and adjusting rather than as prescribing: sociality is formulated as the exemplification of membership (the typification of weakness) which maieutic questioning is seen to violate.

CHAPTER VI

Philosophy

I

If Socrates taught Theaetetus the difference between barrenness and fertility, he must still show him that fertility is not sufficient. Unregulated fertility or eros is destructive — is monstrous — unless it is tempered by a proper respect for paternity. At several points in *The Republic*, Socrates tells his interlocutor that it is precisely those who understand the difference between barrenness and fertility — those who take the risk of fertility — who are most susceptible to 'corruption'.

> Evil is a worse enemy to the good than to the indifferent: so it is natural that bad conditions of nurture should be particularly uncongenial to the finest nature and that it should come off worse under them than natures of an insignificant order.
>
> Qualities like ready understanding, a good memory, sagacity, quickness, together with a high-spirited generous temper, are seldom combined with willingness to live a quiet life of sober constancy. Keen wits are apt to lose all steadiness and veer about in every direction. On the other hand, the steady reliable characters whose impassivity is proof against the perils of war, are equally proof against instruction. Confronted with intellectual work they become comatose and do nothing but yawn.

What is the danger faced by the good, by the keen spirits? They can become unsteady and 'veer about in every direction'. It is the very keen-wittedness and strength of such natures that both frees them from barrenness and makes them vulnerable to unsteadiness. It is because of this risk that the keen-witted are most in danger from the multitude.

The multitude does not refer to 'people' but to *multis*, to manyness. These strong natures are most vulnerable to diversity, difference and variety. They are quick, sagacious, high spirited, intelligent and generous: such qualities propel them into motion, compel them to discourse. While discoursing must not be unregulated it is difficult for those in motion to recollect the centre of their movement. The keen-witted are in danger from *multis* in the way: they can alternate from one occasion to the next; like things, their possibilities for variation appear unlimited. It is the strength of the keen-witted which makes them most likely to treat themselves as things because whatever they are seems to be unlimited by its opposite. The keen-witted are in most danger because they feel free (they feel unlimited), they feel indefinitely changeable.

The fertility of the keen-witted manifests itself in the making of differences. This is the relationship between the strong nature and the multitude: that the strong nature is productive in its making of differences means that the strong nature can make it-self different; having the power of mobility and of being able to change they feel that they have the strength to overcome any limitation. Having risked fertility, the strong nature treats fertility as unlimited.

When the fertility of the strong nature is understood as an interest in making self variable, it is ultimately seen as the making of differences between self and others. The corruption to which the strong nature is most vulnerable — the corruption by the multitude — is reflected in his concern to make differences between him-self and others. It is his very erotic appropriation of honour, property and power (perhaps reflected in the metaphors of timocracy, oligarchy and tyranny) that differentiates the strong nature from the multitude in a way prescribed by the multitude itself. It is the strongest natures — the most fertile ones — who are most vulnerable: after the rejection of barrenness their propensity to treat fertility as an end leads them to celebrate inessential differences as essential. The keen-witted are most corruptible because they are most likely to forget what is necessary and essential.

The corruptibility of the strongest natures means that their acceptance of the multitudinous maxim of freedom — of fertility and the making of differences — guarantees their difference from the multitude. This is only to say that what is Other to the strong nature *is* the multitude. Because such a nature treats him-self as a thing which could be unlike it-self, whatever it is is only limited by what it coincidentally happens not to be. Other is always merely the empirically attainable alternative possibilities which one is presently excluded from (such possibilities — differences — are *multis*). There is then no sense of an absolute Other, of a limitation that is essential. There is no sense of anything different from these differences, for even unity is only the ordering of these differences. There is no conception of something Other in which the idea of these differences and their unification originates. It is the strongest natures who feel most diminished by the notion of something stronger, of an absolute Other.

The strong nature, like Theaetetus — who chooses fertility — runs the risk of accepting a multitudinous version of limitation and alterity. Socrates must save Theaetetus now from philosophy, from the multitudinous version of the necessary and the absolute which philosophy formulates as the common. This appears ironic because philosophy it-self arises to save Theaetetus from *multis* and so Socrates must identify philosophy with *multis*, and he must see philosophy's attempt to save Theaetetus from *multis* as a failure.

II

Anaxagoras' promise of showing mind to be the cause of all things was not fulfilled by his books according to Socrates because the book assigned causes to 'air, and ether, and water, and many other strange things'. These 'strange things' are called 'causes' by Anaxagoras but according to Socrates this is a 'strange' way of speaking, for air and water, or muscles and bones, are not things that are selected because *they* are worthy or esteemed: they are conditions which make possible the selection of the worthy things and as such conditions they only come to life given some idea of their relevance for the worthy things; they are not the worthy things themselves. While no one can deny the value of air or water, or of muscles and joints, such 'things' acquire value for the species as a whole. Their value is to be indiscriminant with respect to persons. They are not the worthy things but the things that are indifferent to worth. In this sense, they are the common things and the common things are different from the things of value. In fact the most valuable thing is to know the difference between the common things and the things of value. That is, the common things have 'functions' and serve 'purposes' but only in relation to the things of value. They are themselves estranged from value, they are the strange things. A man may have firmer or weaker muscles, or more or less water — he may use these things differently — but it is that for which such use is intended that is valuable or not, and it is that aim which shapes and controls such usage.

These 'strange things' only have value in relation to the worthy things and thus, it is a concern for the 'things of value' in which the use of these 'strange things' is grounded. When the theorist speaks of these 'strange things' as causes, he speaks like 'the multitude, groping about in the dark . . . giving it [cause] a name which does not belong to it.' It is 'not to distinguish the real cause from that without which the cause cannot be the cause'.

Socrates ironically claims difficulty in understanding the philosopher. The valuable or worthy thing is that which is necessary, that with which we cannot do without. Strictly speaking it is not a thing at all. Socrates says that what is valuable and worthy is different from these 'things' of Anaxagoras. What is valuable and worthy acquires its value (its Good) because it is needed for life. In contrast, these things of Anaxagoras seem alien to life: while they are conditions or requisites of physical survival, their essentiality is corporeal. The 'things' of Anaxagoras are concrete exigencies, and not essentials. Anaxagoras does not know the difference between survival and life, between life as a thing (e.g., survival, mere existence) which can be this or that, which can become and perish, and the idea of life for which opposition is unthinkable. It is monstrous to say that these things of Anaxagoras are valuable for life, for they are estranged from a proper and weighty sense of life. They belong to conception of life as mere existence or survival.

What is valuable is the 'absolute' or cause, that Otherness which resists our appropriation in the sense that it is not limited by any thing external to it, for its limiting of it-self (its indivisibility) *is* Otherness. The multitude does not think about this cause because the multitude can only think about difference; as far as the multitude is concerned what is necessary (natural and self-evident) is difference, manyness and motion. Because the multitude does not think of difference(s) as icons of the same, it treats every thing it sees as making a difference (as a difference that is made). When the multitude then reflects upon 'cause' — as Anaxagoras does — it can only think of the causes of motion — of making — as moving causes, as differences that are themselves divided through making from Other motions indefinitely. Because the multitude cannot think of that which is absolutely necessary and unchanging, any such conception will always appear to the multitude as an Other moving cause (a 'perspective' or 'opinion'); this is because the only necessity recognized by the multitude is motion as the perpetual making of differences.

The multitude does not itself call air, water and such strange things causes, for this is Anaxagoras' way of speaking. Anaxagoras seeks to impose upon or correct the multitude's way of speaking and yet Socrates says that Anaxagoras is not different from the multitude. Whereas Anaxagoras thinks he makes a difference, Socrates says that there is really no difference. Anaxagoras is different from the multitude in his ability to estrange the many things, to see them as a common thing. Yet, these 'things' are strange for Socrates, they are 'strange' ways of speaking about cause. What is the connection between these strange things — these common things — and their estrangement from value?

Telling us that the causes of Socrates being in prison is the composition and motion of his muscles and joints is 'too absurd' for if it was up to *their* opinions (the opinions of these muscles and joints) he would 'have long ago been in Megara or Boeotia'. The 'absurdity' is that the 'cause' assigns no value to Socrates' action because such causes fail to formulate his action as human conduct in a way that would distinguish a man as a man (unlike what is Other).

Anaxagoras does not know the difference between what is common and what is essential — he is indifferent to that difference — because what is common must be necessary, given his vision of *multis* (of difference) as Other (as limitation). In terms of this multitudinous conception, what is essential must be some concrete common policy, rule, or method which co-ordinates *multis*. Anaxagoras is indifferent to the difference between the common and the essential because he treats *multis* as the limit: such a treatment is itself grounded in his decision not to differentiate life from physical existence. In order to begin to grasp the idea of what is needed, a strong notion of life is itself required. In contrast, if cause refers to the ground or foundation, those things which are necessary for survival could never be causes because they are estranged from the idea of what is essential since they are merely concrete things.

Socrates' critique of the philosopher is organized around the idea that Anaxagoras' failure to distinguish between life and survival accounts for his indifference to the difference between the essential and the common. The philosophical conception of unity makes of oneness what is common to *multis* rather than what is absolute. Where unity makes reference to commonness it acquires its weight by collecting the differences against which it contrasts itself. The neglect of the absolute then establishes these differences as the limits of alterity which their unification collects; there is no thing Other than this relationship between *multis* and its unification. Such a notion of unity makes of it nothing other than the differences which it collects and so, the differences against which such a version of unity contrasts is more apparent than real.

Calling the common thing cause is then like calling *multis* (differences) cause. Man is formulated as acting under the influence of the different things in his environment. Such an environment of 'causes' is an environment of things and things only become causes when man himself is formulated as a thing and his behaviour as an effect or result. Man is treated as a thing when it is said that he can vary, that what he appears as is not limited by its opposite. The formulation of this free man who is essentially in motion personifies the conception of man as a thing, instead of serving as an occasion for formulating and addressing the essent 'man'. Certainly, the thing that is man is influenced by many other things, which is only to say that there are many sources of the thing's motion.

Socrates finds such a conception of man and his environment 'strange'. Socrates means that such a conception is itself estranged from any notion of the thoughtful relationship of man to language. The idea of common causes is grounded in the notion of differences and usage (*multis*) as the original limitation. There is no thing Other than the differences among these differences: *multis* is the limit. Socrates finds strange this indifference to the real and essential difference between *multis* and what is Other. This conception which treats *multis* ultimately as first is strange because the idea of these inessential (*multis*) differences must itself be different from that which authorizes it. There must be some thing ultimately from which these differences (*multis*) differ, some thing that differs from nothing. The idea that *multis* is first is estranged from what must be accepted as necessary, it is estranged from life.

It is then the failure to distinguish between the *idea* of life and its treatment as a thing — Zeno's inability to distinguish between limit and multitudinousness — which leads to the unhappy equation of life with existence or survival. Finally, it is this equation which leads Anaxagoras to identify unity with commonness and alterity with the differences that unity consolidates.

Anaxagoras' things — air, fire, etc. — are then metaphors for the philosopher's common terms, each of them re-presenting a rule or policy for moderating *multis*. Based on the image of exegetical neutrality the philosopher's common things moderate *multis* because they are grounded in an official indifference to anything other than *multis*. They are metaphors for the exigencies.

Socrates finds Anaxagoras' causes strange because they are alien to the idea of life and apply instead to the notion of life as a thing, to the notion of life as survival. When life is treated as survival, it is a contingency whether one survives or perishes and living is formulated as effects, results, products and successes. The notion of cause — like life — is not formulated as an essent, but as a concrete source of what is produced, as a source of effects and of results. The notion of life as survival then generates a version of causation as the concrete interaction between things.

Socrates knows that the good or end of man issues from his very intermediacy and that this intermediacy enunciates man's primary relationship to what is Other than things. The idea of man's fate (*moira*, place) or end as his particular and distinctive value of excellence says that it is his capacity to choose, to value and to work that *is* man's value and that this value is given by the difference between man and what is Other (it is given in man's centrality or intermediacy). If man's end is to formulate his end it is only because man is not first, i.e., that man is the being for whom this work is essential where this essentiality is given by man's need to question and to work (it is given by man's place of intermediacy, by his being central and not first).

In contrast, Anaxagoras' deterministic version of cause treats man as first or as a result and thus, omits what is necessary for its very own formulation. What is so necessary is the requirement for man to work (to value) in order for him even to *be* affected or determined or caused and it is this requirement which is omitted from the formulation. Anaxagoras' causes are then estranged from the very idea of cause because they do not provide for the notion of work which is essential even to his own formulation of man, and by so simplifying man this version of cause tends to treat man as an other thing in motion rather than as one who is different from such things by virtue of his need to work and to value.

Socrates knows that if man's end or place—his intermediacy—is to work, this end is grounded in that which is Other than man, in the vision of life as the requirement to work. It is in this sense that man's work reflects his groundedness and it is in this sense that his work is caused. In contrast Anaxagoras says that common things cause man and yet, if such causes are things they are not part of man's thoughtful relationship to what is Other (to need, value, necessity) but are only external precedents and influences. Such a formulation turns value into a concrete interaction rather than into conversation. These things of Anaxagoras are not proper causes because his man does not value them: or though they might make differences in movement *vis-à-vis* a notion of survival and existence they are indifferent to the difference between survival and life and so, they are indifferent to the place of man. If man's essence is to relate to no-thing, cause must express itself as an instance of this relationship. That which is said to cause man must be seen to be received or welcomed by him if cause is to point to a thoughtful relationship.

Because of the connection of maieutics to value it is essentially linked to difference: the value of speech points to the difference it makes. Socrates raised the demand that speech make reference to the difference *it* makes not in the discrimination of its words, but in its reason for speaking. Speech which is Rational (which makes a difference, which has 'value') is speech which cannot conceive of itself as caused by the common things (the things that are strange to men) but rather, as grounded in the desire for the worthy or valuable thing (for the Good). Rational speech must value the difference *it* makes as a display of the conception of value which differentiates it from the common things. What the theorist and multitude share is the requirement to make a difference; where they differ is in the understanding of how difference is made.

Socrates demands of speech that it orient to the difference it makes — its value — *as* its value. He requires reformulating speech as so orienting and, in this sense, he makes of 'cause' a thing of value. Anaxagoras estranges the idea of 'cause' from value by treating it as any common circumstance which creates a result. Valuable speech does not accept as the limit of its responsibility that it passively typify the fate of any thing, for such speech only thinks of itself as determined, as being grounded in nothing other than the concrete conventional circumstances which precede and condition it. The value of speech is its sense of its own value, its strength and respect for its source as something other than such circumstances. Valuable speech sees its value to lie in its making a difference between the commonplace and the valuable.

III

> I . . . no longer recognize nor can I understand these other wise causes: if I am told that anything is beautiful because it has a rich colour, or a goodly form, or the like I pay no attention, for such language only confuses me: and in a simple and plain, and perhaps foolish way, I hold to the doctrine that the thing is only made beautiful by the presence or communication, or whatever you please to call it, of absolute beauty — I do not wish to insist on the nature of the communication, but what I am sure of is, that it is absolute beauty which makes all beautiful things beautiful.

'It is absolute beauty which makes all beautiful things beautiful' — it may be that one can recognize a friend or enemy of Socrates in terms of how he understands this. The cause of a thing is not to be found in the features common to the thing as a thing (such as form or colour or the like), but reposes instead in the conception of value that enables and brings to life such common things as themselves 'signs' of beauty.

There is a connection between the multitude's capacity to see *multis* and the multitude itself as a personification of *multis*: the multitude sees only division and difference and not unity because the multitude is the many. The multitude is the way they see; it is the look that comprehends only division and difference. The multitude personifies division and difference and sees unity only as the summation of these differences.

The multitude does not see 'absolute beauty' because it sees only *multis* and not unity. The multitude does not appreciate the weight of words, the place of speech within the whole. The multitude does not comprehend the organization of the whole, for the use of the word suggests its limitation by what is opposite to it (beauty would have no weight in a world without ugliness) and the multitude is so obsessed with the difference between beauty and ugliness (with their separation) that it cannot see their necessary relatedness. The multitude cannot see how this difference enunciates the unity of a standard (absolute beauty) upon which its speech draws as it makes its distinctions.

Anaxagoras might see 'absolute beauty' where the multitudes sees only *multis* but his seeing of absolute beauty would only recapitulate the multitude's look. Anaxagoras would see absolute beauty as a common thing (perhaps as a composite of properties or as a collection of predicates) and thus, he would differ from the multitude by seeing what is common to the differences which they conceive. But this common thing that he sees would be an other difference. He would not really understand what seeing absolute beauty means. He would see it as a *concept* and therefore as one of the many things.

Seeing absolute beauty does not mean seeing a common thing — an other object — for seeing absolute beauty means that the multitude's speech about beauty — its practices — requires some decisive conception of beauty. To see absolute beauty is to recognize the essentiality of this: this is the essent, that some conception is essential, is needed; that there is no difference or opposite to this need (that it is essential). On the other hand, Anaxagoras thinks that to see absolute beauty is to see *an* essent and so the absolute beauty he sees as a common thing is not essential because he can always imagine differences or other formulations. He does not see that 'seeing absolute beauty' *is* the necessity rather than the absolute beauty *that is seen*. Differences to the absolute beauty that is seen can always be imagined, but something different from the need to see absolute beauty cannot be imagined. The way in which Socrates understands seeing absolute beauty licenses him to address the roots of this need in life (in language, in that which is not an other thing). In contrast, Anaxagoras' formulation of absolute beauty as a common thing creates his indifference to the difference between common things and anything else. Anaxagoras can be concerned only with the difference (the relationship) between the common thing he formulates as absolute beauty and other common things which it excludes. Anaxagoras must then formulate a notion of absolute beauty sufficiently common to assimilate all differences to it (he must try to complete his speech) and in this sense, he must treat his conception of 'absolute beauty' as one of the many things.

Anaxagoras seems superior to the multitude because he tries to radically assimilate all difference, to reach the point where he cannot imagine difference, and he can only accomplish this through a complete estrangement of his speech from value. Whereas the multitude sees only difference (but not 'seeing difference as difference'), Anaxagoras seeks to correct their perspective by seeing unity in *these* differences. However he does not treat his 'seeing unity' as a Real difference — as a need which because of its essentiality points to what is truly different (what is Other) — for he accepts this possibility as secure and instead treats the difference between the unity that he sees and what it excludes as the real difference (even as he seeks to obliterate *that* difference by radically estranging his common thing from value). That is, Anaxagoras transforms the notion of unity as necessary, as essential, into an idea of unity as common and this is only because — like the multitude — the only necessity he recognizes is the essentiality of difference (of motion).

The multitude treats it-self as the most common thing. The multitude sees it-self as difference and division and when the multitude grasps its unity it can only comprehend this as a reconciliation of these differences. The multitude understands its oneness as what is common to its differences. This is to say that the unity which the multitude comprehends it-self as exemplifying in the organization of a 'society' or 'culture' is a 'thing' much like air or water or ether. When the multitude does look at it-self it can only see an other common thing. This is how Anaxagoras really personifies the reflectiveness of the multitude, i.e., the multitude's looking at it-self.

As an idea, *multis* refers to the point of view of unregulated eros, fertility, and the desire to differentiate through the achievements of honour, property and power. *Multis* refers to the drive for originality, possessiveness, success and production, and to the temporal rather than to the eternal. *Multis* is grounded in indifference to anything Other than these differences and these differences constitute the limit in contrast to which success is achieved. Success as the highest realization of *multis* means the production of an order which collects such differences, a product the realization of which is only possible given the disregard of Other.

That the multitude sees only difference means that it sees what it is (*multis*) as a collection of differences. While it thus appears that the multitude can at least see it-self as the unity which is such a collection, what the multitude here sees is an other difference (it only sees it-self as unified through contrast to what is different, i.e., other societies or cultures). Because it has no sense of alterity that grounds and provides for itself, what is Other for *multis* can only be that which it (empirically) is not, as other empirical differences. In this sense the multitude cannot conceive of its value in any sense other than its being different. In contrast, what is really valuable and good is not a result of difference but is that which makes a difference. That which makes a (Real) difference is that for which no difference can be imagined. That the multitude cannot see that for which there is no opposite means that it cannot see what is essential: since what is essential is what has value (is what grounds the difference) and the multitude can only see that from which it happens to vary, the highest understanding which the multitude can have of it-self is that it is a thing that is different (whether good or bad). Therefore as the philosopher, Anaxagoras typifies the highest understanding which the multitude can have of it-self.

Because the multitude thinks of itself as essentially different — as a thing which could be otherwise — its value for itself consists only in its difference. If the multitude would see its value or good it would comprehend it-self as that which has no opposite (no difference) because what contrasts to it is what is Other (and not different). The multitude's conception of itself as the good society would then not mean that goodness is attached to it as a predicate which differentiates it from other societies better or worse, but that it conceives of itself as drawing its strength (its value) from the idea of Other which it aspires to exemplify.

When Socrates says that the multitude is essentially unphilosophical he means that the multitude sees only difference and consequently, that it can only comprehend unity as the reconciliation of such differences which is itself an other difference.

This is how the multitude can see beauty and ugliness but not absolute beauty itself: the multitude could only see absolute beauty as a 'matter of opinion', as an other difference; they could not comprehend absolute beauty because they cannot understand value — that which has no opposite (as the Good or whole) — as that which grounds and prefigures absolute beauty itself.

Because the multitude sees only difference, when it does approach 'absolute beauty' it can only treat it as an other thing — a common term — as a collection of properties (whether form or colour or the like) that collects beauty as a thing estranged from value. By treating beauty as something that a thing has, it makes the difference between beauty and its opposite (or between having and not having beauty) essential, instead of re-centring attention on the difference between these opposites and that in which they originate. Anaxagoras sees absolute beauty where the multitude does not — where the multitude sees only beautiful things — but he sees absolute beauty as an other thing. Anaxagoras then thinks like the multitude even though he uses different words. Anaxagoras' (the philosopher's) use of the common term seeks to assimilate all difference to the term in order to make the term complete unto it-self. Anaxagoras employs the common term to terminate manyness where such a termination is attempted by radically estranging the term from value so as to allow it to subsume the greatest variety of possibilities. The common thing is a thing of value *because* its segregation from value (from the point of view of what the multitude values) makes possible its radical assimilation of what is different. Yet the common term for Anaxagoras is not that for which no opposite can be imagined (though its very achievement is the attempt to anticipate and assimilate all difference) because the philosopher can still imagine difference. Rather, he is indifferent to the difference which he can imagine: the inclusiveness of the common term permits him to say of the differences which he can imagine that they make no difference. This indifference to difference prevents the philosopher from understanding how the limits of the common term are threatened by 'that which approaches it and forces it to retire' and thus, he does not see the value of the common term to reside in the uncommon which gives it strength to resist extinction. Anaxagoras seeks to protect the common term not by guaranteeing its strength but by weakening (ignoring, obliterating) all difference.

Thus, where the multitude sees only difference and the philosopher sees only unity, he sees the unity as a difference. The multitude and the philosopher are united in their disregard of Otherness. Where the multitude sees only difference, they do not see their 'seeing only difference' *as a* difference (as a requirement produced and grounded by what is truly necessary). Anaxagoras comprehends that the multitude's look is authorized, but not by their desire to see only difference (he does not see *that* as their authorization); rather, he understands their seeing only difference not as a commitment to *multis* but as their failure to grasp what is common to the differences that they see. The difference between Anaxagoras and the multitude is then a matter of degree, that they do not go as 'deeply' as he into the unity underlying the differences which they see and so, while they are united in their commitment to see only difference, the unity which he sees as the reconciliation of their differences is only a difference deeper than theirs.

The difference between the philosopher and the multitude is that his estrangement from value — his neutrality — permits him to see what is presupposed by *multis*. In this sense, he is still limited by *multis* because his horizons end at (and consequently, originate in nothing Other than) *multis* it-self. Anaxagoras' common things are only icons of the 'context' which exegesis always turns up as its version of a 'ground' wherein differences are presumed to originate. Whether the common things are social structure, culture, metaphysics, or world view, the exegetical interest of philosophy always retrieves them as symbols of a unity different in kind from the differences which they presumed to inspire and causally originate.

In contrast, Socrates understands such a difference as inessential since any common thing necessarily shares with the *multis* that it consolidates its character of being a thing. The fact that the common thing is always a thing recommends to Socrates its required alienation from the necessary and the essential and thus, that the philosopher's 'cause' or 'ground' must always be a multitudinous version of that which could be otherwise because it is unlimited and indefinitely expandable. This is how Socrates can say that the philosopher — in his exegetical guise — 'gropes about like the multitude' calling by the name of cause what are only conditions (or — what are concrete exigencies rather than necessities).

Anaxagoras as the philosopher thinks that the multitude sees only the many things and *not* what is valuable, and he equates the good and valuable with the unity or commonness of that which the multitude only grasps as many. Anaxagoras thinks that he finds value in commonness: Socrates accuses Anaxagoras of perpetuating the multitude's look because of his identification of unity and commonness in a way which can only identify the valuable with things that are in motion. What things have in common is that they are achievements and so what is valuable for Anaxagoras is to discern the achieved character in everything. Socrates says that the valuable cannot be what things have in common in that sense, because what is valuable has to surpass things. The necessity of the valuable requires the opposition to it to be unthinkable and since things are indefinitely variable, things are coincidental rather than essential. Socrates says that Anaxagoras' very conception of value is estranged from value because it makes the Good into an other thing, into a source of motion.

Just like the multitude, Anaxagoras does not address the source of his conception of the common as the valuable. Because Anaxagoras cannot imagine the valuable as that which is not a thing, what is valuable can only be that which is common to things. The value of the common thing is that by radically assimilating difference to it-self it promises to diminish the possibility of difference. Anaxagoras' conception of value promises to solve the multitude's problem of seeing only difference which the multitude creates for it-self, by assimilating all difference to the most inclusive standard of unity; Anaxagoras' good can only be a rule. Anaxagoras can only accomplish this reconciliation by perpetuating the very difference which it was intended to assimilate — the difference between his conception of value and that from which it differs — because his rule is always a thing. Anaxagoras can only think of being ruled as the external and coercive moving constraints that *cause* motion. Anaxagoras finishes where he begins — with *multis* — and so Socrates accuses him of thinking like the multitude. Socrates can say of Anaxagoras and the multitude that despite their obsession with difference, they really are indifferent to the idea of difference; that whereas the multitude is unmindful, Anaxagoras rests in the security of his understanding that the indifference of his difference from the whole makes of him the whole (it makes his common things the whole).

IV

Whereas Anaxagoras identifies the common things with the Good, with value, with the essentials, Socrates is concerned with the difference that the common or inessential things make between themselves and that which is essential. Speech is a common thing and Socrates is concerned with the difference speech makes between it-self and that which — unlike it — has no opposite because it is absolute. If speech makes no difference, it is just another common thing like the muscles or joints which men practise for no (good) reason. Speech is 'natural' like air or water or muscles or joints and it is caused like all such things by other things. Socrates cannot accept Anaxagoras' solution that the only difference which speech *makes* is its being moved to come to be for this recommends that man — the speaker — cannot make a difference other than motion.

Socrates asks: how does speech as a thing acquire value by virtue of its relationship to the worthy, the excellent and the valuable? How does speech acquire value through its relationship to what is not a thing? Thus, Socrates' quest for the value of speech, for its reason or for the Good which it fulfils asks for the difference speech makes between the valuable and the common. From this day on, Socrates forces speech to defend itself by conceiving of itself as a contribution to value; he demands of speech that it comprehend its requirements to make a Real difference where such a comprehension is shown in speech it-self *as* the difference that is Real.

If *multis* means the concern with difference that Anaxagoras understands to be unified by the common things, Socrates knows that there is something Other in which the idea of unity originates. What is of value for Socrates is to know this difference where the practice of such knowing as discourse it-self issues from this difference and thus, issues from man's intermediacy. It is intermediacy as the essential difference between speech and that which grounds it which gives value to the knowing of this difference through the practice of discourse.

As a philosopher, Anaxagoras thinks he recognizes the difference but he treats the thing of value (the essential) as the most common things. They only have value because the multitude fails to speak of them, they are rarely spoken. The multitude does not speak of air and water and ether as Anaxagoras does, but this does not make air, water and ether valuable things. There is actually some value in the multitude's silence towards air, water and ether because these 'causes' are alien to what the multitude values. The theorist must listen to the multitude in order to unveil what they value even as he discriminates himself from them. It is possible to hear the essential and the worthy in the multitude's speech about the many things, but this requires thinking about the many things uncommonly. Because Anaxagoras does not truly listen to the speech of the multitude he introduces things that are strange or alien: these things are very common things, but their commonness lies in their being abstracted from and alien to every consideration of value; they are the *most* common things only because he (the philosopher) can estrange himself from all value in order to see the multitude as a heap. The philosopher wants to see them as a heap because his idea of cause formulates the idea as the penultimate source of motion which as a source it-self in motion can only be an Other thing and thus, cannot be essential. The philosopher requires of his cause that it be alien from value. The philosopher differs from the multitude because he can more radically alienate his speech from value, i.e., he recognizes the requirement which philosophy imposes on him to estrange his speech from value. The philosopher's failure to listen to the multitude guarantees that he will speak only of the most common things because the things that are most common are the things that are alien to what the multitude in the concrete particularity of its social existence really value. The philosopher differs from the multitude because he can see unity where they do not. Whereas *multis* does not collect itself in its look, its philosophic realization exemplifies such 'reflexivity' as the multitudinous contrast to 'common sense'.

By starting with security of his difference from the multitude, Anaxagoras ignores the question of *how he could begin* because he sees this question as threatening to dissolve the (analytic) independence of the philosopher into multitudinousness. *Given* this difference, he can only formulate what they are as essentially different from him — as contingently ignorant of that which makes him 'reflective'.

Socrates proposes to reconcile the difference between the many things and the things of value, between the multitude and the theorist. Socrates' invention of ethics means that this is his proposal. The theorist stands to the multitude as a thing of value stands to the many things, as an interest in reconciling their difference stands to indifference to this difference (the multitude). The theorist stands to the multitude not as the custodian of the common things nor as the custodian of the many things, but as the caretaker of *the relationship between the many common things and the necessary and valuable*. Because the theorist guards this relationship between difference and unity, he differs in the way that the caretaker of the whole differs from those who only cultivate parts.

The work of Socrates says that speech must be assessed in terms of its contribution to the whole (that one who speaks about beautiful things is employing a notion of 'absolute beauty'). This requires the speaker to re-direct his attention from the *things* to the whole (beauty), or to the 'cause' of which the speeches are parts. What is suggested is: let us bring from concealment the cause (or whole) in order to convene around it, to discuss it; let us begin to speak about the things of value *through* the many common things.

The problem of the relationship between the many things and water or ether is inexplicable itself because if water merely reported upon the many things Anaxagoras' speech would be the same as that of the multitude (his speech would be 'caused' by the speech of the multitude as itself an other common thing) and his identity as a philosopher would be diminished. Yet, the difference between his speech and that of the multitude must be caused by something Other than what is peculiar to either the multitude or to him, it must be caused by something which both collects and differentiates Anaxagoras from the multitude. This 'something other' — this 'cause' — remains inexplicable to Anaxagoras and so the *value* of his speech can only be to acknowledge his concrete difference from the multitude.

What Anaxagoras does not see is of cardinal importance: 'Will there not be those things, Cebes, which force whatever they are in to have always not its own idea only, but the idea of some opposite as well?' He does not see that *his* difference from the multitude is 'caused' by one of those 'things'. Whereas the multitude does not see the difference between themselves and the philosopher and Anaxagoras does, his seeing — by failing to account for how it and its opposite (the multitude) are caused — does not really see difference either (the difference between these opposites and the 'thing' that causes it). This is how Anaxagoras can differ from the multitude *and* preserve its way of seeing.

V

In a world of many common things there is no notion of what is essential or needed because a difference can be imagined for anything that is thought. There is no idea of the essential as the necessary — as that for which a real (rather than concrete) difference is unthinkable. In such a world philosophy treats what is essential as the requiredness of assimilating all difference to itself even while acknowledging the impossibility of such 'perfection'. If this requirement it-self becomes the only thing that is essential, it becomes the ultimate thing of value, a source the essentiality of which requires *its* being disregarded as a topic of questioning. The conception of language as the indefinite expansion and differentiation of the uses of speech — a conception which sustains this requirement — permeates every philosophical formulation of practice including attempts to 'conceptualize' the requirement itself. Making difference as the producing of motion — of things, of 'changes' — then becomes the necessary law of nature — that whose externality and co-erciveness resists our appropriation as that about which we have no choice — and it becomes the standard and resource for formulating our limits. *Given* the necessity of such a conception of original difference (of language as usage), speech which disregards such a 'matter of fact' (such a fact of nature) will be speech that it-self fails to make a difference. If speech is to make a difference in a way which conforms to this requirement for 'seeing difference' it must respect the essentiality of this requirement; any conception of an Other difference as the Real difference must be repudiated. To make a difference would be to provide a rule or standard for (unnaturally) reconciling such competing usage in a way as to produce (to make) that standard itself as a personification of necessity. The standard that is 'made' must have the same essentiality in its capacity to reconcile differences as the idea of original difference itself; that is, the absolute and required character of the standard (the rule of reconciliation) as a standard must draw its strength from the conception of the absolute and necessary fact of differentiation. All of this by way of saying that where *difference* is natural (essential, necessary) as the difference between things, the idea of unity is always conceived as a solution to *that* problem because unity takes its meaning (as its point of departure) from the requirement to collect and/or combine things in the form of an other thing in a way which necessarily must disregard any thing Other than these things as nothing. To see this anything Other as the thing that is no-thing is not to want to make a difference.

Such a world includes as an essential feature the possibility of interminable argumentation. The limitation of speech to *multis* which endows the method of segregating speech from value with itself the highest value is grounded in the re-cognition of interminable argument as a reflection of original and essential *multis*. In such a world, speech seeks to constitute itself as that which *is* (essential, necessary), or as that for which difference is unthinkable. Value is then discovered *within* speech as a feature of its organization or method rather than in the relationship between speech and what is Other to it. A concern with *multis* means that there are only (many common) things and therefore that there is nothing Other than speech because anything Other is not a thing (is no-thing). That the multitude cannot look beyond it-self means that the multitude creates a world in which *multis* (manyness, difference) is first. The attempt of speech to constitute it-self as that which *is* (and consequently, as 'all') is the attempt of *multis* to organize it-self as what is. The multitude's conception of the social is to organize the manyness and difference with which it starts, as a totality (as a harmony) and so, the harmonic conception of sociality presupposes an original and incorrigible *multis*.

Socrates' remark that 'a harmony can only follow its parts' makes reference to this conception of sociality as the attempt to reconcile concrete differences. Since the estrangement of value from speech is the method for achieving such a reconciliation through the radical assimilation of difference, the social is the most inclusive (common) collection of differences. The social is the species because sociality is equated with commonness through the suppression of difference. Because a harmony cannot rule or lead, but can only follow its parts, the social can only follow or 'summarize' the component differences which it collects. The social then *is* these differences, or in so far as it is anything more than these differences, it is only an organization of them. Sociality is manyness seen from the perspective of organization or of method.

The only difference between the philosopher of the multitude and the multitude itself is that he orients to the harmonic ideal of sociality which is a latent presupposition of their practice as a standard to which his speech must comply. He then personifies the self-understanding of the multitude as the political conception of the limits of language. As the man most estranged from value the philosopher as 'stranger' is indifferent to any one of the many things in a way which permits him to appreciate their unity as a common thing. It is this complete estrangement from value that allows the philosopher to supervise the multitude, since such estrangement emancipates him from commitment to any one of the many practices in lieu of his commitment to universalizing each and every practice in the service of the practice which — because it universalizes — conceives of it-self as different from each and every practice. The sociality of the philosopher *vis-à-vis* the multitude resides in the fact that he commands a view of the requirements of the multitude as a common thing while they can only see themselves (their differences) as the common thing.

The responsibility of the philosopher to the social refers to the demand which the need for harmony imposes upon the speaker. Such a demand expresses the obligation which the multitude ascribes to the speaker as philosopher, the obligation to contribute to the re-constitution of *multis* as harmony. To the extent to which the philosopher redefines his obligation — resists the harmonic ideal — by reformulating the social as a relationship between speech and language he renounces the harmonic conception of value. Such a renunciation shows that the common thing (the harmony) is not the thing of value but only one of the many things. In this sense, the resistance of maieutics is always seen as anti-social.

The conception of the social as the harmony which ought to dissolve and diminish difference formulates the end or Good as the cessation of manyness (as a kind of silence). The achievement of harmony is an achievement of tranquillity that extinguishes the motion and labour of manyness. The multitude's conception of work (of conversation) is then of an interlude to be suffered and endured, which is how conversation can be painfully reformulated as argument. The work of conversation is then detached from the end of tranquillity somewhat as means to an end only because speech (as the multiplicity of uses) is equated with *multis*. The Otherness of language is reformulated as the disarticulation and incompleteness of speech and the fact that it cannot completely assimilate difference is treated as that which must be suffered as the interlude of motion and contingency (practice) which resists silencing in the tranquillity of order.

In contrast, the maieutic conception of the social includes as a feature of the end or Good, a positive conception of work and conversation. The very notion of man's end or aim necessarily entails the understanding that his work — his speech — does not simply and mechanically re-produce itself as an end. This conception of the completeness of the social — that its completeness is necessary and essential — includes within it a notion of the indefinite character of speech not as pain to be suffered *en route* to tranquillity, but as a feature of that tranquillity itself.

The maieutic version of the social requires the continual re-achievement of tranquillity within the motion that is speech. This conception of the social does not generate the need for a solution to the 'gap' between motion and rest (between practice and theory, between difference and unity) because such a need only occurs when motion and tranquillity are conceived as the two 'things' which are respectively the a-social and the social (or, nature and society). The maieutic conception of the social (of 'all is one') includes the relationship between motion and rest — the dialectic of re-achieving tranquillity within motion — as what the social *is*. The social is not a solution to the problem of motion (of difference) for it is the continuous re-collection of the strength to rest within motion (of the tranquillity of thoughtfulness and reserve within conversation).

The difference between Socrates and his enemies — between ethics (dialectic) and the multitude — is that Socrates is indifferent to those differences from which the multitude takes its bearings and is responsive to the real difference (Otherness) which the multitude, even in its philosophical form, disregards.

Maieutics is then not concerned with argument (with *multis*, with reconciling differences) but with conversation. Maieutics which wants to converse and not to argue, makes a distinction between conversation and argument. This is not to say that maieutics evades responsibility for its speech but rather, that it resists the multitude's impulse to only assert, exchange, and reconcile differences (opinions). Maieutics has a continuous interest in addressing (in ascending to) that for which no rejoiner is thinkable (the Good) and it always begins with the commitment to that ascent as its presupposition and ground. Maieutics conceives of conversation as talk that is done under the auspices of such a commitment, talk which is committed to the continuous re-achievement of such auspices.

Socrates then uses the manyness of common things (the multitude's conceptions) neither as limitations to which it must acquiesce, nor as problems for which it must provide satisfaction (pleasure, solutions), nor finally as differences which it must domesticate, but as occasions which invite the formulative work (conversation) necessary to show the dependence of speech on what is Other to it. Instead of exchanging and distributing like argument, conversation formulates and analyses; instead of seeking to silence or dissolve like argument, conversation seeks to sustain and revive; instead of seeking to terminate through rhetoric like argument, conversation seeks to re-collect the authority for its speech. Yet, from the point of view of the multitude (from the point of view of *multis*) it is always Socrates that looks rhetorical, argumentative and authoritarian; because the multitude cannot comprehend the idea of conversation it must always see Socrates as anti-social.

Because Socrates requires the renunciation of argument which the multitude creates as a parameter of *multis*, he tries to show in his speech the reserve and restraint of such a renunciation. Maieutics shows such reserve not by 'escaping' but by conversing (working, analysing). It attempts to teach the positive character of such reserve neither as shyness or silence, but as a reformulation of opinions which resist the multitude's demand for argument. Maieutics then, shows its reserve and resistance through its formulative work itself.

To say that the multitude takes its bearings from argument is to say that it takes its bearings from *multis*; because the multitude does not want to converse (it wants to create the tranquillity and silence of harmony as its communal ideal) it is always involved in arguing (i.e., in asserting, exchanging and assessing opinions). It is actually the argumentativeness of the multitude which leads it to seek to silence conversation because it formulates conversation as argument; it is this very argumentativeness which allows it to see the Socratic abstention from argument as it-self argumentative. This is how the multitude sees Socratic teaching as anti-social. The multitude sees Socratic conversation as argumentative (as anti-social) because Socrates questions *multis* itself and thus declines the invitation to conceive of himself as one of the *multis* (as one of the many). This is maieutic reserve and it is from the perspective of this reserve that the multitude itself appears as argumentative, for its refusal to converse about *multis* (about it-self) shows (to maieutics) as an attempt to preserve and increase what it possesses (to argue rather than to converse).

The criticalness of maieutics — that it looks at the common in an uncommon way — means that it shows its appreciation of the difference between the commonplace and the valuable by speaking in such a way as to demonstrate how such a difference becomes accessible only in conversation. It does not show its criticalness by opposing or objecting to the multitude (through 'non-conformity') as an eccentric affirmation of its right to be different. Rather, it formulates that about which the multitude has stopped thinking in order to teach the multitude to address the question of how dialectical reserve is possible. Maieutics does not 'answer' the questions posed by the multitude, but seeks instead to invite the multitude to deepen the question — to re-achieve the authority upon which the question itself depends — as work which re-collects the question as a question with weight.

VI

The real difference between the theorist and the multitude pertains to how the problem of difference (between speech and language, between the common and valuable) is addressed. By disregarding *this* difference, Anaxagoras converts the problem of difference into the problem of reconciling the many common things; he treats the results of such reconciliations as valuable things. The philosopher's difference from the multitude (demonstrated in his ability to achieve such reconciliations) is grounded in his technical capacity to suppress value, to estrange speech from value. In this sense, the philosopher is the true common man: the philosophical perspective intends to exemplify the radical estrangement from value; paradoxically, the philosopher as common man is the paradigmatic stranger (the one who can methodically estrange himself from value). Even when the philosopher seeks to examine and to cultivate the multitude's many things (their 'point of view') directly, his inspections are always controlled by his aspiration to estrange his speech from value as itself an exemplification of the highest value. This estrangement from value is intended to exemplify the exegetical notion of justice.

If speech is a common thing and if the value of common things lies in their sharedness as instances of becoming — as achievements — valuable speech can only be speech which constitutes or organizes itself as sufficiently inclusive to diminish any difference. This authorization provides the opportunity for the development of logic. Logic brings into sharp relief the multitude's philosophical conception of the requirements of life; that the necessity of difference creates the need for a rule which is not it-self a difference because of *how* the speech is made.

Socrates is said to have invented ethics and Aristotle to have invented logic. Logic is the construal of the speech completely estranged from value. Logic formulates the problem of speech in a way which preserves the multitude's look — as the common thing that reconciles the *multis* of terms, categories, subjects and predicates. Logic then personifies the most complete estrangement of speech from value.

Aristotle also spoke about ethics but always from the perspective of one who demanded the estrangement of speech from value. Aristotle also spoke about 'the good' and 'Being' but always from the perspective of one who demanded even of speech about such things that it be estranged from value.

Aristotle treats speech which makes a difference between the common things and the things of value as divisive, because such a difference can only make of the thing of value no-thing and if the valuable thing is not a thing there will be no way to *produce* value. Unless the thing of value *is* the common thing, our speech will be without value because we would not be able to produce value as a thing. Aristotle's conception of the valuable speech as the thing of value requires him to conceive of its value to lie in its estrangement from value, i.e., in the fact that its estrangement from value can be done, that its estrangement (which is its value) can be produced. Aristotle then identifies value with an art.

Only speech estranged from value will it-self be valuable because it is only such speech that can methodically supervise its own organization as a thing. Thus, if speech is estranged from value it is in the service of the value of such methodic supervision. If 'good speech' is a valuable or esteemed thing — is valid — logic formulates the way in which speech will succeed in becoming a valuable or esteemed thing by conforming to some (valuable) conception of constructing a common thing. The source of value lies in the art of producing it for it is the art which imitates creation in speech it self. In producing harmonic speech such an art co-responds to (or imitates) its image of creativity as the reconciliation of *multis* in unity.

A valid speech will be controlled by a conception of how speech as a common thing is created as a reconciliation of its manyness (of its *multis*) and thus, some vision of the relationship between the *multis* and harmony of speech causes or grounds the making of valuable speech. The relationship conceived in this image is valuable because it pictures the perfect reconciliation of *multis* in a harmony for which no difference is thinkable. Logic's valuation of the value of harmony (as a common thing) is shaped by its conception of speech as the *multis* which needs to be reconciled (re-formulated) as the common thing which it is. Because logic shows that the conception of speech as a common thing grounds the making of speeches as common things, its penultimate value lies in using the relationship which it discerns in and reconstructs from its conception of speech as a collection of differences as a method for reconciling these differences in a harmony. The value of logic is that it can imitate creation — it can recreate recreation — in the human way through the perfect reconciliation of *multis* in speeches.

Speech makes a difference by providing a policy for reconciling the usage of *multis*, where the standard that is provided acquires its weight on the basis of its assumption of the necessity of reconciliation. In this case, where injustice is understood as natural or original, the just speech — as the reconciliation of *multis* — must treat the conditions required for such a reconciliation as absolute necessities rather than as conventions. These regularities of interaction become exigencies. Logic then provides a self-correcting and self-formulating limit for speech from within speech itself by disregarding anything Other than speech as inessential because it cannot be ruled by speech (by policy) given its assumption that only what varies (that only things) can be commanded.

Whereas the multitude uses speech, Aristotle — the theorist — re-collects the speech that is used as an organization of *multis*. Aristotle identifies the limits of the multitude's practices in his inventory of the incorrigible parts of speech (terms, categories, subjects, predicates) and he formulates the relations between these differences (judgments, propositions) as rules to be followed in the construction of a valuable common speech (a syllogism). The philosopher formulates the multitude's practices *as if* they were oriented to his conception of the requiredness of achieving a solution to the *multis* of speech through the making of harmonic speech. Although the theorist cannot imagine an alternative to the value of harmonic speech he can contemplate many different possibilities for reconciling differences as a condition for the achievement of such a valuable speech.

Logic equates the things of value with the common things. The most valuable common thing is the speech for which no difference is thinkable; this speech is imagined as the perfect speech (the perfect reconciliation of *multis*). What is perfect about the perfect speech is that at each stage in its occurrence it assimilates all difference to it-self. It is constructed under the auspices of a desire to make difference irrelevant by constituting it-self as essential (as that from which dissent is unthinkable). The perfect speech silences *multis* by making *multis* unthinkable. The perfect speech makes it-self strong (complete) by rendering *multis* weak (silent). The perfect speech is designed to show at each stage in its accomplishment that there is nothing external to it because what is different (*multis*) has no grounds to speak. It is in this sense that the perfect speech takes its bearings from argument rather than from conversation.

Multis refers to the different ways in which men speak and the multitude's speech is essentially variable in that the way in which men speak is not perfect. In contrast, speech of value is discourse estranged from value and so, logic seeks to exemplify speech estranged from value. Difference stands to unity as beginning to end, as 'imperfection' to completion. The perfect speech solves the problem of *multis* by making *multis* weak because the perfect speech constitutes it-self as essential, thus showing it-self as that for which choice and election is irrelevant; it officially deprives *multis* of will. Since the weakening of *multis* is seen as the strength of perfect speech itself, *multis* is invited to restore its strength through its assimilation to the perfect speech. The communality of the perfect speech resides in its promise of tranquillity, that its weakening of *multis* is actually a strengthening, i.e., a tranquillizing. The communality of the perfect speech lies in its promise to extinguish labour and motion in its creation of tranquillity.

Logic divests speech of value. If men show what they value

through speech they show it through selecting and excluding, through emphasis and indifference, through collecting and segregating. Each speech masks and encapsulates its own decisiveness; each word is an achievement. Logic seeks to create the perfect speech as the speech for which the necessity of action is given, the speech which acquires its value only because it makes the question of the value of speech irrelevant. Logic then seeks to arrest motion in perfect tranquillity — the rest of entailment — because motion reflects choosing, will and election, i.e., motion reflects the labour which produces differences. Because logic transforms value from the end or aim of speech into the inexplicable source (cause) of variability between speeches, it conceives of itself as needing to divest speech of value. The 'problem' which logic sets for itself is then occasioned by its particular conception of value as the cause of (concrete) differences. Yet, logic it-self will have value only because it eliminates the problem of value in its work.

The value of logic is then different from the value which sustains differences, for while these latter are like 'preferences', the preference for logic will not be seen as a preference but as an absolute and essential (eternal) requirement of life. As such a necessity, logic has a higher value than the contingent matters of will and preference which it supersedes — a value so high that it is not strictly speaking a value at all. An option to logic is not thinkable, logic has value because *it* cannot be seen as a matter of preference or choice. What vision of life makes logic so imperative? What image of community — of life — does logic express that it is the only thinkable way of meeting these requirements?

The perfect speech is the speech whose conclusions are entailed, are necessary. The requirement of necessity is rooted in the desire to segregate speech from value, and thus, to assimilate value to speech, because necessity permits no option; it guarantees the inexorable and determinant course of action. The speech whose consequences are so seen is a universal speech because its inexorableness is the same for any speaker. The ideal of necessity is estranged from value itself because necessity formulates a feature of speech whose formality resides in its indifference to differences between speakers. 'Formal' means: indifferent to value. The perfect speech is the speech that makes unnecessary attachment to value. Because the perfect speech takes its bearings from an image of *multis* as the species, the perfect speech is the universal speech (as logic is the universal language).

If the perfect speech is detached from value, the ideal of such a speech is the penultimate value. The value of such a speech is grounded in the value of necessity: necessity is good because it imposes an inexorable order upon the speaker from which he cannot dissent. The acceptance of the value of necessity forces everything else to follow and necessity ought to be valued because the highest good is to have everything follow. If everything follows, the speaker only has to follow and so, necessity diminishes surprise, mistake and risk by confronting the speaker with a determinant order which he only has to 'apply' — to practise, to repeat — but not to recollect and revise. By idealizing rest without motion logic converts labour into rule-following (into competence, into *techné*).

The necessity which the perfect speech commands is discernible as a relationship, a mediating between differences. Things that are alien to one another are domesticated through the arbitration of something they share; things which are separated combine through the mediation of an other difference which presences in each of them in such a way as to guarantee their inexorable integration. Aristotle says: 'A syllogism is an argument which certain things being assumed, something other than these follow of necessity by virtue of the things assumed.'

Whereas the syllogism formulates the movement from what is assumed (the premises) to what follows (the conclusion) as if it is a movement from unity to difference (of drawing out the new from the given or the old), the conclusion is actually first, i.e., it leads to the selection of assumptions which will meet the criterion of generating it. What is assumed is selected in terms of how it promises to show the requiredness of the conclusion and so the principle as conclusion anticipates its selection. Understood properly, the syllogism does not *describe* the discovery of new conclusions from given premises, but is a method of authorizing a principle already secured as true by finding 'right' premises. The correctness of these premises refers to their adequacy in showing the requiredness of the conclusion and in such a showing, of demonstrating (grounding), the conclusion as a common thing.

The conclusion as a common thing invites a relaying of its own grounds through the creation of speeches which entail it or make it necessary, i.e., the principle grounds it-self. Such grounds become assented to as 'assumptions' which generate the conclusion only because the conclusion leads by inviting the search for its ground. Since the conclusion rules the search by requiring its estrangement from value, it diminishes opportunity for hearing it-self as impregnated with value. The conclusion requires that it be heard as a 'universal' or common thing — a sentence affirming or denying one thing or another — in order to secure as an other common thing the *multis* which it collects as that from which it follows. The justification of the conclusion consists in this reconciliation of *multis*, in its re-constitution of *multis* as its ground. Whereas maieutics seeks to open up the conclusion in order to make transparent the agreement upon which it rests, logic needs to estrange this principle from value by treating it as a conclusion whose agreement is secure in order to employ it as a resource for discovering its grounds in other speeches.

Whereas maieutics questions the *value* of the conclusion, logic searches for the method by which the conclusion is produced without respect to value (other than the value of relatedness itself). The perfect speech as the principle which can ground it-self (which is independent and self-sufficient) succeeds by re-creating it-self as the reconciliation of the *multis* which it locates as its ground.

Logic then reformulates the dialectical notion of conversation — the conversation into the value of the speech — as a way of discovering a method which would re-produce the speech in hand as a conclusion (a conclusion whose authority consists in its capacity to show it-self as an achievement of method). Logic then personifies the mathematical re-formulation of conversation by looking at speech as a common object (from the perspective of *multis*): because it needs to examine speech from the standpoint of the reconciliation of *multis* and harmony it conceives of speech as a collection of concrete affirmations and/or denials, a collection of parts indifferent to value, because their necessary relatedness (their harmony, their unity) can only be affirmed or denied if they are estranged from value.

If, as Aristotle says, Socrates invented both common terms and inductive conversation, this means that Socrates invented a conception of theorizing as conversation. Such an invention was not responsive to the need to create a speech that would be unequivocally affirmed or denied (a speech that could be conclusively terminated), i.e., a common speech. Aristotle elected to estrange speech from value in order to create such a common speech. Aristotle required the reformulation of conversation so that the methodicity of the reconciliation of *multis* in harmony would be discernible as a matter to which *multis* it-self could assent or deny. The need to elicit the affirmation or denial of *multis* is shaped by the ideal of harmony as that which is enacted in such a decision. Aristotle differs from Socrates in having a method for creating harmony — for showing the reconciliation of *multis* in unity — in a way that diminishes *multis* itself.

Aristotle's method for demonstrating the necessity of relatedness seeks to reconcile extremes (differences) through the idea of a mediator (the middle term). The extremes are alien or strange to each other and yet, they are familiar with the mediator: the mediator mediates contact between the extremes by being known (common) to each of them. The mediator is truly intermediate — between the extremes — for while he is part of the whole of one (a predicate), he is the whole for the other as a part. The mediator is truly political.

The method of relating aliens is accomplished through the mediation of what they have in common. The mortality of Socrates (the coming together of the two extremes) is accomplished through the mediation of the manliness in which they each participate. The anticipation of the collectedness of the extremes rules the search for what is common and the participation of the common in the extremes reproduces the collectedness of the extremes. The community of the extremes is authorized by the method through which what is common to them is re-collected as that which they both require to commune. That which mediates the extremes can only be re-collected if the extremes are radically estranged from value so as to permit their mediation to be discerned. To sustain the value of the extremes would be to accentuate their Otherness to each other, it would diminish the opportunity for mediation. The extremes are differentiated under the auspices of the desire for and anticipation of their mediation (their reconciliation).

The method asks: how must difference be conceived in order to prepare for reconciliation? The anticipation of reconciliation requires the estrangement of speech from value because differences (extremes) always presuppose the mediator as a standard and the mediator acquires authority on the grounds of its being most strange. The strangeness of the mediator depends upon its inclusiveness, its commonness, that it relates things strange to each other only by virtue of its commonness, where this commonness actually makes the mediator the thing most alien.

If the extremes are strange to one another and if the middle term mediates, how can the middle term be the most strange? Though the middle term reconciles the extremes it can only do so because it is alien to every value except the value of mediation itself. The mediator mediates through its 'objectivity', through its capacity to resist being an extreme. The middle term stands to the extremes as the philosopher stands to the multitude.

The middle term adjusts to not-being-an-extreme, i.e., its nature is to be not-different, not-isolated, not-extreme. The middle term is what it is (it acquires its nature) only through what it is not. The middle term as the moderator takes its bearings from what is different rather than Other, and so the nature of the middle as the mediator is to moderate what it is not.

The moderate does not look up to the highest (to real value) but to the different, and it acquires *its* value on the basis of this renunciation. The moderator moderates through its inclusiveness and the commonality and thus affirms as the value (or nature) of middleness the universality which permits it to lie in safety between the things that it is not. The moderator destroys the idea of the middle as the truly intermediate term between Otherness and speech (between language and the void) by re-formulating the middle as the mediator. The capacity of the mediator to moderate depends on the security of its place between the extreme things rather than between such things and that which is not-a-thing. As the middle term, the philosopher differs from the extremes (from the multitude) by understanding that it is his moderation which differentiates him from those he moderates. As the moderator, the philosopher is estranged from all value except the value of moderation itself.

Maieutics as speech infused with value is seen by Aristotle as dividing and limiting, as differentiating and segregating. Because of its intermediate relation to order, it only sustains difference. In contrast, it treats logic's conception of value as another opinion turned up by the multitude. But then maieutics cannot see anything of value except dividing and differentiating; this is all that it appears to see as valuable — creating and sustaining conversation. Logic understands that conversation must come to an end, that men must subject themselves to an order which diminishes the risk of continuous conversation, of differentiation, of the extremes persisting in their extremities.

The middle term of logic personifies the logistic conception of theoreticity as the need to moderate silence. What the future points to and what the past reminds us of is the necessity of transcending the idea that the ceaseless motion and mortality of speech means that our speech will have no value. What is essential to the continuity and survival of the species is its continuous fertility and re-production, that it continuously re-produce What Is in the form of new things (that it continuously re-produce language in the things that are new speeches). Speech which makes a difference is speech that comprehends the requirement of continuous derivation and thus, which understands the need to re-formulate derivation as discovery, change and difference (as making differences) rather than as re-collection or *anamnesis*. The theorist as middle term — as moderate — is one who exemplifies the understanding that our desire to re-collect must be moderated and thus, as one who can collect differences in such a way as to show his indifference to the difference that re-collection makes. The middle term moderates the concern with anything Other than the relatedness of moving parts on the grounds that such a concern will extinguish the species. The middle term means: to be ruled by a notion of concrete difference(s) as the limit and point of departure for (moderating) theorizing. The middle term is moderate only in relation to the things that appear to differ from it, whereas dialectical moderation is indifferent to *these* differences because it conceives of its moderation as issuing from its place intermediate between all such differences and that which grounds them.

Logic says that what is essential or necessary should not be spoken about *because* it is essential, i.e., that its essentiality means that no thing will change it and so talk will not make a difference. Because what is essential — in this sense — must be disregarded, the most productive talk (the talk that makes a difference) will always be inessential. Yet, the very essentiality of what is essential means that we need and we use it and so, the requirement to disregard what we use commands us to use it in a way that will not disturb it. For logic then, what is essential is to disregard what is essential. However, for dialectic this is a misconstrual of the idea of the requirements of life (of what is essential) because *what is necessary is that which is necessary to re-achieve*. Logic thinks that the inessential differences which it makes (and which it can only make through a simplification of the essential which essentially disregards it) serves as grounds for continuous Real differentiation (productive progress) in a way that promises eventually to crystallize in a re-constitution of the essential. In this sense, logic conceives of the essential empirically as the temporal overcoming of perspective and limit, and each speech justifies it-self as an occasion to invite its own being-surpassed.

Dialectic formulates logic as intending to solve the problem of the value of its speech by manufacturing an abstract notion of difference, opposition and continuity that is concrete and temporal rather than dialectic, and that serves to exempt it-self from any examination on the grounds that the postponement of such an interrogation *is* the only justification, i.e., it is the only way in which speech can serve life. Dialectic says that logic justifies its indifference to difference (reflected in its concrete notion of the oppositional character of the future) by claiming indifference to be essential for sustaining the essential (requirements of life). Dialectic says that such a notion only means that logic sustains *it-self* as essential and nothing more because the conception of life which logic invents as its ruler is only an Other icon of a thing external to life.

Logic and dialectic differ in terms of their conception of the subject to which speech ought to be dutiful. In Aristotle, that which is 'laid down' or 'put under' is the *hypokeimenon*, the underlying thing. Underneath all of its distinctions, what logic in its various forms lays down or puts under is not the principle of identity or that of the excluded middle, but the requirement to segregate speech from value under the auspices of its true *hypokeimenon* which stipulates the value of speech that diminishes difference as the exemplification of an image of complete (divine) discourse. This is the rule which logic follows.

Dialectic understands that this *hypokeimenon* was generated from its opposite — division, difference — and thus, it asks for the true *hypokeimenon* from which both the law of logic and its opposite is generated. In making reference to this true *hypokeimenon* (*arché*), dialectic teaches logic that its very origin is infused with just the kind of 'value' it seeks so assiduously to avoid. Because logic understands its *hypokeimenon* as what it subjects, it thinks of its subject as what *it* lays down or puts under. Logic thinks of itself as what it creates by throwing under. The subject which logic lays down is shaped by the desire of logic to create a course of action with inexorable consequences, and so, the subject is created under the auspices of a desire to assimilate predication to it as a determinant and necessary course of action.

Whereas logic might think of what it lays down or throws under as terms or categories or propositions (assumptions), its true subject is that to which such a thought is it-self subject. The subject of logic is that to which it is subject; it is that which permits it to lay down anything. Yet because that to which logic is subject cannot get it-self laid down and subjected (cannot be treated as a sentence affirming or denying one thing or an other) logic has to be indifferent to the question of the value of its estrangement from value.

It is because logic assimilates origin (*arché*) to predication (in an action shaped by the *belief* in the value of such an assimilation) that it reformulates *hypokeimenon* as that which is a possible repository of predicates. Ethics analyses the demand from which logic's *hypokeimenon* emerges — the demand to estrange speech from value — by showing that this demand and the vision which it exemplifies is truly what 'lies under' logic. In such a lesson, ethics shows further that what lies under logic is only a part of the whole because what truly lies under must lie under both logic and its opposite. While logic is twice-removed from what lies truly under, dialectic can teach logic how its estrangement from value only affirms the value of estrangement it-self, a 'value' which is alien to what truly lies under.

Because logic wants to segregate speech from value, the origination of this desire cannot be addressed by logic. Logic chooses not to address its origin in value because this *hypokeimenon* cannot be limited and determined as a subject of predication. Logic looks essentially cynical because its refusal to speak about its place in the whole is a justification for speaking of itself as the whole. Logic which recognizes that it is a part of the whole repudiates any effort to understand its relation to the whole. Logic's reason for doing as it does remains self-evident until ethics analyses the grounds of logic itself in order to make transparent this reason as the *agathon* of logic. Yet logic cannot be responsive to such an encounter because it cannot assimilate the question ethics addresses to predication. Logic ultimately requires silence of whatever it cannot predicate.

VII

The promise of the corruptibility of Theaetetus — of the strong nature — is heightened by the very decision to reject barrenness. The erotic character of unlimited fertility exposes Theaetetus to *multis* — to the danger of unlimited differentiation, to the competition and jealousy of *multis*. Philosophy arises, in part, to save Theaetetus from *multis*, and theorizing, i.e., Socrates, arises, in part, to save Theaetetus from philosophy (from *multis* in the guise of philosophy). Both philosophy and Socrates accept the need to provide Theaetetus with the difference between barrenness and *multis*; in part they differ in their conceptions of barrenness and of *multis*.

Socrates says that the keen-witted, having rejected barrenness, have first to deal with the problem of unregulated fertility or eros. If philosophy in its exegetical and logistic forms arises to cure the young of barrenness (if exegesis and logic are the two philosophical attempts to control *multis*), as solutions they themselves accept the authority of *multis*. This is to say that both exegesis and logic accept the limits of the very *multis* they seek to control. Socrates also wants to save Theaetetus from *multis*, only he recognizes that philosophy is itself an instance of *multis* and he acknowledges further, that man is saved from *multis* neither by flattering it (exegesis) nor annihilating it (logic) but by understanding its place. Theorizing needs to live strongly and ironically with *multis*, while yet rejecting the monsters of tyranny, withdrawal and intimidation.

Where exegesis is indifferent to any difference other than the distinction between its rule or policy (unity) and its violation (*multis*), it has to equate theorizing with statesmanship. In this guise, exegesis seeks to tame *multis* not by teaching it, but by defending it through the re-formulation of its point of view. The aim of exegesis is to formulate the point of view of *multis* through its just retrieval of the common things that cause *multis*.

Logic stands to exegesis as the paternalism of sky relates to the fertility of earth. Like mathematics, logic abstractly assimilates difference to it-self. Logic knows of and is indifferent towards Other on the grounds that it cannot be assimilated, and so logic still accepts the need to reconcile *multis* as *its* multitudinous limit. While exegesis and logic both accept the multitudinous version of unity and difference, logic attempts to achieve its reconciliation without respect to the point of view which exegesis itself intends to preserve; yet this difference is inessential *vis-à-vis* their common disregard of anything Other than *multis*.

Theorizing must teach the spirited a proper sense of moderation. This means that theorizing must moderate both madnesses of tyrannizing *multis* (e.g., logic), and the nurturance and 'study of its moods and desires' (e.g., exegesis). Socrates seeks to offer an option to either the madness which multitudinously abstracts itself from *multis*, or the madness of *multis*, a way of co-existing with *multis* that still makes a difference between it-self and *multis*.

Theorizing then needs the keen-witted and the high-spirited rather than those who are only reliable. Socrates attempts to teach such youth that moderation is not a deprivation (it is not like the barrenness which they left behind), but is a positive limitation that is both constructive and passionate. He will try to teach these spirits the particular madness of theorizing, of the Desire for analytic justice and the irony and intensity of *sophrosyné* that this work requires. Such a teaching is delicate since the reverence for justice can lead to its own obliteration — it can become abstracted from the work needed to sustain it, turning again into the madness of philosophy. What is needed is the recognition of the link between Desire and work — the idea of the passion of moderation — reflected in the notion that the work of ironically re-formulating the opinions which are *multis* is the just way of making a difference between *multis* and the Good.

CHAPTER VII

The Oracle

I

> I do not know what effect my accusers have had upon you, gentlemen, but for my own part I was almost carried away by them — their arguments were so convincing. On the other hand, scarcely a word of what they said was true.

Socrates opens the *Apology* by distinguishing between beauty and the good, between method and truth. His accusers are artful but their words are not true. Even worse, they use this very distinction between *techné* and truth as a way of characterizing (accusing) him.

> They told you that you must be careful not to let me deceive you — the implication being that I am a skilful speaker . . . [but] I have not the slightest skill as a speaker — unless of course by a skilful speaker they mean one who speaks the truth.

Socrates' defence begins with a comment on the relationship between speech and the whole, between method and the Good. His accusers identify artfulness with truth and it is this identification which he has to confront. His accusers say many convincing things of him none of which is true; the defence opens by raising the question of the relationship between convincingness and truth.

It is the blurring of this distinction that accounts for Socrates' presence in court because the convincingness of their talk makes what they say of Socrates *appear* true. Just as the theorist is committed to reformulate what appears in order to re-collect its source or ground, so must he — at this moment — reformulate what they say of him in order to provide for how it could be said. As an occasion of theorizing the trial is no different from everyday life; opinions must be examined, opinions which appear convincing and secure.

What the trial tries then, is Socrates' commitment to theorizing in so far as it is an occasion to determine whether Socrates will continue to *try* to theorize. The trial tries Socrates' commitment and in this sense, personifies the continuous trial of the theorist as the attempt of genesis to test commitment. That the theorist must resist treating the trial as extra-ordinary *is* his trial in the way in which exigencies continuously try and test his reserve. It is the logos that provides both for Socrates' commitment *and* for the way in which commitment is continuously tried by circumstances and exigencies.

The first opinion that must be examined is the one that says Socrates is a deceiver:

> One thing, however, I do most earnestly beg and entreat of you. If you hear me defending myself in the same language which it has been my habit to use, both in the open spaces of this city — where many of you have heard me — and elsewhere, do not be surprised, and do not interrupt. Let me remind you of my position. This is my first appearance in a court of law, at the age of 70, and so I am a complete stranger to the language of this place. Now if I were really from another country, you would naturally excuse me if I spoke in the manner and dialect in which I had been brought up, and so in the present case I make this request of you, which I think is only reasonable, to disregard the manner of my speech — it may be better or it may be worse — and to consider and concentrate your attention upon this one question, whether my claims are fair or not.

Socrates must examine the opinion that he is a deceiver, a skilful speaker who detaches art from truth. This is the very thing that Socrates claimed of them. Socrates immediately joins his accusers in a discussion of the relationship between speech and the whole. Yet, there is a difference: whereas Socrates says that their deception must be examined and formulated, they urge that whatever Socrates says be discounted because of the way he speaks; whereas he says that they are more than their method, that 'they' re-present an interest in identifying method with truth and in such a re-presentation tend to personify a commitment to an identification that surpasses method itself, they can only say of him that he is identical with his method.

Whereas Socrates begins his defence by seeking to formulate the life of enmity, the life of accusation, they urge that Socrates be discounted on the grounds that listening to him is dangerous. Is it not possible that the life of accusation is the life that says that theorizing makes listening dangerous? The trial is an other re-presentation of the enmity to theorizing reflected in the attempt to test the theorist's Desire in the face of circumstances to which heed must be paid.

An essential feature of Socrates' commitment is that it be tried and so, Socrates must show that he is attentive to the danger posed by the situation. Because Socrates' commitment is-in-part-a commitment to being tried (for that very commitment), he knows that the theorist needs the trial. Socrates must then show his recognition of the need for the trial by resisting making a difference between the trial and life because he knows that a trial tries (is trying in so far as it tries) to make such a difference. Yet, if what is tried is Socrates' indifference to this difference, being tried is still needed: in his attentiveness to this danger Socrates must acknowledge the necessity of the trial through his very indifference to the difference which the trial seeks to make.

Socrates instructs the court on how to listen. He implores them to treat his method as inessential, to resist the impulse to treat his art as central. They who are convincing want to centre attention upon *techné* whereas Socrates invites them to consider *what* he says rather than his method of saying whatever he says. Socrates asks the court to formulate his speech (to seek to listen to it deeply in order to re-collect that to which it is true) because his manner of speaking is a matter of habit. The methods we acquire are results of accident and so should never be treated as essential, the methods we adopt should always be seen as serving other purposes. Because we are all at times strangers to other methods we can only overcome these differences through genuine listening, through the conversation that formulates the justness of speech.

That the life of accusation treats method as essential shows the disregard of that life for justice. That the life of accusation is not interested in what must be, in necessity, but only in what is coincidental or in what happens to be. The danger posed by the trial is that by accusing (categorizing) Socrates it invites him to join in *that* exchange and so, to treat his commitment as a matter of usage. If Socrates were to understand his commitment as a matter of usage (of convention), its being sustained would only depend upon the situation. The theorist's commitment is always tested by seeing if he will continue trying regardless of the situation, if he will permit the circumstances to induce him to give up trying. By being indifferent to the difference between life and the trial (between commitment and circumstances) Socrates is actually challenged to make a difference between exigencies (circumstances) and that which is truly needed. While Socrates needs to be tried, and so the circumstances are needed in *that* respect, he needs the trial (the situation) in order to make a difference between circumstantial limits and real limits. The danger posed by the trial is that it tries Socrates' need to theorize (to work and formulate), it tests his commitment to examine the opinions of *multis* without regard to the circumstances in which the opinions evolve. In this sense, Socrates must try to theorize with those who attempt to test his resolve in trying to theorize.

Socrates must then confront the question of how he appears and the relationship between what appears and what is. He needs to formulate the way in which the life of accusation can treat his appearance as what he is. Socrates then raises the question of his reputation, his repute: how could he be taken to be whatever his repute recommends? Socrates then needs to show that what he is could only be determined in the friendly relation that is conversation; that it is only in the absence of such a relationship that his repute could be identified with what he is.

Socrates asks 'Who is really accusing me?' More 'formidable' than those accusers who are present in court are those who 'filled your minds' when you were young, those who are not present for conversation. These others have told stories about Socrates. Socrates' accusers relate to him in terms of his reputation, they relate to him in terms of how he appeared in the stories told about him, the stories of men who themselves never conversed with him but only heard of him from other stories. Socrates' real accusers are not Anytus and his colleagues but those who have been governed by stories of his repute. To be governed by such stories is to be ruled by the notion that Socrates' method — his speech — is essential.

The life of accusation challenges Socrates to endure and reaffirm his commitment to conversation within the limits laid down by the challenge of the circumstances themselves. Socrates is invited to treat his commitment as an other convention, as that method or *techné* which he uses in a way that depends upon circumstances. Because Socrates is reputed to be such a one — one whose commitment is a matter of *techné* — the trial encourages him to make a difference between it-self (as the challenge of extra-ordinary circumstances) and life by inviting him to be as he is reputed to be. If Socrates' commitment is a matter of convention, the trial invites him to display *this* through his orientation to the trial itself. The trial seeks to force Socrates to stop trying in those circumstances (by urging him to make a difference between the trial and life), and so to confirm the reputation for which he is on trial (as one whose commitment is conventional). Socrates himself must resist such an inducement by addressing the problem of repute. To address the question of repute is to consider how it is that the commitment to theorizing includes as an essential feature its continuous need to endure being tried (a need which takes the form, in this case, of formulating how his commitment invites the accusation itself as the limit with which he must come to terms).

II

An essential problem posed by this trial, then, is the relationship between a man and his reputation. In some sense, the reputation of a man comes to limit him in so far as it serves as an external constraint to which he must come to terms. The externality of a reputation shows in the problem of who owns it, the question that relates to the source of repute. Although a reputation is assembled by those who repute, at the same time its construction is responsible to whatever it takes to be the grounds shown by him of whom it reputes whatever he is reputed to be.

Man is always working against what he is reputed to be in so far as he must work to resist the easy identification of his repute with what he is. This is to say that man must work to clarify the source of his repute in communality — in some conception of the *agathon* or Good — which enters into the construction of his reputation. A man must work to show the relation between self and other which is essentially presupposed in any reputation which is reputed of him. Reputation is then an occasion to make reference to the responsibility of other and, as such, it is an occasion to make a difference between the words and deeds which enter into it and the Good which informs and grounds it. In so far as the trial poses the problem of reputation, it raises the question of the power of exigencies: Socrates must resist treating what repute reputes as a limit because such a treatment would be indifferent to any thing other than the interaction between the stimulus of Socrates' words and deeds and the conventions of communal response.

Socrates must then ask what joins the words and deeds that are 'evidence' (for his reputation) with the words and deeds that enter into the very moderation of what is here so evident? This question asks for something Other than words and deeds, some thing that grounds and guides the collective sense of what Socrates is. If accusation (which derives from the Greek 'categorization' or 'characterization') accuses Socrates on the basis of his words and deeds, these words and deeds become grounds for the characterization of Socrates. Socratic irony must continuously resist accepting such a limit by re-directing attention to the words and deeds which enter into the characterization it-self. Instead of accepting the limit of the relationship between his own words and deeds and that conception of evidence which makes of his practices whatever he is reputed to be, Socrates must address the words and deeds of characterization itself in order to show how some thing Other is required to collect his words and deeds as that reputation which is *his*.

Repute makes reference to what one is known as, what is said of one, the stories that men tell of one. Repute always evolves as part of the narrative structure of the community. The question raised by repute refers to the source of what is said of one. What is taken to be the source for what is said of one are one's words and deeds, and so repute refers to how men collect words and deeds so as to provide a sense for what one is.

Yet a man is not his words and deeds but something more. Examining words and deeds cannot tell what a man *is* because his *whatness* does not reside in the words and deeds *per se* but in the conception of the relationship between whatness and the words and deeds that provide for seeing the words and deeds as informative of whatever he is reputed to be. An examination of words and deeds would not tell what a man is because words and deeds are those practices which any one man (could) shares with many (*multis*).

If men repute of Socrates on the basis of his words and deeds, they must still see some thing Other than those words or deeds, must have some sense of the *agathon* which makes of his words and deeds whatever they are reputed to display. Repute always involves addressing the relation between words and deeds and some thing Other. Whereas the accusers act as if this relationship is self-evident, it only means that they do not seek to re-collect that (Other) which calls into being their own words and deeds (their accusation).

For example, Socrates says that what is reputed of other men (e.g., that they are wise) appears to be based upon their words and deeds in a way that leaves unclarified the relation between these words and deeds and 'wisdom'. Because those who repute men to be wise do so (themselves) in words and deeds, Socrates will examine the words and deeds that enter into such characterizations in order to clarify their relation to the *agathon* of usage (i.e., are they using 'wisdom' in a way that is Good?). Socrates will show how their usage (their words and deeds) is grounded in something Other than usage because in their reputing 'wisdom' of an other they need to draw upon authoritative and decisive conceptions of how the essent (wisdom) is to be understood (in a way that is good). When Socrates finds the one so reputed to be unwise he himself refrains from accusing such a one, but uses the occasion to consider the authorization for the characterization itself. In such a case it is not so much a flaw in the person that is addressed because what needs to be examined is the way in which our *language* is working, the way we re-call how our language collects us. His work is continuously devoted to showing that such usage forgets the ordeal and suffering of its own possibility by acting *as if* the usage (characterization) is not called into being by any thing Other than words and deeds. Because Socrates could not engage in such work (would be no different from *multis*) unless he had a notion of some thing Other than words and deeds, it is important to consider the word or deed to which Socrates was exposed which enabled him to come to such knowledge.

III

At this point Socrates recounts his oracle story. Though the oracle said Socrates was wisest, Socrates knows that he is not wise. Socrates could have disregarded the oracle because he thought he was wrong: he could have dismissed what *he* (Socrates) knew on the grounds that it was wrong. Instead, Socrates sought to understand how the oracle could be truthful and consistent with what he knew. Socrates did not consult the oracle directly because his friend Chaerephon relayed to him the oracle's opinion. Socrates trusted Chaerephon and did not treat his message as a matter of hearsay. It is in this way that Chaerephon initiates the question of Socrates' reputation. But the Delphic oracle is not a story-teller and so, what he says about Socrates must be true ('he cannot be telling a lie: that would not be right for him').

> When I heard about the oracle's answer, I said to myself, what does the god mean? Why does he not use plain language? I'm only too conscious that I have no claim to wisdom, great or small. So what can he mean by asserting that I am the wisest man in the world?

Socrates decides to 'check the truth' of the oracle's remark — to formulate the oracle's pronouncement. What the oracle says must be accepted as truth and not as something reputed to be true. This is to say that for man, *that* the oracle says what he says must be accepted as beyond repute and so, what must be accepted is the necessity of the oracle.

The oracle says that Socrates is wisest but he cannot mean that Socrates' talk is itself beyond repute. Socrates knows that he is not divine and that what he says is what he reputes to be the case. What the oracle must mean is that at the level of the human Socrates is the wisest because he accepts the voice of the oracle as necessary. The wisest human could only be one who acknowledges that the oracle speaks.

If it is an accident that the oracle gives Socrates a sign of something beyond words and deeds, yet what the oracle gives a sign *of* is not the irrelevance of words and deeds but the recognition that in their use words and deeds must always show a concern for some thing beyond word and deed. That this reminder was given to Socrates is what he must treat as good (it is Good to be so reminded) while still acknowledging that the sign (of what is Good, of what is Other than word and deed) only comes to him by word and deed. It is in this way that the oracle reminds Socrates of the origin of life in genesis and particularity.

Socrates executes his task while preserving the difference between the divine and the human. His problem is to re-achieve the truth of what the oracle says. Yet this truth is not identified with the words of the oracle but with the necessity of hearing his words. The truth of what the oracle says is accepted as that which needs to be re-achieved. Socrates proceeds to converse with those reputed to be wise and finds the slightest difference between him and them: that they treat their reputation as what they are while he examines the relationship between repute and what is. The real difference between Socrates and them is that he carries out the oracle's mission, that he rather than they has heard the oracle. The difference between Socrates and these others is that his hearing the oracle becomes his acknowledgment of a necessity that differentiates him from all men. Socrates needs to produce a situation in which his message from the oracle is decisive.

In effect, the oracle said to Socrates that you are the wisest in so far as you heed me. The oracle *made* Socrates wisest by inducing him to listen and it is this listening that produces the wisdom of Socrates. To heed the oracle requires considerable work: Socrates had to treat Chaerephon's report as friendly and the oracle's remark as beyond repute. The friendly relationship between Socrates and Chaerephon freed Socrates to treat the oracle's voice as beyond repute. Only one who can treat the oracle's voice as beyond repute is wise; this is what the voice enunciates. Socrates could not at first understand how he was wisest because he could not comprehend how his will to listen — to treat the oracle as beyond repute — *was* his wisdom. This will to listen depended upon the friendship between Socrates and Chaerephon.

Chaerephon was Socrates' good friend. Socrates accepted his report not because he was egocentric but because he wanted to understand how Chaerephon's report of what the oracle said could be true. It is in this very Desire that Socrates fulfilled the truth for which he was searching. Socrates came to understand that his particular wisdom could only reside in his continuous effort to hear the oracle by re-achieving the truth of what he said.

The oracle said that he who was wisest must accept that which is beyond repute. Further, that such acceptance lies in questioning the relationship between repute and what is. Such questioning is a decisive acceptance of what is beyond repute (the oracle) and yet, it continuously risks appearing (being reputed to be) it-self (its method) as that which is beyond repute. What is beyond repute is *that the oracle speaks.* In addressing the relationship between what is and what is reputed to be, Socrates himself runs the risk of reputing to be beyond repute. Socrates must be indifferent to his reputation in that repute is in the service of what is beyond repute while nevertheless realizing that the task which the oracle set is impossible. The oracle's task is impossible because if Socrates is charged with teaching men to accept what is beyond repute, these men must relate to Socrates in the same way in which he relates to Chaerephon, in a spirit of friendship. Yet, the men with whom Socrates is enjoined to converse are not necessarily friends.

If the oracle's message recommends that it is the theorist's very acknowledgment of this message which distinguishes him from others, this distinction serves to render him strange in the eyes of those who do not hear the oracle.

The oracle's naming Socrates occurs by accident and because of this serves as a reminder of the place of genesis and exigency in life. If the oracle is important in so far as he speaks and if he speaks to Socrates by accident, it is still necessary that some sign be given, that some voice be heard. If the oracle re-presents the accident of life as the memory of genesis, this accident acquires its necessity as the sign that man needs in order to theorize.

That the oracle names Socrates guarantees his strangeness to those who have not been named and Socrates' acceptance of the oracle is an acceptance of this guarantee (of this risk). This is the contract in which Socrates entered. The theorist's acceptance of the oracle renders him strange; this is the price paid for his wisdom, his difference. The oracle then says, because you are the wisest, Socrates, you will appear strange: your strangeness will *appear* in your attempt to acknowledge the voice of the oracle. The oracle tells Socrates that his strangeness will consist in his acceptance of the necessity of having heard the oracle. It is the necessity of Socrates' acceptance that will then appear most strange.

The oracle provides the sign through which the needfulness of grasping the source of speech is apprehended. If the logos is common to all, it only 'lives' in so far as it is re-collected as what is common to all. This gathering or collecting which calls 'all' into being must it-self be continuously re-called. What must be re-called is how this collecting calls and binds where this re-call is it-self a binding or collecting of how what is common calls. The capacity to re-call *that* the logos binds and calls (all into being) is itself a feature of the binding and calling which is the logos. The logos generates both its being needed and needlessness for what it calls (into being) is the necessity of its not being re-called. This tension which *is* logos provides then for both Socrates and *multis* and it provides for the difference as the accident of the sign (of the oracle). The logos needs a sign of it-self, an appearance of it-self that is not identical with it-self, and such a sign (like the oracle) makes reference to that which calls *it* (into being) as both what it is and what it is not. The sign then makes reference to logos as part of what it is and as what is other. The sign without Socrates (without one to apprehend it) or without logos (without that which it must re-call) would be nothing, whereas Socrates (thanks to the grant of the logos it-self) could still be (*multis*) without the sign. Logos without the sign would be abstract and lifeless because it is only its sign that enables its call to be re-called by man.

IV

Socrates says that he must do what is right, regardless of his reputation. What is the source of this imperative, of this eccentric need? Doing what is right is necessary for Socrates; he *must* do what is right. This necessity is unconditional. Though Socrates could technically do other than what is right, he *needs* to do what is right. But since Socrates is not a god (and his acceptance of this is part of doing what is right) what he reputes to be right will often not be right. For Socrates to do what is right is not for him to continuously *do* what is right all of the time because the human is one for whom the relationship between repute and what is is itself in continuous question and so can never be appropriated; rather, it is to seek to address the relationship between what is reputed to be right and what is right. Socrates says that what he must do is Desire to do what is right where such Desire takes the form of addressing the relationship between what is reputed to be and what is. What Socrates must then do is preserve his dedication to what is beyond repute even as this dedication appears disreputable.

Socrates' need to do what is right is his need to endure his commitment's continuous trial by circumstances. These circumstances will try Socrates' affirmation of having heard the oracle by inviting him to treat this necessity as a convention which he has elected. Socrates' desire to do what is right is then an attempt to resist this invitation; rather than seeking to *do* any one thing, he needs to keep alive the fact of the oracle's voice in the face of the challenge of circumstances. This need was apprehended in the accident of a sign.

The imperativeness of Socrates' commitment cannot be altered and this appears strange. He *has* to do what he does. This wilful Desire is what distinguishes Socrates from *multis* and is that which accounts for his strangeness where this distinction is itself grounded in his having heard the voice. Yet the way in which Socrates goes about his task is homely and familiar. Socrates questions others and addresses the grounds of what is reputed to be through speech. Socrates must be familiar with usage for he needs to be sociable in order to do what he must. Where the strangeness of what he must do is apparent, his method is often familiar and recognizable.

Socrates' method of speaking is inessential; it is conterminous with his place, custom and habit. If these habits are seen as what is essential to Socrates, his distinctiveness will not be understood. In these habits he resembles all men for he shares with all men the practised repetition of usages. The familiarity of Socrates' behaviour is grounded in the strangeness of his necessity, a necessity which is strange because it compels him to estrange himself from accepting exigencies as limits.

Socrates must face the charge of corrupting the young. The charge questions Socrates' effect upon the young. But he can only have a deleterious effect if the young treat his method — his speech — as essential. These others treat Socrates as if *he* was an oracle (as if he was beyond repute) or an artist (one whose method is essential) and so, they miss what he is (that he *is* the one who is committed to acknowledging his having heard the oracle). Socrates runs the risk of being treated apparently because the very familiarity of his activity invites its being viewed as a convention which he elects. What is not seen is the necessity of his having to do as he does.

The charge of corruption can only be made if Socrates' dedication to doing what is right is not understood as what Socrates is. Socrates does not deny the possibility that he might have done harm, but whether or not he does harm is not essential. It is impossible for a man not to do harm: what is essential is Socrates' need to do what is right. When a man does harm he must be seen to do it unintentionally; because Socrates is a man he knows that he could do harm. If a man does harm he must be instructed or enlightened because he could only do it unintentionally. The proper way of relating to one who does harm is to instruct and formulate him through conversation. Whereas Socrates relates to his accusers and to the life of repute as if its harm was unintentional, they relate to him with enmity as if his harm was intentional. Their accusation seeks to silence and punish him only because they see what is distinctive of him to be that which is inessential. If they would see his dedication as essential they would seek to instruct and enlighten him. Socrates advises the court: 'Do not stop the mouths of others but make yourselves as good men as you can.'

Intentionality becomes central in so far as the practices of a man do not necessarily distinguish him from any other man because essential difference is displayed in the necessity that guides and organizes such practice. Socrates *is* his acknowledgment of the necessity to do right (to seek to resist the challenge of circumstances to relax his grip upon this necessity) regardless of whatever he happens to do in the circumstances. A man's doing what he does must be seen as guided by a necessity which anticipates whatever he *happens to do* to be his solution to the problem of needing to do right. Community requires of any man that this need be assumed whatever the man happens to do: community then requires the good faith of assuming of a man that his 'actual' departure from what is right is a feature of his conception *of* what is right and so, that this conception must be addressed (enlightened and instructed) instead of assuming the man's intention to do wrong. To assume intentional wrong-doing is to assume that a man is whatever he happens to do.

Those whom Socrates is reputed to corrupt are like the accusers. That is, they are young men who did not truly listen to Socrates, those who did not seek to formulate whatever he was doing as his method of making reference to his need to do what is right. Among these youth were 'those young and wealthy ones — ones with leisure — who listen to me and try to imitate my talk with others, those ones who enjoy hearing others cross-questioned because it is amusing.' It is not Socrates who corrupts these youth because the way of attending to him presupposes that corruption. They use Socrates' method (as what is essential to Socrates) as a way (a method) of maximizing their reputation. It is Socrates' acceptance of the necessity of the sign of the oracle that itself generates the circumstances in which the necessity of his commitment is tried.

V

Socrates is encouraged to give up theorizing or die. Socrates says that his acceptance of the oracle includes as a feature the risk of enmity, of death. Socrates cannot imagine a reason for giving up theorizing since having to do what is right is inextricably bound up with the nature of man. To give up theorizing would be to give up being a man. This commitment is beyond repute and so, what Socrates is invited to choose is a life that relinquishes any concern with what is beyond repute. Socrates cannot conceive of giving up on the life that is beyond repute because he cannot envisage a life that is other to that. It is in this sense that Socrates accepts as his limit that there is no life Other than the life that is dedicated to that which is beyond repute. This is why Socrates says that it is necessary for him to theorize.

The life that is beyond repute is the life that acknowledges the fact of the voice of the oracle, it is the life that re-cognizes that what is given in the oracle's sign is the need for a sign. Though the appearance of the sign is accidental, it serves as a reminder of the need for what it signifies — that the accident of life needs something other than accident or convention. It is the very accident of the sign that reminds man that he needs a sense of necessity — of some thing Other than accident it-self — if he is to endure the accidental and circumstantial. This need is beyond repute in the sense that it can only be acknowledged by one who does not conceive of it as a ratification of what is reputed to be because it originates in an apprehension that is both particular and necessary.

The particularity of the sign — of the oracle's voice for Socrates — guarantees its necessity for him as that with which he must live. The accident means that it is necessary for Socrates to speak with those who have not heard the oracle and so, that it is necessary for this difference to be tried in such circumstances and by the circumstances themselves. The acknowledgment of the sign is an acknowledgment of the need to live up to the sign in the face of circumstances that try this need by inviting its relaxation.

Accepting the necessity of his commitment is accepting the commitment's trial by circumstances that will seek to induce him to accept circumstances themselves as his limit.

Socrates speaks about the fear of death. Death appears strange. Death seems to be estranged from value, it appears to be alien or detached from what is good. What is strange is what is indifferent to Good. The strange-like 'nature' is that condition or exigency that seems to be indifferent to our Desire to do what is right.

Socrates says that the strange ought not to be feared because one can only fear what one knows and the strange or alien is enigmatic. To tame the strange is to formulate it in a way that preserves its enigma. Socrates knows that it is man's fate to live among the strange and that the need to do what is right is accepted under the auspices of what is here known. Death presents only an other example of the strangeness with which man *has* to live, a strangeness which theorizing has to tame.

Socrates says that his acceptance of the oracle was simultaneously an acceptance of the need to live with the strange. Living with the strange is living with the trial of circumstances, it is living with the need to make circumstances serve what is good and so, to resist the idea that the circumstances limit the good. Living with the strange means trying to do what is right with the very circumstances that compel one to give up trying to do what is right. The work involved in listening to and in accepting the oracle was itself an effort to tame the enigmatic. The oracle said that the re-achievement of this truth would always reside in the work which tames strangeness and that this work could only be carried out strongly through the acceptance of what is beyond repute as what needs to be. The oracle said that this acceptance is a continuous contest with strangeness.

What is strange to Socrates is the life that chooses not to hear the oracle. This choice cannot be intentional and so it must result from ignorance. What is strange about ignorance is that it chooses to detach itself from that which is good. Socrates will seek to instruct and enlighten this preference by formulating its source: his work of formulating — of conversing — will itself be a testimony to the difference between wisdom and ignorance as the work involved in resisting the impulse to disregard the voice of the oracle. Socrates will then find ignorance both strange (because it chooses what is bad) and familiar (in its preference to make that choice). Socrates himself only heard the oracle by accident. (It seems to me that he is not referring literally to Socrates, but has merely taken my name as an example, as if he would say to us, the wisest of you men is he who has realized, like Socrates, that in respect of wisdom he is really worthless.)

The oracle intended that Socrates be an example of theorizing. That it was not necessary for Socrates to be the example is the strangest thing of all. Socrates' gratitude must then preserve the memory of his sharing what all men share before he was called. Being named by the oracle provides Socrates with a sense of his fate, of his necessity, a fate which appears at once strange and familiar. What is strange is that Socrates was named; what is familiar is that he is only an example, that he might not have been named. That Socrates was named is inessential because what is essential is that the one who *is* named carry out the command. Socrates must seek to understand and so, to preserve the life that does not hear since that life lives within as a part of him that could have resisted but for the accident of *his* having been named. This means that the oracle is a sign of the memory of genesis as the co-existence of need and particularity, of accident and order, of the Good *and multis*.

Socrates does not want complete clarity because as a man he cannot pretend to divine why he was named. His being named must always appear enigmatic. Socrates' being named reminds him of the origination of life in accident and of the need of life for a sign of some necessity that is not accidental. It is accident that reminds Socrates that he needs a notion of necessity to be other than *multis* because he only differs from *multis* by virtue of the accident of the sign. He can only domesticate this enigma by 'checking upon its truth'. He then works in a way that will clarify the truthfulness of the oracle's statement. Socrates treats his being named as both strange and familiar, as the limit which he will re-achieve: the limit is strange in that *he* (Socrates) was called, and it is familiar in so far as his being called is now part of what he is (so much a part of him that he can envisage no-thing Other).

The oracle tells Socrates that the strange is not a barrier but rather a reminder of the necessity of decisiveness. If the acceptance of the oracle is the acceptance of the continuous presence of the strange, the strange itself reminds us of how we need that acceptance in order to understand our place.

The oracle tells Socrates that his acceptance of what is beyond repute includes an acceptance of the place of strangeness and thus, includes an acceptance of theorizing as part of the whole and not as the whole. What is beyond repute for man is that theorizing is not the whole *and* that it needs to be desired as the human way of reconciling its relationship to the whole. In a sense, the dedication to doing what is right (to theorizing) is continuously engulfed by that which is indifferent to value (the strange) and so, what the dedication means is that it is committed to understanding the place of the strange. The dedication dedicates itself to its continuous trial by strangeness.

The oracle then tells Socrates that his difference from others resides in his knowing that the strange cannot be known. This means that Socrates knows that the strange cannot be possessed or appropriated (and so, ought not to be feared). Socrates is different in his knowing when to stop, in his knowing that he cannot achieve complete clarity. The oracle tells Socrates to seek to tame the strange through conversation, to ask of what is said (what is wanted, what is feared) how it could be; to seek to envisage the life of the speech. The oracle tells Socrates to imagine every speech as a way of making reference to the living problem of needing to do what is right.

The fact that Socrates was named is strange and, as such, shows better than anything the place of theorizing within the whole. Regardless of how comprehensive or detailed, Socrates' perilous project of seeking to do what is right cannot comprehend why Socrates was named. What Socrates knows is that theorizing itself cannot conquer or appropriate the strange just as Socrates cannot know why he was chosen. Socrates' knowledge as the highest form of human wisdom knows that why *he* was called cannot be known. Socrates' project is then designed to re-achieve a sense for what is strange, a reading or rationality for his having been named. To re-collect a sense for the strange is Socrates' mission. In this sense what Socrates knows is that a sense for the strange must be provided; Socrates knows that this is what we need.

VI

In naming Socrates the oracle calls to his attention the need to re-call the call that collects and gathers together what is. As one of *multis*, Socrates himself is summoned by the call that collects and binds all men together. Those who belong together are gathered by virtue of their being called and all who are so gathered have an opportunity to re-call how they are called and bound together. Thus, all can take the opportunity to (re)integrate with logos.

But, what does integration with logos mean? All have an opportunity to re-call the collectedness of the collective; all men have the opportunity to re-call what manliness gathers together and collects as what man is and what man is not. The logos which collects and binds all together provides in its very collectedness for men re-calling how they were called, just as it provides in its very collectedness for men not re-calling how they were called. That life includes both necessity (the need to re-call being called) and heedlessness (*multis*) means that being a man — being one of the many who are collected by the call — is to exist as one who does not necessarily re-call the ordeal of being called. It is because the call of the logos does not necessarily invite its re-call that it requires the conjoining (the binding) of work and accident for a man to Desire to re-call being called. Such a man must always work through the resistance which logos itself provides for its call being re-called; the logos makes it necessary *and* difficult for such a man because the need to re-call being called must always be re-achieved in the face of the resistance of dispersion against which the collectedness of man is.

Through the accident of the appearance of the sign to him, Socrates in particular was chosen to respond and to be responsible to the call that collects the collective. The chosen man is the true social or communal man in so far as the accident of his being chosen appoints to him the task of re-calling the collectedness that binds all together and to sustain and re-achieve that collectedness in his work. The one who is chosen needs to re-call being called by continuously showing how this can be done in his showing how accident can be transformed by acting towards it as a way of affirming responsibility to the summons of collectedness.

The oracle tells Socrates that though all are called, only the one who hears his voice will suffer the ordeal of being called to re-call; though all are collected, the collecting itself provides for *its* re-call as a suffering because what it collects in its call is the limitation of what is by what is not. The one who is chosen must suffer the work of re-calling the source of life as the call which gathers and collects what is (and what is not as the contrast and limitation upon what is that re-calling what is has to consolidate as what *is*). What Socrates must suffer or endure is that the re-collecting of collectedness must always work as a binding together of what is dispersed by showing through the dispersion of the work itself, how binding together is needed and good.

Socrates is chosen — is called the wisest — because he needs to show how binding-together — how re-calling being called — is Good. What is Good (and needed) is the need to show the Good of re-collecting collectedness in the face of the dispersion of circumstances that try this need. That Socrates can show the need — the good — of re-calling being called in his very failures and that he can be seen to generate these failures *through* his need to re-call being called shows throughout the dispersion of the circumstances that try him how one must continue trying to show the good of re-calling being called. Socrates is the wisest in his suffering; he is the wisest in so far as he shows his responsibility to affirming the good of re-collecting collectedness in his very encounter with the circumstances that invite his dispersal; his wisdom consists in his recognition that *he needs* to persist in re-calling the call even as his intention produces the very circumstances that try this need.

VII

The oracle tells Socrates that he is the wisest. Socrates knows that he is not wise because he knows that he cannot conquer the strange, he knows that he cannot possess the enigmatic. Socrates then understands the oracle as saying that it is in *that* (knowledge) respect that he (Socrates) is the wisest.

But Socrates is the wisest by accident; the oracle happened to name him. This accident is the strangest thing of all. Then, Socrates' being named the wisest because of his knowing that the strange cannot be conquered must be exemplified in the very response Socrates makes to the enigmatic accident of his being named. Socrates' wisdom is inseparably tied to his being named: his being named creates the opportunity for him to exemplify that which he is named to exemplify.

Socrates embarks upon a project designed to 'check the truth' of what the oracle says. But the oracle does not lie, 'that would not be right for him' and so, Socrates' project seeks to re-achieve the sense of what the oracle says ('to check the truth' means to ask how what the oracle said could be said). Although the naming of

Socrates as wisest is strange, he can understand its reason. Socrates is named the wisest because he is the one who continuously asks how what is said can be said. Those who work in this way are those who desire to do what is right. This is to say that Socrates is not wise because he is the one who continually embarks on this project, but that his wiseness — the assignment of the name of wisest to Socrates — confers upon him the responsibility to examine or test what the oracle means (and what the oracle means is that the wisest is one who embarks on this quest).

Which comes first — Socrates' attempt to do what is right to which the oracle 'responds' by naming him as the wisest? Or, does the oracle first decide that wisdom is the attempt to do what is right and then assign this name to Socrates who proceeds merely to carry out the task? The strangest thing about having to do what is right is that questions such as these cannot be answered. What is strange about Socrates being named the wisest is that the source of this accident must remain inexplicable.

The work of trying to do what is right is inseparable from being named the wisest. That is, to be the wisest means to attempt to do what is right. Socrates is wisest not because of what he does or practises but because of his Desire or incentive: wisdom as the Desire to do what is right makes of such a Desire what is good and necessary. Socrates' wisdom (Desire) means that he must endure not giving up in re-calling the call because he knows that to keep trying is good. Knowing the good of trying (and so, of having his effort tried) is good and it is in this knowledge that Socrates appears the 'wisest'.

Being named the wisest is treated as an accident even though the oracle might have intended to reward Socrates for his having done what is right. However, in such a case, Socrates could rest upon his laurels, he could treat himself as a prizewinner and the point of Meno's question would have greater force. Socrates must treat his being named the wisest as inessential because he regards it as a test: what Socrates will examine or test is his wisdom. Socrates will engage in examining for himself the wisdom he is reputed to have; yet, since the oracle is beyond repute, *that* Socrates is the wisest is not in doubt. Socrates will seek to examine how it is that he is the wisest. Being the wisest is bound up inseparably with the need to examine how it is that what is said can be said. This means that being the wisest is essentially connected to conversation. Socrates will seek to examine how it is that he is the wisest but since *Socrates* is the wisest by accident he will seek to examine not how much wisdom *he* happens to have, but rather how it is with wisdom. If Socrates treated his being named the wisest as essential, then he would have no grounds for continuing the work which is essentially bound up with doing wisdom.

Socrates will test his wisdom by continuing to do what is right in all circumstances that try his Desire; his need to do what is right will show itself as the need to show how re-calling the call (how doing what is right) can be done even when his need is shown in his failures or is shown to produce those very failures. Socrates can only fail to do what is right then, when he fails to show the need to do what is right and so, his Desire should be discernible throughout his concrete practices. True failure for Socrates would then be to give up trying to show the need to do what is right.

The oracle says: the one I happen to name is charged with the task of seeking to understand how it is with wisdom. He will live up to the name (the accident) through his seeking to do right by it. The one who is wise is the one who seeks to do right by the name that he happens to have. The oracle says: those who want to live up to the name which they happen to have must Desire to do what is right. The oracle then says: what these ones must accept is that their name and the need to do right by it is beyond repute, that it is shown by their use of words and deeds to make reference to that which is other than words and deeds. The oracle says of these that they will devote all of their time to seeking to do right instead of attempting to know and to possess the mysteries of the various empirical conditions which happen to be assigned to them. It is only then that they will make reference to the good of collecting collectedness as what is needed to re-call the dispersed back to their source.

Socrates will then not treat his being named the wisest as the essential source of his difference from *multis* for that is an accident. Those who treat the accident of their name as essential are ones who confuse repute with what is. What essentially differentiates Socrates from *multis* is not his being named the wisest but the fact that he — unlike they — seeks to do what is right for any name he happens to have and that this work is his necessity.

It is this Desire that differentiates Socrates from *multis*. But this Desire is not an abstract 'ideal'. Socrates' re-cognition that he *has* to do what is right is not a search for some 'goal' or 'end' from which he currently is deprived; rather, the necessity of his doing what is right is bound up essentially with the being of Socrates as that need from which he cannot detach himself. In this sense his need is both strange (the way he was named) and familiar (an essential part of him). Compared to Socrates, *multis* refers to those who luxuriate in the freedom which accrues from their resistance to re-cognizing that need.

But if Socrates knows that he has to do what is right, he also knows that the accident of *his* being named denies his divinity. Only the human is controlled by circumstances (by accident, contingency) in that only the human must confront as an essential feature of his environment the place of the strange. Socrates then knows that being human requires a commitment to understanding the impossibility of total appropriation and penetration of the whole. Socrates knows that the accident of *his* having to do what is right (of his having to examine himself as his way of life) means that he cannot *necessarily* do what is right. Wisdom — what Socrates knows — is that he cannot necessarily do what he needs to do. The oracle named Socrates as one who will Desire to do what he cannot necessarily do.

Socrates then understands that whether or not he does what he needs to do is controlled by the strange and that he needs to Desire to do what he must do in so far as he lives among the strange; what he needs is to understand the place of the strange in the whole. Socrates knows that his self-examination shares with all practice its character as work. He knows that questioning shares with all work its character of not being necessary. Socrates then knows that it is not his work (his method, his practice, his dialectic) that distinguishes him from *multis* because all work is engulfed by the strange. Socrates knows that it is his need to do what is right by accident that is itself right, that what is right is to show the good of doing what is right by accident. To do what is right by accident is to bring out the best of whatever happens to be the situation, where the 'best' refers to how the need to do what is right can be shown as what is good. What marks Socrates off from *multis* is his re-cognition of the essential not as the strange but rather, as the need to understand the strange.

If Socrates treated his work as essential he would risk treating the practice of theorizing as extraordinary. But, theorizing shares with all human practice its character as work, that its being done is not necessary because it is as strange as the enigma of Socrates having been named the wisest. Socrates knows he has to do right by theorizing because theorizing, like every practice, is part of the whole. Socrates shows this knowledge by reformulating theorizing as that decisive grasp of the need to do what is right — of the necessity of doing what is not necessary as a way of re-calling the collectedness of the good.

VIII

Socrates tells the court that his service to God makes him valuable for the city. This means that he is charged with testing and examining his fellow citizens and that they should follow his example and seek to examine him rather than accuse him. He says 'you will not easily find another like me'.

In saying this Socrates is not indulging in self-praise for that would be to act as if his being named was essential rather than accidental. What he intends is this: that since his being named is an accident, the presence of the theorist in the city is likewise an accident. The city ought to act toward the accident of the theorist's presence in the way that Socrates acted towards the accident of his being named. Whereas Socrates organizes his life around the endeavour to re-achieve ('to check') the truth of the oracle's saying, the city ought to organize its life around the endeavour to re-achieve ('to check') the truth of the theorist's presence. It is not at all necessary for the theorist to be in this city just as it was not necessary for the oracle to name Socrates rather than an other.

The co-presence of Socrates and this city is an exigency which ought to be placed, it is an accident that can only be understood through the wilful dedication to a conception of limit that surpasses the particularity of Socrates' existence in this city. If the theorist needs a place — if he has to be some place — wherever he happens to be is still an accident. If *this* city be inessential, it is still essential to be in the city. Given this accident, a sense must be re-achieved for it. It would be altogether wrong for Socrates to question this accident — to seek to know and to appropriate it completely — just as it would be wrong for him to seek to conquer the enigma of *his* having been named. The accident must be lived with and its sense must be re-achieved partially through the moderation of the impulse to conquer it.

Socrates offers as proof of his dedication, his poverty. He has neglected his private affairs, busying himself on the city's behalf, seeking no fees or pleasures. Only one who needs to do right will neglect those activities which accrue to high repute: that Socrates needs to address the relationship between what is and what is reputed to be is shown in his indifference to his repute. Such a one is poor: in resisting the drive to 'know' the enigmatic, he shows his wisdom as a knowledge of the limits of knowledge itself. This is the theorist — the one who knows the limits of theorizing — and as such, he is always reputed to be poor. The theorist is poor in so far as his strength resides in his acceptance of the necessity of what he does: the acceptance of the need to do right guarantees his poverty (that what he knows is the necessity of resisting the possessive attempt to know) because what he accepts in this acceptance as his necessity is the need to do what cannot necessarily be done.

The theorist is poor because he needs — his necessity is — to do what he cannot necessarily do. He risks the humiliation of *willing* to suffer the strange. Socrates' suffering — his poverty — is his proof of his having been charged with a divine mission. He asks — is my suffering of the strange not proof of my having to do what is right? Is my poverty not proof of my necessity? Socrates asks — would I endure (suffer) the ordeal of needing to re-call being called if I had not been chosen? Would I not have been one of *multis* if I had not heard the oracle?

Socrates' suffering (his proof) points to this: that he has neglected politics: the one who truly champions justice — who Desires to do what is right — must confine himself to conversation (to social life) and must leave politics alone. Socrates says that no one dedicated to justice can escape with his life in politics. One who needs to re-call being called cannot live in politics for he will always be accused on the basis of his words and deeds.

Politics is the life that identifies what is reputed to be with what is. It is the life of accusation, the life that wants to characterize rather than to instruct or enlighten. The life of conversation is the opposite of the life of politics. Socrates is being accused by politicians, an accusation which the theorist necessarily risks.

Yet, though the risk of accusation is a necessary risk, Socrates must treat it as inessential. This is to say that he will not differentiate between the trial and any other occasion: he will seek to converse with — to formulate — the life of accusation. The danger of such a life is that it re-cognizes no limit upon repute because it accredits no-thing beyond repute. Better — the only thing beyond repute for the life of politics is that there is no thing beyond repute.

Socrates says that one who re-cognizes that which is beyond repute (he who hears the oracle) must neglect the life which recognizes no limit upon repute. Socrates offers his suffering — his poverty — as proof of his life. What he must suffer in his conversation with politics is that his words and deeds will be treated as essential rather than as that which is striving to make reference to the need to re-collect collectedness. Consequently, his speech will be heard to serve his conventional interests. This is why Socrates addresses the relationship between speech and the whole.

The life of politics treats the necessity by which Socrates lives as inessential, as an accident. Socrates tries to teach them what it means to be named. His being named by accident charges him with the necessity. He says that since humans are always named by accident, that is not the essential issue. What is essential (what is necessary) is to seek to do right by the name. It is necessary that the life of politics cannot understand what it is to be named. They can only see his acceptance of an accidental limitation as a need that is necessary — they can only understand this acceptance as corrupt or perverse, as an intention to do harm.

The life of politics can only see the acceptance of this necessity as conventional, as that which could be otherwise, These men would leave their city — their sex, their race, their families — if it displeased them. In contrast, though it is an accident that Socrates happens to be in Athens, he is charged with doing right by that accident even if Athens displeases him. What the necessity of Socrates necessarily risks is his being seen as a corruptor: because what he wills is seen as a mere preference, he himself must be seen as one who intends harm.

Socrates will be seen as one who prefers to be governed by a limitation — a need — that could be exchanged. In this, Socrates' true moderation is not comprehended. It is a divine pretension to treat the accidental as essential: that humans must seek to do what is right by their name means that they must moderate their preference to treat a difference between conditions as an essential difference. Humans must seek to do what is right by 'checking the truth' of whatever they *happen* to be named as. Though Socrates was named by accident this is not what is essential about Socrates.

What is essential is how he understands the accident of his being named by accident. To be named by accident is then to accept responsibility for working to clarify what it could mean to be so named. Such work is realized in its concern for doing what is right by the name.

Socrates *must* do as he does. Socrates must dwell at the place where he is named. Such dwelling exhibits patience and reserve: seeking neither complete clarity about the source of accident, nor exchanges between accidental conditions in order to restore a preferred relation, it intends rather to do right by the place at which it dwells. To do right at such a place is to formulate — to converse — the place (its end or aim). What Socrates must do is continuously seek to re-achieve in conversation a lively sense of the end or aim of whatever usage with which he happens to cohabit. When Socrates says that he is valuable for the city he means that his Desire to re-collect that which collects them all is a Desire ignited by accident and which is good. He asks the city to respond to his accident as a sign, to make of his co-presence something good.

IX

That which is said to Socrates (e.g., the oracle) must be treated as strange. To treat speech as strange is what must be done. To treat speech as strange is not to seek complete clarity or control: rather, it means that the truth of the speech must be checked and examined. Yet, to examine the truth of the speech presupposes that in some sense it is not strange; it must be known in a way — it must be familiar — to be available for such an examination. Perhaps, what is strangest of all is that speech must be treated as both strange *and* familiar.

Socrates knows that he needs this: he knows that he needs the necessity of what is (here) beyond repute. If what is said is not examined it only reputes to be what is. Whereas the life of accusation *characterizes* what is said, and in so doing, preserves as its limit what is reputed to be, in addressing the relationship between repute and what is Socrates asks how what is reputed to be can (itself) be. In this move — in his need to do this — Socrates distinguishes himself from *multis*.

What is beyond repute — that which needs not be examined —

is that Socrates *needs* to do this. There must be something beyond repute — something Other — if the relationship between repute and what is is to be examined. The life of accusation wants Socrates to *characterize* what is beyond repute as if he possesses it. The risk Socrates runs is that his subscription to what is beyond repute (his need to check the truth of what is said) will always appear to be (characterized as) what he reputes him-self to need.

What is first must be the acceptance of the strangeness of having been named. This acceptance acknowledges the unalterability of what is first. *Because* it is accepted, its very Otherness (that it cannot be penetrated and possessed) means that it cannot be otherwise. This acknowledgment affirms the alterity of that which cannot be altered, it confirms the other*ness* of that which cannot be other*wise*. In this resides the strangeness and familiarity of Other.

Socrates' need to theorize is then neither preference nor exigency, whereas whether or not Socrates does theorize is governed by a *multis* of alien conditions. Whether or not theorizing is done is controlled by the exigencies and in this sense, theorizing is familiar in its sharing with all work its governance by the exigencies. Yet, the *need* to theorize is not an exigency in so far as it grounds and provides for suffering the exigencies as a feature of its life. To suffer the exigencies — to neglect politics and to live the life of poverty — is to need to check the truth of what is said. The acceptance of being named is then identical with the acknowledgment of the *need* to converse (the need to resist accusation and characterization) as that which cannot be otherwise because it is Other (it is both strange and familiar).

To say that theorizing needs conversation is then to say that it needs friendship. Conversation (formulating) as a checking of the truth of what is said can only occur among those who resist the impulse to accuse (to characterize). That impulse is one which we all share because the fact that one of us is named to do the work of disregarding it is an accident. *That* we know our need to disregard this impulse could be otherwise and so, the impulse itself is only something from which we are saved from accident, needing as it does continuous work to put it in its place. This is to say that it is necessary that what we are saved from by accident can re-occur and strike us by accident. The difference between the oracle and man guarantees our being continuously disturbed by the resistance such an impulse offers for our work; accepting the oracle is an acknowledgment of this distance — it is an acknowledgment of the strangeness of our need to resist the life of accusation and of how this strangeness *must* be socialized.

Socrates' need for conversation is then a necessity — an imperative — and yet, whether or not he will obtain satisfaction is it-self subject to all of the exigencies that fortuitously govern human practice. In this sense, Socrates is one of the *multis*. Socrates needs to practise conversation and so, he needs to dwell among friends, he needs to dwell among those who will be indifferent to the exigencies which promise to extinguish conversation. Socrates' friends are those whose need to converse shows itself as a practised indifference to the exigencies that threaten conversation, an indifference that is practised as itself a conversation about the relationship between the exigencies and the whole.

Yet, if the most important exigency upon which conversation depends is friendship and if the friendship is a practised indifference to accusation and characterization, whether or not friendship is present is a continuous and ongoing feature of the conversation itself. Conversation then requires friendship as a resource and it addresses friendship as its concern. What is examined (as in the saying of the oracle) is how it can be said (how it is true to say) that we are in the presence of friends?

The oracle does not converse. He says what is true (because 'it would not be right for him to lie') and thus, he depends upon human labour to 'check the truth' of what he says. In contrast, man converses and, because he is man rather than divine, depends upon other men to engage with him in 'checking the truth' of what is said. Whether or not he is co-present with friends is both that which his work addresses and that which it cannot guarantee. Dissatisfaction and unhappiness with the result(s) of conversation derive from man's thinking him-self an oracle, from his thinking that he has the power and glory to name an other who will hear him as the oracle names Socrates.

The work of conversation in which Socrates is engaged is done with the knowledge that it must continuously, regularly and repetitively release back upon itself the accusation which it Desires to enlighten and instruct. The work is done with a practised indifference to the exigency of accusation and characterization that it invites, an indifference that shows itself as the Desire to converse with enmity.

Socrates knows that the young will imitate his methods (that his work will *appear* as the strange and inexplicable result of 'nature', that it will *appear* as a result of genius, or magic, or a sublime artistry). He also knows that the old will treat him as having divine pretensions ('whenever I succeed in disproving another person's claim to wisdom in a given subject, the bystanders assume that I know everything about that subject myself'). Socrates knows that his need to converse will not be seen for what it is, and that they will repute of him what he is not. Socrates knows that his necessity will appear as an adjustment to natural exigencies (e.g., as stoical), or as mere preference (e.g., as cynical). What Socrates knows is that his work must live with the essential humiliation of appearing self-interested and so, that his work must suffer the exigencies in order to Desire what is necessary.

Conversation must live with the enmity that it seeks to tame and whose absence it needs to presuppose as an incentive for its continuation. This enmity is strange because it is alien from and indifferent to what is Good. This enmity is strangest in so far as Socrates shares in it, that he was named (or 'cured') by accident. In fact, Socrates' recovery is as strange as the sickness from which he recovered, a condition which unites Socrates with all men and which differentiates man from God. As a man, Socrates speaks of his work as an attempt to apply 'the healing touch'.

Since the health of Socrates is a result of accident, it is fragile. He needs to show his gratitude as the Desire to engage in work that is faithful or true to his good fortune. He can only maintain his good health by administering 'the healing touch' to his fellows. Socrates' gift from the oracle must be repaid through his sociability, through his work: this work belongs-together with the gift as its essential requirement. In accepting the gift, Socrates accepts as his limit the necessity of what the gift requires (the dedication to conversation)—the commitment to a life devoted to resisting characterization by attempting to do what is right — as its way of expressing his gratitude. This *way* is the only way open to the human — the social way — for it respects the accident of its good fortune by seeking to improve the fortunes of others with respect to what is good. Such work requires conversation about what reputes to be good fortune and what is truly good.

The health of man is precarious. In applying the healing touch Socrates seeks to maintain *his* good health. In another context, Socrates speaks of the fragility of this work in his comment upon a line from the poet Simonides.

> For he speaks on what follows a little further on and if he meant to argue prosaically that although there truly is a difficulty in becoming good, yet this is possible for a time, and only for a time. But having become good, to remain in a good state and be good, as you . . . affirm, is not possible, and is not granted to a man; a god only has this blessing, 'but man cannot help being bad when the force of circumstances overpowers him'.

Socrates says that only those who become good (for whatever reason) can become bad. Since *multis* is always 'overpowered by circumstances' it is necessarily bad, but it is an essential feature of the life of the good man (the theoretical life) that he 'become bad' because 'becoming bad' only has meaning for this life; 'so that when the force of circumstances overpowers' the man of resources and wisdom and virtue then, he cannot help being bad. . . the words of the poem can be shown that on the one hand a man cannot be continuously good, but he may *become* good and may also *become* bad. And again that 'they are the best for the longest time whom the gods love'. Success and failure are then not constituted by the practices which men call 'doing good' and doing bad because even good men will, on occasion, do what is bad. It is because the good man is a man and not a God that circumstances are always trying his Desire to do what is right. It is the good man who has to work most strenuously to maintain his resolve even when the circumstances 'overpower' him and disperse his Desire. *The good man then does what is right by resisting giving up on the Desire to do what is right regardless of what the circumstances compel him to do.* The struggle of the Good man is then not with the circumstances *per se*, but with his preference for relaxing Desire — with not heeding the need to re-collect collectedness — in his encounter with the circumstances. While the circumstances try the goodness of the good man they can never make him bad unless he gives up trying to be good whatever he comes to do, for it is the good man who shows his goodness even as he is overpowered. The good man can only be truly bad when he gives up trying to do what is right.

In order to do what is right the theorist must be disturbed by the bad. That is, he must share in the very preferences which he desires to instruct and enlighten. In this sense, the theorist needs to moderate his preference for treating his work as extraordinary by showing *sophyrosné* towards the strangeness which his work shares with all human practice. The theorist's work is strange because whether or not it is embodied in a particular action depends upon conditions that are estranged from value. In this respect, the strangeness of the work of theorizing relates it in a familiar way to all human conduct. The theorist must resist this work as extra-ordinary, as that unique practice which can be penetrated, which can be completely clarified and possessed (which can be 'known'). What Socrates *knows* in his ironic knowing that he does not know is that human activity is ordinary and not extra-ordinary because it is human. Socrates knows that the social stands to the divine as the ordinary stands to that which is extra-ordinary.

Yet is there not something extra-ordinary about that which Socrates here knows? In a sense yes, for what Socrates knows is in its way the most extraordinary thing for a human to know. This is 'wisdom' and as such, it makes reference to the extra-ordinary limits of the ordinary. Although Socrates' work is familiar, what he knows is — in some sense — strange. Yet, what Socrates knows is not estranged from value because what he knows is the place of estrangement (*its* value, *its* good) in the whole.

What Socrates knows is the extra-ordinariness of knowing the place of work in the whole. Knowing this is knowing that he must suffer the preference for thinking of work (of theorizing) as the whole because what is extra-ordinary about what he knows is that understanding the place of suffering is the only human cure. What Socrates knows decisively and imperatively is that conversation must be done as the way of suffering the work needed to formulate the place of suffering within the whole. What such work continuously suffers and risks is the charge of *multis* (the accusation) lodged both within and without that the work cannot domesticate the strangeness (the alterity) of its being named.

To say that Socrates has the strength to stop theorizing is to say that he knows the place of theorizing within the whole. Socratic wisdom as knowledge of the limits is then a knowing of what is needed, what is necessary. We say that Socrates knows what it is to be decisive, he knows that strength (health) is gathered from knowing this. To maintain his health requires Socrates to supply a myth whenever he feels the itch to exegesis. The myth is intended to preserve his health when 'the force of circumstances threatens to overpower' him. The myth is Socrates' way of directing attention to the requirements of decisiveness — of the decisive life

— as that work which needs to be suffered in order for one to do what is right.

Socratic wisdom strives to re-collect collectedness; this is Good. Yet, what is collected in this very collectedness is the necessity of the good man *becoming* good. This means that what the collectedness collects is the necessity of its not being re-called. The collectedness collects both the need for its being re-called *and the necessity for its collectedness not to be re-called.* This tension or inclusiveness of the logos provides for its very corruptibility.

Whereas the bad man (the heedless) is necessarily bad (*multis*), the good man (the theorist) is not necessarily good, for like *multis* he must intermittently do the same things as the bad man. We will not find the difference between theorist and *multis* (between good man and bad man) in these practices. That only the good man can (on occasion) become bad tells us that 'good' makes reference to something other than these practices. The good man might do bad things but he only becomes truly bad when he ceases attempting to show the good of re-collecting collectedness. What the logos guarantees is that such a cessation is not shown in other words and deeds *ad infinitum* as if we could have a final solution to the problem of 'failure' and so, that it is tried most severely by the man himself who struggles with the need to do what is right against his impulse to terminate such a struggle.

It is the logos which provides for this struggle as its very tension. The logos which needs its call to be re-called actually invites in its very call the opportunity for not suffering the ordeal of re-calling its call. The danger for Socrates is then not that he will abandon his 'position' (that he will be inconsistent, or that he will equivocate in his words and deeds but, rather, that he will understand 'giving up his position' as his real danger. Yet, the real danger is that Socrates will forget the difference between courage and wisdom, that he will forget that words and deeds are his method(s) for sustaining what must not be given up. The danger for Socrates is that he will stop trying to show the good of doing what is right (that the occasion will stop him from working upon and formulating those who are trying him).

The difference between Socrates and *multis* is that only Socrates is in a position to fail deeply (in the same way that only the good man can truly become bad). That Socrates is in such a position is an accident and so, the theorist owes what he is to accident. In order to be in such a position (in order to comprehend the necessity of re-calling the call), the man of *multis* needs a sign, he needs to hear a voice. What is absolutely necessary is that a sign is needed to be in such a position and so, if being in such a position is good (and revives a sense of what is necessary), it depends upon that which is strangest, most concrete and indifferent to value; it depends upon the accident of a sign.

The collectedness that the logos calls and needs, re-called, then includes as an essential feature the need for a sign. The very sign that it needs to re-call what it calls it not identical to what it collects in its call: this very need joins logos with genesis, goodness with *multis*, as the tension which is the Good (as the co-existence of necessity and accident). *That* Socrates is in this position by accident means that his work to maintain that position must continuously suffer the force of accident; being chosen by accident means needing to tame accident by showing that what is needed is to Desire something other than accident. If the sign reminds Socrates of the accident of life, it joins this re-cognition to the idea that some thing Other than accident is needed and good for re-collecting the collectedness that includes *both* this cognition and its dispersion.

X

The relationship between Socrates and the oracle personifies the relation between man and Other. That relationship is mediated by conversation, by friendship (by Chaerephon). Socrates hears the oracle only because he accepts what Chaerephon reputes to be as what needs to be examined. This means that Socrates does not passively hear the oracle's words and then submit by living out what is ordained, because he prepares actively for such hearing through his relationship with Chaerephon. Through his work with Chaerephon Socrates provides his friend with the incentive to report to him what the oracle said. In fact, the sign appears to Socrates as a confirmation of his having prepared to heed it, for the sign can only come (by accident) to those who are 'open' to what it signifies.

Socrates does not seek to 'know' or to possess the oracle's words; he does not seek to describe the 'point of view' of the oracle. The strangeness of the oracle for man resides in his not having a 'point of view'. Yet Socrates wants to know 'what the oracle could mean'. This Desire expresses man's effort to comprehend the whole by conceiving of strangeness as friendly, as that which has a place. Socrates starts from the requirement that what is said must be good, that it would not 'be right for the god to lie'. Socrates then begins by accepting as the human necessity the need for decisiveness, the need to accept the oracle's words as a sign of what is absolutely needed. In this respect, the difference between Socrates and the oracle is the need of the human to accept a sign of the necessity of the god — an acceptance that occurs in the face of the *multis* of sensual testimony.

Because this need is prepared by friendship — by the conversation in which what is reputed to be is addressed — Socrates' acknowledgment of the sign can only be developed through the work of investigating how what is here acknowledged has to be affirmed as the human way of resisting the trial which genesis puts to man. In the sense that the human necessity is prepared by sociality, we can think of man as originally social.

We assume that the gods speak for a reason, for a reason that is good. Whereas Socrates needs a friend to hear the gods, the gods themselves need only messengers or oracles to carry their words. The difference between man and the gods (between Socrates and the logos) can be seen in the way in which the gods speak to man (in which the logos appears to man through a sign). The oracle talks and man listens, the oracle utters and man labours to 'check the truth' of the utterance, the oracle speaks enigmatically rather than explicitly and man assigns good faith to the speech assuming that it is good and 'cannot lie'. The difference between man and god is that man needs a sign of the god so as to Desire to work strenuously and positively in the relationship. The god gives man such a sign in the oracle for which the god provides as a reminder of it-self as the collectedness that collects both what is needed and what is strange.

What the oracle tells Socrates is that he is what he is by accident. Without this accident Socrates would be *multis*. The oracle is a sign of the reminder that whatever one is, results from accident. The oracle speaks for genesis by reminding us of the source of life in accident. Yet, if this is the force of the oracle's voice, the reminder of life's origination in accident requires us to re-call some thing other than accident. The logos calls into being the oracle to remind men of what they truly need in order to live with what they are. The oracle's reminder of how anything could be otherwise is simultaneously an invitation and an incentive for one to re-call the source of the sign in that which is unalterable and eternal.

Whereas Socrates without the sign would be *multis*, the logos without its oracle would be abstract, without the oracle, man and God would relate to each other as *multis* to impersonal creator and so, the oracle is needed to join man and god together in the work of needing to re-collect collectedness as the human way of doing what is right. In reminding *multis* of the need for necessity and in displaying the need of necessity for *multis* the oracle gives a sign of the necessary trial of man by genesis: in giving this sign the oracle points to what is needed (by *multis*) to suffer this trial (re-calling logos) and thus provides an opportunity for the relationship between man and god to be personified in the theoretical life. The oracle gives a sign that theorizing is possible, indeed, that theorizing is good and necessary, in its very reminder of the accidental source of life. In this reminder, the oracle gives a sign that something other than philosophy (abstract logos) and common sense (unreflective *multis*) is needed.

The enigma of the oracle's speech incites man to search for its reason. Because of his distance from the strange, man's work is devoted continuously to providing a ground or a foundation for what is said. In providing such a ground, man's work takes the form of preserving the essential strangeness of the whole, that the oracle's reason cannot be given but reason can be re-achieved. The work of re-achieving reason resists the impulse to *describe* the oracle's reason as it must if the distance between god and man is to be preserved as a feature of this work. The essential Otherness of the oracle to man means that he cannot be treated as an alter (as an other man, an object to be known and possessed) because his alterity guarantees his resistance to appropriation. The strangeness of the oracle's words is actually an incentive for man to try to do what is right by strangeness by re-calling its collectedness in that which is necessary. Whereas the very strangeness of the sign reflects the dispersiveness which collectedness collects, it shows that the source of strangeness and accident must itself be re-called in that which is necessary. The sign of strangeness invites Socrates to re-call the need of man for that which is unalterable and friendly.

Decisiveness is a problem for man and not for gods. Yet, man's decisiveness is a problem for the gods. It is in the human acceptance of the limit of collectedness upon genesis that the gods are re-cognized. Yet again, these would be poor gods indeed if they required human recognition in order to be. Man's decisiveness is a problem for the gods only because the gods are friendly to man — they Desire him to do what is right — and this is possible only through man's acknowledgment of the sign. To do what is right is to sing the praise of the gods for it is only in such song that the deeds of the gods are acknowledged as beyond repute.

Man's decisiveness means that he accepts as his necessity the need to sing of the gods as his way of taming the strange and the accidental. Such song preserves man and gods in their proper places and so, reconciles the relationship of parts to the whole. In requiring man to sing of the gods, the gods place great burdens upon man, for man must endure the work of distinguishing between words and deeds and that which collects words and deeds by showing through his examination of words and deeds — by showing in word and deed — his need to re-call the call that collects them. This work is to be endured or suffered because the distance between god and man guarantees that the goodness of the god will always be in some sense strange to speech — it will always require a sign — and so, that man must continuously work to make reference to that goodness. What the gods enjoin of man then guarantees that the work of speaking will ultimately be inventive or mythic in regards to what is required because of the very largeness of the subject. As the subject of speech the gods *subject* man to endure speaking about the Good in a way that is not necessarily good. Man's speech is not necessarily good because he is man and not god. Man can please the gods but he cannot be a god.

Man's manliness which makes him other than a god, requires him to have a sign, to hear the oracle, as the accident which joins him to the gods by seeking to revive their presence as the collectedness that collects all. Through the sign, *multis* acknowledges that the needs of man and god are mutual — that the need of collectedness to be re-called and the need of what is collected to re-call are joined. In the acknowledgment of this sign, *multis* receives the opportunity to be something better — to theorize — and the gods benefit by becoming something better — to be friendly and collectable; yet, the gods enjoin that this community depends upon the intervention of an external other

— a sign, an accident — in order for the need to re-collect its collectedness to be re-called.

The very goodness of the Good means that speech is not adequate to it, it means that the adequacy of speech — its highest end and fulfilment — is realized in its re-cognizing this limit. The re-cognition of the limit of god upon man is it-self the positive human good; this re-cognition sings the praises of the Good — in the human way — by re-calling the limitation of god upon man. In re-calling this limitation man does right by what he is as he suffers the work of making reference to what is Good. This limit is re-called through the reminder of the sign.

This wise man desires to please the gods by showing in conversation his need to resist the human preference to imitate the gods. To seek to imitate the gods is to act as if they are completely known and appropriatable. Such a preference ignores the co-existence of necessity and genesis, it ignores the oracle. This contest between Desire and preference — a contest which is continuously practised as the work of conversation — is what characterizes the end or place of man. For man to engage in this contest strongly he needs to accept that what the gods require is beyond repute. That the gods require man to please them is absurd, for the gods are self-sufficient: and yet, man needs to conceive of the gods as requiring his work. One of the forms in which *multis* appears is its preference for thinking of the gods as self-sufficient. The necessity of the good man is limited by his conception of what the gods need. This myth enables man to place the strange by understanding his relationship to the whole. Man's desire to take his bearings from what the gods need it-self always needs to suffer the temptation to think of the gods as self-sufficient. It is in this sense that the work of Socrates always invites the charge of paganism because Socrates' conception of man and gods is limited by the decisiveness of his commitment to what life needs. Life needs a conception of the whole that neither obliterates the gods nor overpowers man.

When the oracle named Socrates, Socrates showed his respect by accepting the essentially enigmatic character of his speech. The oracle gives his gift to Socrates through Chaerephon. The oracle tells Socrates that a proper conception of the relation between man and god is what (human) life requires. In inviting Socrates to listen to him, the oracle gives a sign of that relationship. The oracle then reminds Socrates to take his bearings from a notion of what is necessary to life. The oracle reminds Socrates that the relationship between god and man must be placed and in this reminder he points to something Other than god or man, to the idea of life. The oracle teaches Socrates that man must listen to speech as he (Socrates) listens to his friend Chaerephon's words about the oracle. The lesson of the oracle is that man must be dedicated to 'check the truth' of what is said as his way of showing how one needs to do what is right, as his way of showing how needing to do what is right can be done (how the need for such a need is good and unalterable).

To hear the Good depends upon how its reputation is developed among men. What it is reputed to be must be addressed in conversation. The inclusiveness of the Good means that whether or not it is heard depends upon the accident of hearing the oracle. Because the Good is all-encompassing it can be reputed to be anything and everything. Man must continuously work to address the difference between what the Good is reputed to be and what it is even as his work is always realized in a way that makes of what *it* says a matter of repute. The need for man to work decisively, however, cannot — for man — be a matter of repute for it is the absolute and unconditioned necessity which man *must* project life to require him to accept as that which is beyond repute.

XI

The oracle does not teach Socrates because the oracle is a sign. As a sign, he reminds Socrates that the human way is the way of teaching. The work which the oracle 'enjoins' Socrates to do is the work of teaching, but the oracle oraculates — he does not teach Socrates what it is to teach. We might say literally that the oracle 'calls' Socrates to teaching, that he 'calls' Socrates from physics to teaching. What the oracle calls Socrates from is the use of words and deeds to disclose the nature of things in a way that is heedless of their own nature. The oracle calls Socrates to pay heed to (to need to examine) the collectedness that collects words and deeds. The oracle calls Socrates to re-call the collectedness that binds the collective. That the call was heard by Socrates is as accidental as the teacher's appearance to *multis*. The teacher will then call *multis* to pay heed to the collectedness that collects words and deeds.

Among those who are present to this call, will be some few who will Desire to pay heed (these will be 'students').

Yet the difference between the oracle and Socrates — between the sign and the teacher — is that the teacher must endure or suffer his vocation as the oracle does not. As a mechanical sign or reminder, the oracle appears and evokes: in so far as he appears he guarantees that he will be heard. The oracle does not need to suffer conversation because he is a sign and not a teacher. That the sign is strange — is indifferent to value — guarantees that the truth of what it says will be checked. Since the sign is as it is — it cannot lie — it does not generate its own trial by exigencies because what it signifies is the origin of life in exigency and as a sign, *it* is the exigency.

In contrast, the teacher is not a sign. The teacher must suffer his vocation — his being called to re-call collectedness — as the oracle does not. Because the oracle is a sign (of logos) he is called but not to re-call. As mechanism, the oracle does not have to suffer the need to re-collect, for his is as he is. The oracle is pure instrument, tool, or medium used by the logos to give man a sign of the need to re-call. Without the logos or man the oracle would be nothing and that is his impersonality, whereas logos or man without the oracle can deeply fail and so, can still be (can be abstract, or can be *multis*). That the sign cannot fail shows its indifference to value, its strangeness (it shows what accident and nature is). The sign then, does not have to endure the tension occurring from the resistance of what it could be (what it is not) to what it is (what is needed) whereas the teacher must suffer this as a feature of his being called.

Socrates being named guarantees the identification of theorizing with teaching; it guarantees that the life of theory will be forever devoted to the work of teaching. The way in which Socrates was named — by accident — guarantees that the difference between teacher and student will forever be inessential (since Socrates could have been the student and the student could have been named).

In this way, the event of Socrates' being named — that decisive event — guarantees that the work of theorizing — teaching — must forever suffer the risk that the difference between teacher and student will appear as essential. Suffering that risk is what it means to teach. What the risk means is that the difference between teacher and student will be seen as decisive — as necessary, as essential — even though Socrates was named by accident. The risk means that the need for decisiveness to which Socrates Desires to point (which he needs to re-achieve in conversation) will be forever treated as a 'problem' or topic of the conversation itself, and in such a treatment will *appear* as that which decisiveness is reputed to be rather than as that which it is.

The problem of the Good — of the collectedness that collects its own need to be re-collected — is that man will always treat the need to engage in such re-collective work as a matter that is within his control rather than as being a feature of the very collectedness of the Good it-self. Man must come to see how his heedlessness of what calls him is an other sign of the comprehensiveness of that call and so, whether he heeds or is heedless, that he must always live with the opportunity to attempt to respond to what is right.

The decisiveness that is required of the student means that he must come to acknowledge the theoretic life as grounded in the sign which points to a need for some thing beyond itself. It is the teacher who must suffer with him his resistance to acknowledging the need for a sign; while the teacher is not a sign, his work is designed to show the need for a sign in order to see what is needed and the need of what is needed for such a sign. That this work — teaching — can only be done through word and deed means that it must suffer the charge (the accusation, the characterization) that *its* words and deeds claim to be what is needed.

What is risked in teaching is that the decisiveness of its commitment will be viewed as a condition of the interaction itself, that the need for decisiveness as what is essential and good will be forever viewed as if it was a condition (a characterization) particular to the words and deeds of Socrates which separate him in essential ways from the student (from *multis*). What is hidden is that the need for decisiveness is shared-in-common as an opportunity for re-collecting that which collects all. The risk of teaching is that the teacher will be seen as extra-ordinary (e.g., as defendant, genius, or oracle) and in this way, that the god will be forgotten. The sign preserves the extra-ordinariness of the co-existence of accident and necessity as that which needs to be re-achieved (to be re-called), whereas to be heedless (not to see the sign) is to treat the teacher's labour as what is most extra-ordinary. What is needed is to re-member the need — the decisiveness — of teaching as a part of the whole and not to resuscitate the teacher as a particular embodiment of decisiveness. The teacher then knowingly risks being seen as an embodiment of decisiveness rather than as an example of the need (the good) for decisiveness.

The work of teaching, in so far as it endures the risk of conversing with those who are not friends, commits itself to suffering accusation. The strange origin of this relationship guarantees that the friendship which it requires will continuously and provocatively lie ahead of it as the uncertain and unattainable 'object' of its interest. The risk of teaching appears as an embodiment of the co-mingling of Desire and enmity — of wisdom and ignorance — which continuously needs to be suffered as a practice of conversing that is indifferent to the making of decisiveness into a problem.

What teaching re-cognizes is the need to dispense with (to be indifferent to) the essentially problematic character of decisiveness even as it seeks to re-achieve the truth of the need for decisiveness. This indifference shows itself as work which begins with what decisiveness is reputed to be (with the divisiveness of the *problem* of decisiveness as that which needs a solution) and continues by sustaining conversation into the question of the end or aim of decisiveness it-self (with the unity or sociality of the *need* for decisiveness as that which is perfect in itself and which requires no-thing Other). Teaching then must always suffer the enmity which it invites when it seeks to resist accusation and to ask what is true to life.

Theaetetus has to be saved from the exegetical conception of necessity which is to say that Socrates has to teach him the difference between looking up to and taking one's bearings from exigencies (circumstances, conventions) and from what is needed (re-calling collectedness) even while he can only impart this lesson by invoking the exigency of a sign. It is this tension itself which enables Socrates to show how collectedness collects both what is needed and what happens to coincide. To see the belonging-together of what belongs together requires Theaetetus to understand that philosophy's dream of perfection (of conquering strangeness) is at its inception segregated from the need to re-collect collectedness in so far as collectedness collects the indifference to re-collecting collectedness it-self as part of what collectedness *is*. The strange cannot be conquered as it is itself always a sign of the call that collects it as the dispersed and the accidental. Theaetetus must learn how the strange is addressed, that it can only be related to with strength by using it to re-call the need for that which collects the strange.

The corruptibility of the Good then comes to this: that what is needed (to re-collect collectedness) will be treated as a convention or a preference that always comes into conflict with the exigency of the strange, rather than as that need which is animated *by* the strange and tried by the strange. The need to re-call the call endures the strange by striving to re-call that which is familiar as its means of arresting the dispersion of the strange. To show this need is to show how one Desires to re-call the call as a way of making reference to that which is needed because it is good and familiar.

Theaetetus must come to see that nostalgia, idealism and philosophy are the first steps in the degenerate comprehension of the Good, even after he has seized the opportunity of fertility to become — as a student — one who wants to be something other than *multis*. He must come to see that the need to which the Good makes reference is not a source or reservoir of fantasy, but that it must be accepted as the unalterable and so, that it must be Desired because it is Good. Theaetetus must come to see that what is unalterable about the unalterable is that it must be continuously *used* to sustain its liveliness as the source of communality (a usage which *appears* paradoxical since if it was truly unalterable it would not be affected by discourse, and if it could be so effected, it would appear to be variable).

The Good essentially and eternally lays down the possibility for obliterating the sense of distance and work necessary for its re-call as that which lays down this very possibility. In this sense, the Good is always putting man on trial to live up to the opportunity which it gathers by making it necessary for man to be heedless to its call while giving him the sign that paying heed is truly needed. In so far as man is man he is always being tried by the Good whether he knows it or not; but, the severest trial is for the man who understands that one must keep trying and that this is what is being tried. As distinct from *multis*, the good man knows that what is being tried is his resolve in trying to act upon the opportunity which the Good lays down for him as his initiative and trial.

The trial is then a test not of Socrates' reputation, but of his understanding of what is good. Yet, in so far as Socrates' reputation is produced by his need to do what is good, the trial tests his resolve. If Socrates is reputed to be one who will not stop theorizing, those who accuse him think that such resistance is bad. While they are indifferent to the relationship between such conduct and what is good (and thus, are not interested in addressing the question of the Good), they can still serve as instruments for testing him without respect to what is good. At best, the accusers can test Socrates' courage but not his wisdom, for that would involve a conversation about what is good. This perhaps represents the highest understanding which *multis* can have of the theorist — that he is courageous — because the words and deeds of *multis* have no place for the wisdom for which Socrates was named.

Notes

Chapter I Theory and life

1 Cf. Leo Strauss, *Liberalism: Ancient and Modern*, New York, Basic Books, 1968, p. 3, for this exegetical opinion of the 'great minds' — the teachers who are not pupils toward which Socrates is so ironic.

Chapter II Hedonism

1 J. Locke, *An Essay Concerning Human Understanding*, London, Dent, 1947, Book 1, chapter II, paragraph 5.
2 J. Locke, *Of Civil Government*, London, Dent, Lecture 46.
3 J. Locke, *An Essay Concerning Human Understanding*, Book 1, chapter II, paragraph 1.
4 Ibid.
5 Ibid.
6 Ibid., Book III, chapter 1, paragraph 1.
7 Ibid., Book III, chapter 10, paragraph 23.
8 Ibid.
9 Ibid., chapter XI, paragraph 11.
10 Ibid., Book II, chapter XXXII, paragraph 11.
11 Ibid., Book IV, chapter XII, paragraph 4.
12 Ibid., Book III, chapter XI, paragraph 26.
13 Ibid., Book IV, chapter XVI, paragraph 4.

Chapter III Exegesis

1 J. Locke, *An Essay Concerning Human Understanding*, London, Dent, 1947, Book 2, chapter XXI, paragraph 31.
2 Ibid., paragraph 33.

Index